Working
with children
in the early years

Working with Children in the Early Years is an accessible introduction to early years theories, policy and practice, offering practitioners in a diverse range of settings the opportunity to develop their knowledge, understanding and skills for working with young children. This fully updated second edition builds on new government agendas and interests in supporting quality provision for young children and their families. Bringing together current research and thinking in a broad range of areas, it covers:

- the diversity of practitioner roles and multi-agency working
- working with families
- listening to children
- observing and assessing
- developing professional roles
- health and well-being
- curriculum and pedagogy
- the importance of play and learning in the early years.

All contributions are strongly practical and underpinned by relevant theory, and will support students and practitioners studying in the field of early years and early childhood studies as well as those aiming to achieve Early Years Professional Status. The book will also appeal to training providers, equipping them with a valuable and unique source to support a range of early years courses.

Carrie Cable is Senior Lecturer in Education at The Open University and Director of a DCSF funded research project into language learning in primary schools.

Linda Miller is Emeritus Professor of Early Years at The Open University.

Gill Goodliff is Senior Lecturer and Head of Awards for Early Years at The Open University.

This Reader, along with the companion volume *Supporting Children's Learning in the Early Years,* 2nd edition (edited by Carrie Cable, Linda Miller and Gill Goodliff) forms part of the Open University course *The Early Years: Developing practice* (E100). This is a 60 point, level 1 course for anyone working with young children in public, private, voluntary and independent childcare and education settings.

Details of this and other Open University courses can be obtained from the Student Registration and Enquiry Service, The Open University, PO Box 197, Milton Keynes MK7 6BJ, United Kingdom: Telephone +44 (0) 845 300 6090, e-mail general-enquiries@open.ac.uk.

Alternatively, you may wish to visit the Open University website at http://www.open.ac.uk, where you can learn more about the wide range of courses and packs offered at all levels by The Open University.

Working
with children
in the early years

Second edition

Edited by Carrie Cable, Linda Miller and Gill Goodliff

LONDON AND NEW YORK

First published 2002 by David Fulton Publishers

This edition published 2010
by Routledge
2 Park Square, Milton Park, Abingdon, Oxon OX14 4RN

Simultaneously published in the USA and Canada
by Routledge
270 Madison Ave, New York, NY 10016

Routledge is an imprint of the Taylor & Francis Group, an informa business

Published in association with The Open University, Walton Hall, Milton Keynes,
MK7 6AA, United Kingdom.

© 2002, 2010 Compilation, original and editorial material, The Open University.
See acknowledgements for copyright holders for other sections.

Typeset in ITC Garamond by RefineCatch Limited, Bungay, Suffolk
Printed and bound in Great Britain by the MPG Books Group

British Library Cataloguing in Publication Data
A catalogue record for this book is available from the British Library

Library of Congress Cataloging-in-Publication Data
Working with children in the early years / edited by Carrie Cable, Linda Miller, and
Gill Goodliff.
    p. cm.
1. Education, Preschool—Great Britain.   2. Preschool children—Services for—
Great Britain.   I. Cable, Carrie.   II. Miller, Linda, 1946–   III. Goodliff, Gill.
LB1140.25.G7W67 2009
372.210941—dc22

                                                            2009002008

ISBN 10: 0–415–49698–5 (hbk)
ISBN 10: 0–415–49699–3 (pbk)

ISBN 13: 978–0–415–49698–8 (hbk)
ISBN 13: 978–0–415–49699–3 (pbk)

Contents

Acknowledgements

We wish to thank those who have written chapters for this Reader of who have given permission for us to edit and reprint writing from other publications. Special thanks to Caroline Davies (Course Manager), Liz Santucci (Course Assistant) and Gill Gowans (Copublishing Executive) for their help in preparing the manuscript.

Grateful acknowledgement is made to the following sources for permission to reproduce material in this book:

Chapter 1: Jones, C. and Pound, L. (2008) 'The roles and responsibilities of leaders in leadership', *Leadership and Management in the Early Years: From principles to practice*; Maidenhead: McGraw-Hill Open University Press. Copyright © 2008 C. Jones and L. Pound, reprinted with the kind permission of Open University Press. All rights reserved. Edited for this edition.

Chapter 2: Cable, C., Drury, R. and Helavaara Robertson, L. (2008) 'A day in the life of a bilingual practitioner', newly commissioned for this volume. Copyright © 2009 The Open University.

Chapter 3: Owen, S. and Haynes, G. (2008) 'Developing professionalism in the early years', *Professionalism in the Early Years*, ed. L. Miller and C. Cable; London: Hodder Arnold.

Chapter 4: Read, M. and Rees, M. (2000) 'Working in teams in early years settings', updated version of this chapter from *Looking at Early Years Education and Care*, ed. R. Drury, L. Miller and R. Campbell; London: David Fulton Publishers.

Chapter 5: Miller, L. 'Professional roles in the early years', updated version of Kardstadt, L., Lilley, T. and Miller, L. (2000) 'Professional roles in early childhood', *Looking at Early Years Education and Care*, ed. R. Drury, L. Miller and R. Campbell; London: David Fulton Publishers.

Chapter 6: Jones C. and Pound. L. (2008) 'Leadership in a multi-agency context', *Leadership and Management in the Early Years: From principles to practice*; Maidenhead:

McGraw-Hill Open University Press. Copyright © 2008 C. Jones and L. Pound, reprinted with the kind permission of Open University Press. All rights reserved. Edited for this edition.

Chapter 7: Miller, L., Devereux, J., Page-Smith, A. and Soler, J. (2002) 'Approaches to curricula in the early years', updated version of this chapter from *Working with Children in the Early Years* (1st edn), ed. J. Devereux and L. Miller; London: David Fulton Publishers. Copyright © 2003 The Open University.

Chapter 8: Waller, T. (2005) 'Modern childhood: contemporary theories and children's lives', *An Introduction to Early Childhood: A multidisciplinary approach*, ed. T. Waller; London: Paul Chapman Publishers/Sage Publications. Copyright © 2005 Tim Waller, reprinted with the kind permission of Sage Publications. Edited for this edition.

Chapter 9: Underdown, A. (2002) 'Health inequalities in early childhood', *Working with Children in the Early Years* (1st edn), ed. J. Devereux and L. Miller; London: David Fulton Publishers.Copyright © 2003 The Open University.

Chapter 10: Holland, R. (1997) '"What's it all about?" – how introducing heuristic play has affected provision for the under-threes in one day nursery', *Working with the Under-3s: Responding to children's needs*, ed. L. Abbott and H. Moylett; Buckingham: Open University Press. Copyright © 1997 R. Holland, reprinted with the kind permission of Open University Press. All rights reserved. Edited for this edition.

Chapter 11: Shirley, I. (2007) 'Exploring the great outdoors', in Austin, R. (eds) *Letting the Outside In*; Stoke-on-Trent: Trentham Books Ltd. Edited for this edition.

Chapter 12: Whitehead, M. (2007) 'Hi Granny! I'm going to write a novel', *Early Years Foundations: Meeting the challenge*, ed. J. Moyles; Maidenhead: McGraw-Hill Open University Press. Copyright © 2007 M. Whitehead, reprinted with the kind permission of Open University Press. All rights reserved. Edited for this edition.

Chapter 13: Duffy, B. (2006) 'Creativity across the curriculum', *Supporting Creativity and Imagination in the Early Years*, 2nd edn; B. Duffy, Buckingham: Open University Press. Copyright © 2006 B. Duffy, reprinted with the kind permission of Open University Press. All rights reserved. Edited for this edition.

Chapter 14: Owens, P. (2000) 'Children growing and changing: the interpersonal world of the growing child', *Looking at Early Years Education and Care*, ed. R. Drury, L. Miller, and R. Campbell; London: David Fulton Publishers.

Chapter 15: Albon, D. and Mukherji, P. (2008) 'Promoting healthy eating in early years settings', newly commissioned for this volume. Copyright © 2009 The Open University.

Chapter 16: Young, S. (2006) 'Playing with song', *Early Childhood Practice: Journal for Multi-professional Partnerships*, 18(1): 20–29. Edited for this edition.

Chapter 17: O'Hara, M. (2008) 'Young children, learning and ICT: a case study in the UK maintaining sector', *Technology Pedagogy and Education* 17(1): 29–41. Reprinted with the kind permission of Taylor & Francis. Edited for this edition.

Chapter 18: Fabian, H. (2007) 'The challenges of starting school', *Early Years Foundations: Meeting the challenge*, ed. J. Moyles; Maidenhead: McGraw-Hill Open University Press. Copyright © 2007 H. Fabian, reprinted with the kind permission of Open University Press. All rights reserved. Edited for this edition.

Chapter 19: Wood, E. (2007) 'Listening to children: multiple voices, meanings and understandings', *Developing Reflective Practice in the Early Years*, A. Paige-Smith, and A. Craft, ed; Maidenhead: McGraw-Hill Open University Press. Copyright © 2007 E. Wood, reprinted with the kind permission of Open University Press. All rights reserved. Edited for this edition.

Chapter 20: Kenner, C., Arju, T., Gregory, E., Jessel, J. and Ruby, M. (2004) 'The role of grandparents in children's learning', *Primary Practice, The Journal of the National Primary Trust*, 38 (Autumn).

Chapter 21: Browne, N. 'What can we learn from listening to girls and boys talking about their play?', newly commissioned for this volume. Copyright © 2009 The Open University.

Chapter 22: Nutbrown, C. (2006) 'Watching and listening: the tools of assessment', *Contemporary Issues in the Early Years: Working collaboratively with children* (4th edn), ed. G. Pugh, and B. Duffy; London: Paul Chapman Publishers/Sage Publications. Copyright © 2006 C. Nutbrown, reprinted with the kind permission of Sage Publications. Edited for this edition.

Chapter 23: Hancock, R., with Cox, A. and Griffin, S. (2008) "It's not like anything Joe and I have experienced before": family workshops at Tate Modern'. Copyright © 2009 The Open University.

Chapter 24: Hurst, V. and Joseph, J. (1998) 'Parents and practitioners sharing education'. *Supporting Early Learning: The way forward*; Buckingham: Open University Press. Copyright © 1998 V. Hurst and J. Joseph, reprinted with the kind permission of Open University Press. All rights reserved.

Chapter 25: Draper, L. and Duffy, B. (2006) 'Working with parents', *Contemporary Issues in the Early Years: Working collaboratively with children* (4th edn), ed. G. Pugh, and B. Duffy; London: Paul Chapman Publishers/Sage Publications. Copyright © 2006 L. Draper and B. Duffy, reprinted with the kind permission of Sage Publications. All rights reserved. Edited for this edition.

General introduction

Carrie Cable, Linda Miller and Gill Goodliff

> ...*if* today we really believe that care and education are inseparable, that children are
> active learners from birth, that services can and should provide a range of services for
> *all* children and families irrespective of parents' employment – then we need a new type
> of worker for these services: a worker who can combine many tasks and work with the
> whole child and her family; a worker who is a reflective practitioner, able to think and act
> for herself, rather than a technician trained to do as she is told, a worker on a par with
> school teachers in terms of training and employment conditions.
>
> (Moss 2003:5)

All those working in the early years are all too aware of the rapid changes in policy,
provision and practice in recent years. Recognition of the role and contribution to
children's learning and development of those who work in the early years is long over-
due and welcomed, although the contentious and unresolved questions of employment
conditions and status still need to be addressed. Keeping up-to-date with change can
seem like a time consuming task and one that impacts on the time available to spend
supporting children's learning and well-being. As Moss suggests, it is important for
practitioners to do more than just keep abreast of changes if they are not to find themselves in positions where they follow guidance and carry out tasks without thinking
about why they are doing something and how it meets the needs of the children and
families they work with. In choosing to read this book or to follow a course of further
study, you are seeing yourself as the new type of worker Moss refers to above; as
someone who wants to engage with 'why' and 'how' questions.

In England change and developments have been driven by the *Every Child Matters*
(DfES 2003) agenda, the 10 Year Childcare Strategy, the Children Act in 2004, and
the Childcare Act in 2006; this has led to the restructuring of services for children at
local authority level. The increased regulation of services through registration and
inspection, the development of a more coordinated approach to services for children
and families and inter-agency working are key elements of this developing agenda.
The new *Early Years Foundation Stage* (DCSF 2008) provides the framework and
guidance for practitioners to use in achieving the key outcomes of the *Every Child
Matters* agenda: staying safe, being healthy, enjoying and achieving, making a positive
contribution and achieving economic well-being. An integral part of this reform process

is the move to rationalise and professionalise a diverse workforce through the development of a *Common Core of Skills and Knowledge for the Children's Workforce* (DfES 2005), an Integrated Qualifications Framework and the endorsement of qualifications such as Foundation Degrees and new roles such as that of the graduate Early Years Professional.

Each of the other countries in the UK is following its own pathway to reform through similar developments in policy, provision and practice. For example Wales, Scotland and Northern Ireland has each conducted, or is conducting, reviews and consultations relating to pre-school education, curricular guidance and workforce reform. In 2006 Northern Ireland published a Ten Year Strategy for Children and Young People and in the same year Scotland published a National Review of the Early Years and Childcare Workforce. Different theoretical positions, value and belief systems and policy initiatives means there are significant differences in the curriculum frameworks provided by the different countries. For example both Scotland and England have frameworks for supporting the youngest from birth to three, while in Wales and Northern Ireland there is no specific framework or guidance for this age group; although Northern Ireland has curricular guidance for three to four year olds. The Foundation phase for ages 3–7 was introduced in Wales in 2008 while four year olds in Northern Ireland follow the Northern Ireland Curriculum as they start school at four. In Scotland the curriculum guidance for 3–5 year olds is under review.

Practitioners in all four countries (and in other European countries) are working within agendas for reform, which recognise the need to recruit and train a well qualified workforce in order to have high quality early childhood services (OECD 2006). Practitioners, lecturers, researchers, local and national officers and managers and policy makers are all involved in on-going debates and discussions about what early years provision should look like in the 21st century. This debate includes a consideration of the values, principles and practices which should govern work in the early years, and the knowledge, skills and attributes those who work in the early years should have or aspire to. As Moss notes above, a new kind of worker is needed to engage with this debate; one who can reflect on their own practice and their taken for granted views and assumptions, one who is open to change and willing to question. We hope that the chapters in this Reader will support you in this process. They have been chosen to stimulate and challenge your thinking while providing an overview of some of the key changes affecting the lives and working relationships of those who work in the early years.

References

Department for Children, Schools and Families (DCSF) (2008) *The Statutory Framework for the Early Years Foundation Stage*. Nottingham: DCSF.

Department for Education and Skills (DfES) (2003) *Every Child Matters*. Nottingham: DfES.

Department for Education and Skills (2005) *Common Core of Skills and Knowledge for the Children's Workforce*. London: DfES.

Moss, P. (2003) *Beyond Caring: the Case for Reforming the Childcare and Early Years Workforce*. London: Daycare Trust, The National Childcare Campaign.

OECD (2006) *Starting Strong 11. Early Childhood Education and Care*. Paris: Organisation for Economic Co-operation and Development.

Part 1
Roles, provision and practices

Carrie Cable

Introduction

The chapters in the first part of this book provide insights into the changing roles of practitioners in the UK in the 21st century and aim to support you in reflecting on your own role and those of others you work with in the diverse settings encompassed within early years provision. Themes that are considered in these chapters include: the policy context for developments in early years services; different types of provision; professionalism and professional roles and responsibilities; working in teams both in and across settings and agencies; and the nature of leadership in the early years. A variety of settings and approaches are drawn on by the authors to enable you to compare and contrast your own experiences and practices.

In Chapter 1 Caroline Jones and Linda Pound discuss the range of tasks, roles and responsibilities that all those working in the early years undertake whether or not they are in leadership positions. They examine the specific nature of the roles and responsibilities associated with leadership and explore the concept of distributed leadership as one of particular significance in the early years context. The examples and case studies they provide should support you in reflecting on the different roles you carry out and different leadership styles. Becoming an effective leader in the early years is seen as an on-going process; developing professionalism is central to this process and is supported by experience and reflective practice.

In the next chapter Carrie Cable, Rose Drury and Leena Robertson examine the role of bilingual practitioners who support bilingual children, their parents and other practitioners in making connections between home and school. Many young children growing up in the UK speak one language at home with families but will be learning English at school or in their early years setting. The chapter considers the reasons for supporting children's bilingualism and the varied roles of bilingual staff. A case study of a 'day in the life' of one practitioner is provided for readers to reflect on. The authors argue that many bilingual practitioners adopt a mediating role in supporting the development of shared understandings of children's experiences and learning.

Chapter 3, by Sue Owen and Gill Haynes, offers a review of developments in the policy context of early years services over the last ten years, and then concentrates on the more recent policy and strategy developments linked to the *Every Child Matters* agenda (DfES 2003). The second half of the chapter reviews the background to workforce reform before focusing on the policy related to recent workforce development in England, including the introduction of Early Years Professional Status. The authors discuss these issues in the context of the development of professionalism in the early years workforce and pay, conditions and rewards.

Working together is a key aspect of professional life in early years settings. In Chapter 4 Mary Read and Mary Rees provide theoretical and practical insights for early years practitioners into ways of working together successfully. They highlight the importance of communication in forging and maintaining professional relationships and consider how to develop and manage strategies for dealing with conflict within teams. They conclude by discussing the personal and professional development of individual team members and pose helpful questions for leaders and managers of teams.

In Chapter 5 Linda Miller explores the nature of professionalism for early years practitioners. She discusses reforms in the children's workforce across the UK and considers the developments in each nation for raising the standards and qualifications of those working in the early years. She considers different training and professional development routes and examines the discussions and debates surrounding the requisite knowledge and skills practitioners will need. She argues that the challenge for practitioners undertaking further professional development is to develop a critical and analytical perspective towards their practice in order to uncover new professional insights.

The theme of Chapter 6 is team work but this time within multi-agency contexts within early years provision. Caroline Jones and Linda Pound outline the challenges and emphasise the role of negotiation in establishing and maintaining good working relationships across what were previously seen as professional boundaries. The Common Assessment Framework is considered in some detail as a tool in developing shared understandings. The authors argue for an inclusive approach to collaboration which cuts across professional boundaries and embraces different perspectives. This inevitably means people moving outside their comfort zones and reflecting on their taken-for-granted assumptions.

In Chapter 7, the final chapter in this part of the book, Linda Miller, Jane Devereux, Alice Paige-Smith and Janet Soler consider five approaches to early years curricula. Two of these examples consider what we have to learn from taking an historical perspective (Steiner and Montessori). More recent approaches (Schema, TeWhaariki and Reggio Emilia) offer a contrasting perspective on the more centralised models which are being developed in a number of countries, including England. The authors argue that a consideration of alternative approaches enables us to look at the work of others and have insights into our own practice.

Reference

Department for Education and Skills (DfES) (2003) *Every Child Matters*. Nottingham: DfES.

Chapter 1

The roles and responsibilities of leaders

Caroline Jones and Linda Pound

> Caroline Jones and Linda Pound discuss the range of tasks, roles and responsibilities that all early years practitioners, whether designated leaders or not, undertake. The specific nature of leadership roles and the parameters of the responsibilities of a professional leader are examined. The authors argue that becoming an effective leader in the early years is a developmental process. Developing professionalism is central to this process and is supported by experience and reflective practice.

We are all parties to leadership. Although it helps to have a sympathetic position leader . . . we shouldn't wait for the go-ahead. There can be acts of compassionate leadership in every step you take. You may collaborate with others as soon as you begin to value their interests. You can be a collective leader when you vow to serve others and your community . . .

(Raelin 2003: 252)

Introduction

As changes occur in the way in which schools and other early years settings are organized; childcare needs are addressed for children above and below statutory school age; as government priorities shift, the roles taken on by practitioners in all sectors of provision will need to change too. Those of you who have been designated leaders (or as Raelin terms it above, 'position leaders') will be well aware that what is expected of you changes all the time. Your title and salary may remain the same but your role frequently changes, as circumstances are altered by both national and local contexts. In this chapter we explore the changing roles and responsibilities of leaders. We consider the range of tasks, roles and responsibilities which early years practitioners have to assume and the relationship between them. We explore the specific nature of leadership roles and responsibilities in the 'leaderful community' (Raelin 2003) of early years settings and identify the different groups to whom leaders in this sector are accountable. Responsibilities to and for the team with whom you work are examined and the chapter concludes by considering the responsibilities a professional leader has in terms of self-development and reflection.

Tasks, roles and responsibilities

We begin by considering not only the roles and relationships which leaders (and indeed all early years practitioners) must undertake but also the tasks that everyone is involved in and how these relate to their roles and responsibilities.

Case Study

Claire is an assistant head in a children's centre which was formerly a maintained nursery school. Claire's role has changed and developed over several years. When her children were small and attending the nursery school she volunteered as a parent helper. Because she already had a qualification equivalent to NVQ3, Claire was able to take on a wider range of responsibilities than other parent helpers. She felt comfortable, for example, playing maths games with the children and was able to contribute ideas for art and for design technology activities. When a post in the nursery class became vacant, Claire applied for it and was appointed. Her roles in the centre inevitably broadened, and she began to take responsibility for ensuring that resources were well maintained, and that all areas of provision were inviting and stimulating. She took on areas of responsibility beyond the setting and was able to take a lead in community involvement and work with parents.

When it was decided to introduce an extended day scheme, Claire was very enthusiastic and sometimes helped out by covering for staff absence or other emergencies. She enjoyed the opportunity to spend time with children in a more relaxed atmosphere and found that this helped her to build a strong relationship with them. It also meant that she was able to meet parents that she would otherwise be unable to see on the regular and informal basis which she enjoyed with other parents. Working alongside the extended day team also gave Claire an opportunity to build a stronger relationship with staff there. Overall she was able to act as a bridge between home and school and between school staff and the extended day team.

When the nursery school was designated as a children's centre, Claire applied for an assistant head's post, with overall responsibility for children up to the age of 3. In this role she worked closely with other senior managers to set up and implement plans to provide full day care for a group of babies and toddlers. She was also given responsibility for the day-to-day wrap-around care for older children.

In spite of this high level of responsibility, Claire felt that some additional qualifications would help her to fulfil her roles more effectively and she enrolled initially for an early years foundation degree course. The successful completion of that course spurred her on further and she undertook the NPQICL course. She has found that her developing ability to reflect critically on her work has given her both new insights and increased confidence. These in turn have enabled her to gain support for aspects of provision which have sometimes been regarded among some team members and managers as peripheral to their work.

During her time at this centre, Claire has held a number of different roles. In those roles there may well be a high level of overlap in the tasks she undertakes – but her responsibility as she undertakes different tasks may vary. For example, in most of the roles which Claire has been in, she will have undertaken simple cleaning tasks.

- As a parent helper, her motive or sense of responsibility will have something to do with simply being the extra pair of hands, and something to do with demonstrating to her own child her commitment to the setting.
- As a member of staff, Claire may have decided to get involved out of a sense of responsibility to the team but may also have been driven by her sense of responsibility to children. She may have noticed that the child who was asked to mop up some spilt water is becoming frustrated and is on the verge of a tantrum, and clearly needs support to complete the task successfully. In her role as an educator she may have sought to promote a child's self-esteem, acknowledging her responsibility for supporting all-round development.
- However, as an assistant head seeing water spilt in a corridor, Claire might mop it up in order to demonstrate her responsibility for the smooth running of the school as a whole; for the safety and well-being of children; or to act as a role model for staff and children. Alternatively, if as assistant head Claire were, for example, showing the centre to a councillor, it might be more appropriate for her to exercise responsibility as a senior manager and request that someone else do the task so that she can concentrate on acting as an advocate for the centre by bending the politician's ear.

Claire has a large number of roles within the centre, contributing to the well-being or care of children throughout their time there. In collaboration with the qualified teacher she supports children's learning and development across the curriculum. She liaises between different teams within the centre, and between parents and staff. She takes responsibility for developments within the setting and beyond. She demonstrates leadership in a number of important aspects of life in a children's centre which is also a school – using both formal mechanisms where she has been given specific roles and responsibilities and informal ones where she must use influence to contribute to change within the institution.

Table 1.1 summarizes the varying roles and responsibilities assumed by Claire and her team as they undertake similar tasks.

Within differing roles, leaders undertake a wide variety of different tasks. The sense of responsibility involved in carrying out even apparently similar tasks may vary. Beth, for example, regularly works in a nursery alongside other members of her team. At different times she may see a simple task like reading a story as part of her role as officer in charge, maintaining day-to-day contact with children so that she can fulfil her responsibility to have a clear overview of the children's needs and interests. Sometimes she is

Table 1.1 Roles, responsibilities and tasks

Tasks	Roles	Responsibilities
Playing a (maths) game	Parent helper	To own child, demonstrating commitment to what goes on in the setting To children playing the game
	Carer	To children who may have needed a diversion or some quiet time away from the crowd
	Educator	Responsibility for mathematical development, with a focus on accurate counting and/or developing appropriate strategies
	Pedagogue	Responsibility for mathematical development but strong focus on personal and social development
	Team member	Responsibility to other team members to address curriculum plans and learning objectives
	Assistant head	Demonstrating responsibility to parents, children, team and community. Playing the game may be part of monitoring provision, or it may simply be a way of demonstrating involvement to parents, staff and children
	Student	Responsibility to governors and staff who have given permission to undertake courses. While playing the game, the insights obtained about children's learning and development create an additional responsibility to act on those insights and enhance the quality of education. Study also requires a sense of responsibility to self – taking time to study properly, acknowledging the gains for the centre as well as self. Not taking appropriate amounts of time for study and reflection sells everyone short
	Leader	Responsibility to children and staff, acting as role model to both groups
Changing nappies	Carer	To the well-being of the child, fulfilling responsibility to parents
	Pedagogue	To the well-being of the child but with a recognition that talking and singing as you undertake the task, the way in which you touch the child and so on, all contribute to the child's care and education
	Team member	Covering colleague's absence
	Assistant head	Responsible to child, parents and team but in addition may act in capacity as strategist and be trying to determine how to improve procedures for children and staff
	Leader	Responsibility for staff development, acting as a role model

covering a staff leave or absence. Her role and prime responsibility in that case will be to take on the roles and responsibilities of the missing team member. At other times she may want to observe a particular child about whom a parent has expressed concerns – her role may be that of an observer or assessor and her responsibility will be to the child and family. In all of these cases however, Beth is acting in her role as a leader and whatever her focus, she recognizes her multiple roles and responsibilities to staff, to children and families, and to society in general.

Leadership roles

Leadership has been described as a 'differentiated role' (Pierce and Newstrom 2006: 9). This description contributes to the view that everyone in an early years team has sometimes to act as a leader. In the view of Pierce and Newstrom, different members of a team act in response to the needs of the group and take on different leadership roles. It then becomes the role of the designated leader to orchestrate the work of the group in achieving its aims. In short, the role of leaders is seen to be evolving into 'leading others to lead themselves' (Pierce and Newstrom 2006: 11 citing Manz and Sims 1991). This fits well with a proposition put forward in the National College of School Leadership's framework for leadership development (cited by Crow 2005: 71–2) which states that 'school leadership must be a function that is distributed throughout the school community'.

Shared or distributed leadership may take a variety of forms (Gronn 2003). Leadership may be shared in the sense that everyone working in a centre sees themselves as being leaders by representing the centre to the outside world as well as 'reflecting pictures of the outside world back into the system' (Gronn 2003: 34). This has the distinct advantage in complex early years and integrated centres of not needing what Yukl has called a 'heroic leader' (1999 cited in Gronn 2003: 34) because the team can undertake all the necessary roles, actions and functions.
[. . .]

Ideally, distributed leadership should be the result of conscious and deliberate action by the designated leader. Often it occurs spontaneously and the wise leader will nurture this. In a children's centre Laura, an experienced nursery officer, took a strong lead in improving the quality of interactions with children. Her skill in talking to children and in communicating with them was recognized by the whole staff, her advice was sought and she was acknowledged by all as being a leader in this area of work. The head was frequently asked to talk at national conferences and to write articles about the centre's high quality of work in intervening in children's play. She began by involving Laura but over time, as her confidence grew, writing and speaking on the subject was delegated entirely to Laura.

Gronn (2003) also describes some distributed leadership as intuitive. The way in which, within groups, different roles emerge and different people take up different roles has been well documented. Belbin (1981 cited by Handy 1999), for example, identifies eight distinct but unofficial roles which emerge in effective groups. These include the chair (whom Belbin describes as working through others); the shaper – the spur to action, passionate and dominant; the company worker, who is methodical and good at setting up administrative systems; the team worker (not always noticed except when he or she is not there); and the finisher, who makes sure that deadlines are met.

There are many difficulties in having the role of a designated leader. Not least among these is that others hold particular expectations of you as a leader. Anne, a newly-appointed headteacher in a nursery school, held strong views of distributed leadership and was keen to encourage others to exercise decision-making. However, she was taking over from a long-standing and very traditional headteacher who had made all the decisions. In the first week of her headship, Anne was approached by a member of staff who asked whether the children should be brought in from the rain. She replied that she would be happy for the members of staff in the garden to make that decision. This was not well received since the nursery nurse involved felt unable to take responsibility. It is very easy to see how the expectations of others can lock you into certain behaviours or responses.

[. . .]

It may also be the case that designated leaders misuse the notion of distributed leadership. Amy, for example, is a manager who talks at length about her belief in distributed leadership – believing that in handing out responsibilities her role is finished. But designated leaders have responsibilities to team members to support them in taking on additional roles, to give constructive feedback on how things are progressing and above all to notice improvements and developments. Amy does not do this and as a result her team, initially happy to take on new areas and new initiatives, are left feeling disaffected. A vicious circle of disaffection has developed – Amy does not emerge often from her room and therefore does not even see developments let alone comment on them. It is important to be clear that the purpose of distributed leadership is not to make the leader's life easier but to provide a better service – by using everyone's talents to the full.

The gender of leaders in early childhood settings is interesting when considering roles, expectations and conflicts. Women may suffer from the same problem as women leaders in many other sectors – being expected 'to fulfil at one and the same time the expectations attached to being a woman and the expectations attached to a male stereotype of successful executives' (Handy 1999: 65). Men working as designated leaders in early years settings, on the other hand, may also have to contend with the fact that the care and education of young children is not always seen as an appropriate area for men to be employed in. Moreover, the expectation is that they will:

- act as role models for boys in undertaking traditionally male and female tasks;
- provide a balance within the ethos of early childhood care and education which is dominated by women.

Role ambiguity can be particularly troublesome when, as is so often the case, there is more than one view of what the leader's role is or should be. This is likely to occur in situations that are fluid and subject to frequent change – as many of your roles are likely to be. Role ambiguity leaves you uncertain about your actual areas of responsibility and others' expectations of you. It can lead to uncertainty about how your competence is judged or valued. This in turn may make you feel insecure about whether you will be considered for promotion (Handy 1999).

Many leaders also suffer from role overload (Handy 1999). Again this is particularly prevalent in situations involving high levels of change. Gronn (2003) suggests that with change, leaders may find themselves being given more and more roles to fulfil. Any salary enhancement becomes like an overtime payment as leaders struggle to deal with all that they are asked to do.

[. . .] While management may be one of the roles of a leader, it is by no means the whole story. Pierce and Newstrom (2006: 11) remind us of this when they write:

> an increasing number of management gurus are suggesting that many of today's organizations are 'over managed and under led.' Increasingly, organizations are modifying the role of yesterday's manager, changing the role to that of a leader charged with the responsibility to gain follower recognition and acceptance and become a facilitator and orchestrator of group activity, while also serving as coach and cheerleader. It is feasible that many of those roles (e.g. servant, teacher, coach, cheerleader) will become a common part of the conceptualization of leader and leadership as the twenty-first century continues to unfold.

The responsibilities of leaders

Everyone involved in work with children and their families carries a heavy burden of responsibility. It is important, amid all this talk of responsibilities, to remember that in working with children, practitioners have the privilege of working in a rewarding and hopeful area of work. In dealing with the most vulnerable and impressionable members of our society, we clearly have a responsibility to the children themselves. As the emphasis in early childhood care and education has shifted to focus on the needs of working parents and the Extended Schools Initiative has emerged, the debate about the extent to which practitioners' responsibility is to parents or children has also developed. In addition to these day-to-day responsibilities there is a broader responsibility to society at large which is sometimes seen as more nebulous.

As a member of a staff team, you have responsibilities not just to your line manager, but to the rest of the team. Increasingly, as you develop and take on more responsible roles, you will become aware of the need to take responsibility for the development of staff and many complex aspects of the setting itself. You should also not lose sight of the fact that your developing role brings with it the responsibility to develop your skills and competence as a leader, in order to maintain 'the excitement and enthusiasm' for learning, which Whalley (2005) suggests is an important aspect of both effective leadership and pedagogy.

Accountable to society or children?

Although the accountability provided by inspection can sometimes seem removed from day-to-day concerns, the debate focused around *Every Child Matters* (DfES 2003) has sharpened the level of accountability to aspects which clearly impact on children's well-being. In the 2005 version of the Ofsted framework (in England) for nursery and primary schools (Ofsted 2005), self-evaluation forms (SEFs) were introduced as an important step forward in promoting a professional approach to self-assessment. Leaders are asked to take increased responsibility for assessing their own performance. Head-teachers are asked to comment in their SEFs on a number of things, including the extent to which learners:

- adopt healthy lifestyles;

- feel safe and adopt safe practices;
- enjoy their education;
- make a positive contribution to the community;
- prepare for their future economic well-being.

The final point is replaced for non-maintained early years settings by a focus on the effectiveness of the organization of childcare. [. . .]

Responsibilities to children and families

Practitioners' responsibilities to children are so much an inbuilt part of day-to-day practice that it can be difficult to take the necessary time and space to reflect on what is entailed in addressing those responsibilities. Elfer *et al.* (2003: 8 citing Manning-Morton and Thorp 2003), for example, identify a list of tasks or roles that a key person working with children under 3 needs to undertake if he or she is to meet the full implication of his or her responsibilities. The list includes the need for key persons to develop trusting relationships with children and parents; interacting with children in ways which build on their preferences and ensure that they feel safe enough to explore the world around them; acknowledging all their feelings including those that are seen as negative; settling children gently and being with them at key points, such as eating and toileting; and seeking support to ensure that key workers' emotional needs are also addressed. This range of responsibilities indicates just how complex the role of a key person is. It involves taking a high level of responsibility for all aspects of the children's development and well-being but inevitably will involve overlap with the responsibilities of parents and principal carers.

[. . .] It is important to recognize that young children are closely bound to their parents, emotionally. Part of all practitioners' responsibility for children's development is the need to work in partnership with parents. Failure to do this can place unnecessary and unhelpful pressure on the children themselves (Jowett and Baginsky 1991). Both as a leader and as a practitioner, your role will be to take a lead in this, modelling good practice and providing training for other staff members who find this difficult (Moylett and Holyman 2006). [. . .] You should also take responsibility for ensuring that policies are clear and explicit since these make expectations clear to parents and provide support for staff. When they act outside policy, staff may lay themselves open to criticism from parents.

Whalley (2001) praises the role of the *Start Right* report (Ball 1994) in acknowledging the importance of parents' contributions and commitment to their children's learning and development. [. . .] Manning-Morton and Thorp (2003) add that practitioners need to examine the attitudes they hold towards families if they are to develop warm and trusting relationships.

Responsibilities to the community

While in a small village it may be possible to define a community, in large cities this may be more difficult to achieve. Even in rural areas many members of the community

may travel long distances to work in neighbouring areas, giving a dislocated feel to what are often termed dormitory towns and villages. In large towns and cities, a sense of community may not exist because residents may move frequently, may not know their neighbours and may prefer to keep themselves to themselves. The community that you, as a professional, serve may not live in a single geographical area but may be widely scattered, perhaps defined as a community because they are working parents or because of high levels of socioeconomic need or disability.
[. . .]

Responsibilities to society

Traditionally the responsibilities of practitioners working in the field of the care and education of young children have been seen as relatively narrow, focusing mainly on children and their families. The government's childcare agenda, which is primarily designed to support working parents, has broadened the level of responsibility since this has been set in a context of broader social and fiscal policy. [. . .]

Developments in the 1990s, such as [. . .] the creation of Ofsted inspections, were an attempt to monitor (on society's behalf) the way in which schools were addressing their responsibilities. [. . .]

Ofsted's field of work has always included nursery and Reception classes in maintained schools but in 1997 its sphere of influence was extended. [. . .] From that point on Ofsted inspections occurred in not only maintained setting but in non-maintained private and voluntary settings where free education places were offered for 4-year-olds. Funding was dependent on an inspection process devised and managed by Ofsted. Since that time there have been a number of changes in the process of inspection and its scope, including the introduction of free education places for 3-year-olds. [. . .]

Responsibilities to and for the team

Even as a leader, you are likely to be a member of one or more teams. [. . .] Frequently practitioners find themselves in a range of teams – an extended day team, a management group, an action committee and so on. [. . .] The responsibilities of leaders include both responsibility *to* the team and responsibility *for* the team. In taking responsibility for the team, you will, for example, take a lead in:

- promoting positive relationships;
- creating an ethos in which staff feel valued and want to learn more and develop further;
- keeping core values at the heart of the setting's work;
- monitoring, maintaining and developing the quality of provision.

In addressing these responsibilities you will be taking responsibility for the team but also demonstrating your responsibilities to the team, for developing effective practice.

These things cannot be achieved by the leader alone. Sam, recently appointed head of a small day nursery, was anxious to ensure that her staff team were fully engaged in a shared responsibility for what happened throughout the setting. She was greatly inspired by the work of Goleman *et al.* (2002) on the subject of emotional intelligence and leadership, and decided to begin team meetings with a reminder of the need to ensure that everyone stick to the point. She asked team members not only to monitor their own behaviour but also to monitor what others said and did so that meeting times were purposeful and productive. This is important in all areas of work but particularly so where shift work is involved since it is often very difficult to get every-one together. Staff came to value this approach and became highly disciplined and skilful in raising questions about procedures and building on the contributions of one another.

Responsibilities to and for yourself

It has been suggested (see, for example, Whalley 2004) that the purpose of education, including the care and education of young children, is transformation. An approach to leadership which results in transformation places 'self-examination' at its heart. This, it is claimed, can inform a range of new ideas; will build competence and confidence; support plans and their implementation; and enable leaders to take on new roles and evaluate and act on feedback (Whalley 2004 citing Mezirow 1975, 1982).

Self-examination involves reflective practice which is the subject of many current publications. [. . .]

An effective process of reflection is inevitably linked to action, or as Freire (2005: 15), a highly influential educationalist of the twentieth century, suggests, 'authentic reflection cannot exist apart from action'. John Dewey, again a highly influential writer working in the early part of the twentieth century, expresses this slightly differently: 'Reflection', he suggests, 'involves not simply a sequence of ideas, but a consequence' (Dewey [1910] 1991: 2). Observation is an essential element of reflective practice. However, as Drummond (1993) reminds us, looking and listening are not neutral or objective activities. The observer's mind or perception of a situation may create errors in observations.

Sometimes observations can become formalized and lead us to a form of practitioner or action research. Rodd (1998: 174) comments that 'research is also important for leadership . . . because it is a recognized means of gathering the facts and information which carry weight in arguments for change'. Clark and Moss (2001) make the point that research brings responsibilities – meaning that if you have identified problems or issues for the child, then you have a responsibility to act on the knowledge. Mary, as part of her foundation degree study, gave a group of children disposable cameras to photograph the aspects of provision which were important or significant to them. She was shocked to find that several of them took photographs of the bathrooms – which they said they found dark, and even scary. Mary realized that she had to convince senior management of the need to redecorate and refurbish this area.

Graham, responsible for under 3s in a children's centre, was studying for the NPQICL and was anxious to develop his ability to reflect on his practice, and that of his team. He found the leadership or reflective journal which he was required to keep increasingly helpful.

[. . .]

In addition to written reflection, Graham found that he was more aware of things going on around him. He observed interactions between staff, or between staff and parents, more accurately. He found that he was more likely to take responsibility for his actions and to consider their likely outcomes more fully, and was more likely to question and analyse what would previously have been automatic and largely unquestioned decisions.

Developing professionalism

Rodd (2006: 54) has identified three stages of professionalism in leadership in early childhood services: direct care/novice; direct care/advanced; and indirect care. For each of these she identifies two sets of roles and responsibilities. She suggests that the roles and responsibilities of the novice professional are:

• to deliver and be accountable for a quality service;
• to develop and articulate a philosophy, values and vision.

Thus, even inexperienced or novice practitioners can only be seen as professional if they are both accountable and sufficiently reflective to engage in developing a vision which informs their practice.

Lucy had recently completed an NVQ3 qualification and was working in a private nursery. She demonstrated a warmth which children, parents and fellow team members alike found attractive. She was willing to take the initiative but also ready to ask advice when she needed to. Leadership qualities showed themselves in situations where she acted as a mentor for students undertaking work experience – not merely indicating what had to be done, but explaining the particular importance of helping children to feel secure, competent and valued.

As Lucy became more experienced she undertook an increased range of roles and responsibilities (described by Rodd as advanced direct care) and was appointed deputy head. In this role she was able:

• to engage in a collaborative and partnership approach to leadership;
• to engage in ongoing professional development and to encourage it in all staff.

She demonstrated good administrative capabilities, getting letters out on time, maintaining records efficiently and responding in good time to requests for information. Staff felt that she dealt sympathetically and fairly with issues which they raised and she was able to communicate effectively. In this role Lucy also undertook an increasing amount of responsibility for financial management.

The third stage of professionalism identified by Rodd, namely that belonging to those not directly responsible for day-to-day care, demands the ability:

• to be sensitive and responsive to the need for change and to lead change effectively;
• to act as an advocate for children, parents, carers, staff, the profession and the general community.

Lucy's line manager was ill for a period of time, and during her months of absence Lucy was given the opportunity to lead the team. She found that she enjoyed the experience and was good at helping the team to embrace change. She gained a great deal from the opportunity to raise the profile of the setting in the wider community.
[. . .]

One key role for an early years professional in transforming both self and institution lies in exciting the enthusiasm of other practitioners, both within and beyond the team. McGregor (2003: 126) suggests that 'the role of leadership is . . . in facilitating engagement, imagination and alignment'. Crompton (1997) suggests that community leadership requires commitment and Owen (2005) highlights his view that effective emerging leaders focus on three Ps – people, positivity and professionalism (which he suggests includes loyalty and reliability).

It is clear from this that becoming a professional is a *process*. Experience and reflections gradually lead the aspiring professional towards becoming what have been called mature or influential professionals (see Pound in press). According to Pound, the characteristics of these professionals are that they:

- have 'long experience in a range of roles and functions';
- 'hold composite, high level, professional leadership roles';
- 'strive for "professional insight, perspective and realism" '.

Gardner offers yet another stimulating perspective on the nature of professionalism. He differentiates between those who are members of professions and those who act professionally. He writes:

> Many individuals designated as professionals and dressed in expensive suits do not act in a professional manner; they cut corners, pursue their own interests, fail to honor the central precepts and strictures of their calling . . . On the other hand, many individuals who are not so designated officially behave in an admirable, professional-like manner. They are skilled, responsible, engaged, themselves worthy of respect.
>
> (Gardner 2006: 129)

For Gardner, professionalism of this sort involves what he terms 'an abstract attitude – the capacity to reflect explicitly on the ways in which one does, or does not, fulfil a certain role' (2006: 130). Leaders in the early years have a responsibility to ensure that they develop this capacity not only in themselves but in those they lead, since their ultimate responsibility is towards society's youngest and most vulnerable members; the future of society itself.
[. . .]

References

Ball, C. (1994) *Start Right: The Importance of Early Learning*. London: RSA.
Belbin, R. M. (1981) *Management Teams*. London: Heinemann.
Bolton, G. (2005) *Reflective Practice*, 2nd edn. London: Sage.

Clark, A. and Moss, P. (2001) *Listening to Young Children: The Mosaic Approach*. London: National Children's Bureau/Joseph Rowntree Foundation.

Crompton, D. (1997) Community leadership, in S. Kagan and B. Bowman (eds) *Leadership in Early Care and Education*. Washington, DC: National Association for the Education of Young Children.

Crow, G. (2005) Developing leadership for schools facing challenging circumstances, in M. Coles and G. Southworth (eds) *Developing Leadership – Creating the Schools of Tomorrow*. Maidenhead: Open University Press.

Dewey, J. ([1910] 1991) *How we Think*. New York: Prometheus.

DfES (Department for Education and Skills) (2003) *Every Child Matters*, Cm 5860. London: The Stationery Office.

Drummond, M-J. (1993) *Assessing Children's Learning*. London: David Fulton.

Elfer, P., Goldschmied, E. and Selleck, D. (2003) *Key Persons in the Nursery*. London: Fontana.

Freire, P. (2005) *Education for Critical Consciousness*. London: Continuum.

Gardner, H. (2006) *Five Minds for the Future*. Boston, MA: Harvard Business School Press.

Goleman, D., Boyatzis, R. and McKee, A. (2002) *The New Leaders*. London: Little, Brown.

Gronn, P. (2003) *The New Work of Educational Leaders*. London: Sage.

Handy, C. (1999) *Understanding Organizations*, 4th edn. London: Penguin.

Jowett, S. and Baginsky, M. (1991) *Building Bridges: Parental Involvement in Schools*. Windsor: NFER Nelson.

Manning-Morton, J. and Thorp, M. (2003) *Key Times for Play*. Maidenhead: Open University Press.

Manz, C. and Sims, H. (1991) Super leadership: beyond the myth of heroic leadership, *Organizational Dynamics*, 32: 1.

McGregor, J. (2003) Collaboration in communities of practice, in N. Bennett and L. Anderson (eds) *Rethinking Educational Leadership*. London: Sage

Moylett, H. and Holyman, K. (2006) 'Don't you tell me what to do', in L. Abbott and A. Langston (eds) *Parents Matter: Supporting the Birth to Three Matters Framework*. Maidenhead: Open University Press.

Ofsted (Office for Standards in Education) (2005) *Are You Ready for Your Inspection?* Short version, ref 2447A. Ofsted Publications Centre.

Owen, J. (2005) *How to Lead*. Harlow: Pearson Education.

Pierce, J. and Newstrom, J. (2006) *Leaders and the Leadership Process*, 4th edn. New York: McGraw-Hill.

Raelin, J. (2003) *Creating Leaderful Organizations*. San Francisco, CA: Berrett-Koehler Publishers Inc.

Rodd, J. (1998) *Leadership in Early Childhood: The Pathway to Professionalism*, 2nd edn. Buckingham: Open University Press.

Rodd, J. (2006) *Leadership in Early Childhood*, 3rd edn. Maidenhead: Open University Press.

Whalley, M. (2001) *Involving Parents in their Children's Learning*. London: Paul Chapman Publishing.

Whalley, M. for the National College for School Leadership (NCSL) (2004) *Participants' Guide: Book 6, 'Developing the Practitioner Researcher Research Stages 1–8', National Professional Qualification in Integrated Centre Leadership*. Nottingham: NCSL.

Whalley, M. for the National College for School Leadership (NCSL) (2005) *Programme Leaders' Guide: National Professional Qualification in Integrated Centre Leadership*. Nottingham: NCSL.

Yukl, G. (1999) An evaluation of conceptual weaknesses in transformational and charismatic leadership theories, *Leadership Quarterly* 10(2): 285–305.

Chapter 2

A day in the life of a bilingual practitioner

Carrie Cable, Rose Drury and Leena Helavaara Robertson

Many young children growing up in the UK speak one language at home with families but will be learning English at school or in their early years setting. In this chapter Carrie Cable, Rose Drury and Leena Helavaara Robertson consider the reasons for supporting children's bilingualism and the roles of bilingual staff. They discuss theoretical perspectives underpinning a socio-cultural view of support for bilingual children's sense of identity and learning of English. They argue that many bilingual teaching assistants adopt a mediating role in supporting the development of shared understandings of children's experiences and learning.

Introduction

During each working day teaching assistants engage in a range of different activities to support children's learning. Bilingual teaching assistants engage in many similar activities. However, in addition they draw on and use their language expertise and knowledge and understanding of other cultures to support bilingual children and their parents' knowledge and understanding of the culture and working practices of schools and settings and children's learning. They also strive to support practitioners in developing their knowledge and understanding of the cultures and practices of the families and communities children belong to. In this way they act as mediators of learning and understanding, facilitating communication and knowledge exchange, building bridges and relationships. The extent to which they can do this varies from setting to setting and is influenced by a setting's approach to children's bilingualism and the extent to which the setting considers itself a learning community. In this chapter we consider the reasons for supporting children's bilingualism and the roles of bilingual staff and draw on data from small-scale research projects which involved interviews with bilingual practitioners and the filming of 'a day in the life' of one assistant and talking to her about her role.

Bilingualism and biculturalism

The vast majority of people in the world are bilingual, or indeed multilingual, and see the use of more than one language as a normal part of their daily lives. They may use different languages for different purposes and may be literate in one language but not in another. Many children growing up in the UK, for example, may speak one language at home to parents or grandparents but be learning English at school or in their early years setting. Some parents may be encouraging children to become literate in their home language through teaching them at home or through attendance at community schools. Bilingual learners are diverse in terms of their backgrounds and experiences – they are not a homogeneous group and each child and family will have a different understanding of their home or community language and how and when it is used. Language use is also constantly changing as children come into contact with other language speakers and cultures (Harris 1997). However, in England we tend to use the term bilingual learner to refer to any child who is growing up in a home and community where the use of more than one language is a part of their daily lives.

An important part of being bilingual is learning how to live and behave in different cultural contexts. In schools and early years settings children need to learn about the routines, ways of being and expectations of the adults and other children they come into contact with in order to thrive and learn successfully. They have to learn more than the language in order to do this and the journey that this involves will impact on their self-esteem and their sense of identity. This can prove particularly challenging for some young bilingual children (Brooker 2002, Drury 2007). The way the setting and those that work there respond to them will play a large part in whether this is a positive, affirming experience that supports children's ongoing learning and development.

Children's home or community languages play an important role in the learning of English. There is a wealth of evidence that shows that supporting children's use of these languages is important in terms of their learning, their learning of English and their ability to learn within the formal context of the setting or school (Baker 2006, Cummins 2000, 2001). Languages are also an important part of an individual's identity and respect for children's languages and cultures is an important part of the *Every Child Matters* agenda (DfES 2003) and the *Early Years Foundation Stage* guidance (DfES 2007). In addition, with increasing globalisation, people with the ability to speak more than one language are an important resource who can make a significant contribution to a society's economic and social development and understanding of diversity.

Jim Cummins, one of the foremost thinkers and writers in this area lists the following reasons for supporting the development of children's bilingualism:

* Bilingualism has positive effects on children's linguistic and educational development.
* The level of development of children's mother tongue is a strong predictor of their second language development.
* Mother tongue promotion in the school helps develop not only the mother tongue but also children's abilities in the majority school language.

- Spending instructional time through a minority language in the school does not hurt children's academic development in the majority school language.
- Children's mother tongues are fragile and easily lost in the early years of school.
- To reject a child's language in the school is to reject the child.

Summarised from http://www.iteachilearn.com/cummins/mother.htm
(accessed 03.12.2008)

In spite of the clear research evidence referred to above and guidance in official documents (DfES 2007, DCSF 2007) that bilingualism is an advantage and that supporting the development of children's bilingualism will support their learning of English and their learning overall, the prevailing view held by many monolingual and bilingual practitioners in England is that support for home and community languages is to provide children with access to English and to support the transition to school. Bilingual staff still tend to be seen as a resource to meet the 'transitional needs' (DES 1985, p.407) of young children starting school much as they were over 20 years ago.

In schools and settings in the UK bilingual staff can support children, parents and practitioners in developing their ways of working and interacting to enable children to retain and develop their sense of identity as bilinguals and as people involved in a joint endeavour to develop children's bilingualism for its intrinsic value and in supporting children's learning of and through English. Learning together and seeing this as an ongoing process are important elements in socio-cultural views of learning. The work of Jean Lave and Etienne Wenger (1991) has been influential in developing the thinking underpinning this view of learning. The notion of 'communities of practice' is derived from their work. A 'community of practice', a school or setting and all those involved in learning in our context, is not perceived as static but as a dynamic place of ongoing change, learning and development dependent on the knowledge, understanding, contributions and negotiating skills of those involved. In some situations ways of thinking and doing things may have developed over time and then got stuck – a sort of 'well that's the way we do it here situation'. There may be no shared understanding of why things are done in a particular way, why things are as they are and no space to question or make suggestions about alternative ways of thinking or doing. Certain aspects of official guidance and policies or the views and approaches of one or two individuals may be used as the justification. A key role in challenging taken for granted views or ways of working is played by individuals who can broker or mediate new meanings and shared understandings (Wenger 1998). Bilingual staff have specific knowledge and understanding of other languages and cultures but in order to become brokers the 'community of practice' needs to develop a shared understanding and commitment to supporting children's bilingualism.

Mediators of learning

Many bilingual assistants act as mediators of children's learning and provide a crucial interface between home and setting and setting and home. For some children and parents this role has been described as a 'lifeline' (Drury 2007). Jill Bourne suggests four roles commonly undertaken by bilingual assistants in primary classrooms. These include: acting as a role model for bilingual pupils, acting as the 'teacher's helper', assisting in the assessment of bilingual pupils and providing a link between the home and the school (Bourne, 2001, p.262). These are undoubtedly roles that bilingual assistants will recognise with varying degrees of pride and frustration. The importance of a role model is often referred to by (monolingual) staff as one reason for employing bilingual staff, although in reflecting on this 'role' one bilingual assistant one of us spoke to preferred to see it in the following way:

> My perception of this is they relate to you, you are possibly somebody who is one of them, especially if you are an only child coming into school. It's [school] very much monolingual, very much white, culturally, linguistically, in every way. I think they probably feel a sense of belonging – that's OK. Like saying to this child – I'm going to bring my sense of identity to this; it's normalised something for them. I think that's important.

> (Cable 2004)

Moll et al. (1992) and Gonzáles et al. (2008) write about the 'funds of knowledge' in homes and communities and the importance of teachers, many of whom do not come from or live in the local community, knowing the child as a whole person and gaining this knowledge through 'the analysis of the funds of knowledge available in local households, in the students they teach, and in the colleagues with whom they work' (Gonzáles et al. 2005, p.127). Developing this kind of knowledge will enable practitioners to build on what children already know and can do, and underpins holistic approaches to children's learning and development which are endorsed in *Every Child Matters* (DfES 2003) and the *Early Years Foundation Stage* (DfES 2007). Even where bilingual staff do not speak the same language as members of a local community, some consider that their bilingualism and their biculturalism can provide them with insights which they can draw on in their support for learning and relationships with parents. Another bilingual assistant one of us spoke to put it like this:

> So long as they know that there is someone else whose language is not only English, you know, but who has a different language or who understands them. Because, usually, if I don't understand the language at all, it is possible they come from a country where we have similarities in doing things so the fact that there is another person whose first language is not English brings confidence to them, they talk to you.

> (Cable 2004)

What kinds of mediation?

Teasing out what is distinctive about the roles of bilingual assistants in mediating children's learning can help practitioners to move towards a better understanding of how they can develop shared understandings of children's experiences and learning. As part of a small research project we filmed 'a day in the life' of one bilingual assistant, Razia, and interviewed her at the end of the day to gather her impressions of the events and exchanges she was involved in. We then viewed, discussed and analysed the video material and compiled a 30-minute video of extracts which exemplified the kinds of activities she was engaged in with children, parents and other practitioners. This kind of qualitative, case study research (Cohen et al. 2000) can provide detailed descriptions of the lived realities of peoples lives which support reflection and questioning of assumptions and taken-for-granted truths.

Razia is employed as a bilingual teaching assistant and works in two schools each week in a medium sized town in the south of England. She works with nursery and reception children and has worked in one of the schools for the last eighteen years. Pahari is her mother tongue but she also reads and writes Urdu and can speak and understand Punjabi and Hindi. A number of the children joining the nursery speak Pahari at home but there are also a large number of other languages spoken in the school. Recently, children who speak Portuguese and Polish have joined the nursery and reception class and there are other bilingual staff who also speak these languages. Razia lives near to the school and so is very much part of the local community. What follows is a brief summary of her day.

The day begins

The day begins with Razia and other staff greeting parents and welcoming children at the school door. Information is exchanged and messages passed on as Razia moves easily between languages. When all the children are inside and the parents have departed she moves into the main room drawing children on to the carpet ready for the start of the day. Razia takes a seat at the back of the group gently encouraging children to sit down, stop fidgeting and pay attention to the teacher using English or Pahari. Her role is to keep the children focused and sitting down. At the end of registration there is a brief time for 'show and tell'. Razia encourages some of the bilingual children to move near to her so that she can translate what the children are saying.

The first session of the day is a speaking and listening activity involving a puppet. Razia sits between four bilingual children and when the puppet reaches them she repeats the instructions in Pahari and encourages the children to say their names and the name of their favourite ice cream. The next activity is drawing a picture of themselves and Razia sits with a mixed group of bilingual and monolingual speakers, including Pahari and Portuguese speaking children. She explains the activity again, moving between languages, helps the children to select different coloured pencils and responds to their questions.

Story time and singing

The teacher reads a story and Razia and the other bilingual teaching assistant sit behind the children and listen and encourage the children to pay attention and sit down. They translate individual words and ask questions to support understanding. During singing Razia sits on the floor near to some of the bilingual children and joins in the singing and models the actions.

Working with individuals and groups

During the 'Free choice' session Razia helps children to settle to their chosen activity, put on aprons, roll up sleeves etc. and then sits down to talk to one boy who has chosen to play with the 'play dough'. While he rolls and cuts out 'cakes' they have a conversation in Pahari and English about friendships and what he likes doing at school and home. Razia also spends time in the home corner joining in children's play and supporting children in learning the names of utensils in English.

Supervision

Razia supervises snack time with a group of children during which they talk about what they have been doing and then they go outside to play. After playtime the children sit on the carpet again for a music session before getting ready to go home.

Home time for the nursery children

Razia helps the nursery children to put on their coats, collect their bags and sit down. She translates the teacher's instruction to the children about bringing library books back the next day and repeats this to parents, in Pahari when appropriate.

Literacy support for reception children

Razia joins the teacher and class to listen to the end of the whole class teaching session. Then she takes a group of five children to an area outside the main classroom for a phonics session. The group includes Pahari and Portuguese speakers. The session focuses on revision and reinforcement of initial sounds, using cards with a picture on one side and a letter/sound on the other. There is also a 'sound machine' which the children post the cards into to support the focus on each sound. Razia encourages the children to tell her the names for the objects or animals in their home language as well as in English and she uses Pahari to support children's involvement in the activity.

Feedback and planning

At the end of the morning session Razia meets up with the teacher and reports back on what each child has been able to do in the phonics session and how they behaved. The teacher then goes over what the plans and objectives are for the afternoon session and Razia confirms which group she will work with on a writing activity.

More literacy activities

After lunch the children gather on the carpet while Razia checks through resources she will need. The teacher introduces the children to the nursery rhyme 'Sing a song of sixpence' which is projected onto the white board. During the whole class teaching session Razia translates the words and explanations for the Pahari speaking children who sit close to her, and tries to keep them focused. Group work involves writing their own lists of ingredients for 'Blackbird pie'. The children in Razia's group speak Pahari, Polish and Portuguese but the activity provides few opportunities to use the first languages.

After a snack Razia works with the same small group on a reading activity based on a book about the five senses. They look at the pictures and read the text together. Razia encourages the children to tell her the names for the parts of the body and the senses in their first languages and provides some artefacts for the children to touch, smell and taste.

The end of the day

During a brief 'free choice' period Razia sits and chats about home and school with one monolingual child while she does two jigsaws. At the end of the day Razia meets two new parents and talks with them in Pahari about the school and helps them to fill in forms.

Roles in mediating learning

Most teaching assistants working in the early years in school settings will recognise many of the aspects of Razia's day – working with groups and individual children, sitting on the carpet and listening to another adult, maintaining children's attention and focus, feeding back to the teacher about what children have done, brief planning meetings, preparation of resources, sitting with children at snack times, supervising outside play, greeting parents and bidding children goodbye. However, there are also distinct features of the role of a bilingual assistant that bilingual assistants will be able to identify. Using the first language to greet parents, listening to information parents need to convey and then passing it on to other adults and passing on information that the school wishes to convey to parents at the beginning and end of sessions. Meeting individual parents to tell them about the school and helping them to complete forms. This role of mediating communication between parents and the school and the school and parents is a key aspect of her day as Razia outlines:

> . . . if the parents have any questions for school, teachers have any messages for the parents . . . I'm here; my role is . . . partnership with the parents, the school . . . I'm a middle person, I'm a bridge for them too, and I also translate important letters for them in Urdu . . . And if the teachers have any messages, important messages though, which cannot wait until end of day, I sometimes phone the parents as well, so I get that time for that.

Using the first language to help children make sense of the activities they are expected to engage in is another key role, especially when children are new to English and the English school system. Modelling expected behaviours, whether it is sitting and listening to the teacher, sitting on the carpet, joining in actions, taking turns, sharing, answering questions, putting your hand up, while providing a commentary and encouragement in the first language enables children to learn the social expectations of the setting and the expectations of the teacher.

> If we look at the registration, very first session, that session was all about, you know, . . . talking to one another . . . encouraging children to listen to one another, taking turns, speaking and listening . . . and it gives the teacher time to see how the children are listening or not

listening or behaving on the carpet, or . . . are prepared to share their experiences with other children. So that gives the children some support and they feel it, you know, comfortable about sitting and listening to others . . .

. . . . and later on when we have lesson time on the carpet, that is, that is the time when the teacher can teach them, and my role is to make sure the children are sitting and listening. In my language, I try to sit nearby and . . . (a) keep them focused on the listening and speaking side of it and (b) make sure they are understanding. Sometimes I . . . try to translate it there and then, other times I just make notes. Sometimes in my mind or on a piece of paper, so I can take them away and go through that lesson briefly again so they understand.

Another aspect of the role involves helping children to make sense of the learning by encouraging children to draw on their experiences, making links with their home environment, using and thereby valuing their knowledge of another language and utilising the experiences the children are engaging in to introduce new words in English.

. . . all children . . . in our school are from different backgrounds, you know, and they bring, really they are very knowledgeable, and they bring lots to school. Culture wise they have been, like if I take an example of a little boy who's new at school, he, he knows a lot about science, you know, the science area, and in maths he's very good. He can, he talks about back home, his culture there, how they had lovely open spaces so, many days they can go out to play. And that sort of [thing], I think that, I see that as strength, you know. He had real opportunity to play with the real materials out there, even though maybe it's not sitting down [at a] desk writing or reading, but he really is very rich, very rich, knowledge wise. He knows, for example, where clay comes from, what is clay. The other day I was working with them and asking, and he knew what clay is, where it comes from, and what you can do with it. And other [things], like fruit being grown on trees, he'd seen them really growing, the oranges on the tree. And, you know, when I ask children where the oranges come from, these are lovely oranges, where do they come from? A lot of children, very able children say they've come from Tesco's and shops and all that. But he said no they grow on the trees. So that's one example. They do bring lots of strengths and lots of good experiences to the school . . .

Working with groups on literacy related activities with reception aged children, in this case phonics, reading and writing, is not uncommon although the degree of formality and adult direction may vary from setting to setting. In the examples from Razia's day she has little control over what she is required to do at these times as this is determined by the teacher's planning and as she says by the 'National Curriculum'. She has some control over the choice of resources, selecting a 'sound machine' to support the phonics activity and artefacts to support the reading activity on senses. In these two activities Razia encourages the children to draw on their first language knowledge and to name objects in their first language and English but she also tries to provide visual support and scaffolding for these children and those in the group whose languages she doesn't speak.

I always try to make [it] visual and practical as well as, you know, the reading, the writing . . . So before practical activities using the real materials, like this afternoon I used a book, and we looked, and we read the pictures, we tried to read the words, but I gave them a real apple to smell. We were reading a book about senses, five senses, so we used an apple for an example

. . . You always try to make it real for the children, for the children who do not speak my language or English, to give them access to the activity or to the curriculum.

At the same time Razia's comments suggest that she tries to utilise opportunities such as 'Free choice' to support children in developing their social and language skills through their interactions with her and other children and that she sees this as an important part of their learning and socialisation into the culture of the nursery.

> Then we have free choice, when the children can have fun, no, learn, again, we always have activities which are related to the curriculum . . . the day's topic, whatever we are learning on the day. So they can make choices, play with them, again sharing and interacting with one another, and listening to one another. I think the social skills come through that; they're very important for young children. Some children don't have that sort of opportunity outside school, you know, maybe they're from a one child family or they haven't got proper places [to play], so I think that is very important for them to have hands on activities and learn through that, learn through play. For example if they're working in water, they can listen and they can use all their senses in listening . . . And normally we have small groups . . . about four, no more than four children on one activity.

She also utilises 'supervision' times when she is with a group of mixed monolingual and bilingual children which provide opportunities for modelling behaviours and language to develop children's social skills and their speaking and listening skills as she describes in the following comment.

> After free choice we have a drink and snack. Again that's a very good way of sharing . . . behaviour learnt from one another, and that is our sort of normal, quiet, calm down time. We have a snack, a piece of fruit, and we do encourage all the children to take a piece of fruit and have something, have a taste. Even though they don't like it, we try to encourage them to taste. And they do, most of the children after a few weeks they'll start eating, and they need it because it's a long session, so they have a drink. After a drink we have recall time, where we reflect what the day was like. You know, what we did, what we enjoyed. So every child takes a turn speaking, and others are listening, I really like that activity. That gives them the opportunity to listen to other children and see what they've been doing, and maybe they'll join in next time . . .

Mediating learning

The various mediating roles that many bilingual teaching assistants carry out (see also Cable 2004, Cable et al. 2006) can be summarised as:

- Mediating communication between home and school and school and home.
- Supporting transitions for children new to school and to English.
- Providing access to the expectations and culture of the school including rules of behaviour.
- Facilitating access to English through use of the first language.
- Supporting and mediating children's learning.
- Utilising their cultural knowledge and understanding to draw on and validate children's knowledge and skills.

- Enabling teachers to deliver curriculum entitlement to all children through use of the first language.

In a small number of settings some assistants are also able to:

- Utilise cultural and linguistic knowledge to influence policy and practice.
- Support the ongoing development of children's first language skills and biliteracy.

However, all too often the knowledge and understanding that bilingual assistants bring to their role is not fully recognised and integrated into the policies and practices in settings or schools nor used to inform the experiences and activities children engage in. Bourne (2001) considers the constraints that primary practices and pedagogic approaches place on the contribution that bilingual assistants can make to children's learning and teaching. In particular she suggests that the discourses and routines teachers employ mitigate against assistants in utilising their languages to support learning (see also Martin-Jones and Saxena 2003). As we saw in the description of Razia's day, a key use of the mother tongue was for encouraging what were seen as acceptable behaviours in whole class sessions. The constraints placed on teachers, and therefore assistants, by the requirements and structures of curriculum guidance and the interpretation of these in practice (e.g. the structuring of a list writing activity based on a reading of 'Sing a song of sixpence' described above), can make it even harder to make learning meaningful for children new to English and new to settings or schools.

Bourne (2001) describes the role of bilingual staff in providing a link between home and school as a 'buffer'. As we see above, Razia sees her own role as more of a 'bridge'. Both images imply some sort of gap that has to be filled which raises serious questions about what happens when there are no bilingual staff to fulfill this role. What do bilingual children and their parents do? It also of course raises serious questions about an educational system that is not communicating with and, by implication, catering for or including all children and parents or meeting the requirements for inclusion in the *Statutory Framework for the Early Years Foundation Stage* (DfES 2007).

Conclusion

All the bilingual teaching assistants we have met have been enthusiastic and conscientious practitioners who believed in the children they taught and the settings they worked in. They had a key role in facilitating communication between home and school and school and home. They also saw their role as helping children to adapt to the requirements of the setting, to learn the rules and procedures. Whenever possible they tried to help settings, schools and teachers to understand more about the lives, experiences and communities of the children and parents they particularly worked with. However, they did not perceive their role as supporting the development of children's bilingualism or biliteracy although they saw a role for the use of the first language in supporting pupils' transition to English. We have moved a long way from the days when English was the only language spoken (or indeed allowed) in schools in England (and other parts of the UK), many early years settings and schools now employ bilingual staff, but we still have a way to go before they are enabled to use the full range of their knowledge and skills to support children's learning of their first as well as their second, or third, or fourth language. They need to become (and be enabled to become) members of the 'communities of practice' where they work in order to contribute to the development of shared understandings about the importance of bilingualism in the lives of children, their parents and society.

Acknowledgements

We would like to thank Razia for allowing us to talk to her and observe her at work. The funding for this project was provided by the OU Centre for Excellence in Teaching and Learning – Practice Based Professional Learning.

References

Baker, C. (2006) *Foundations of Bilingual Education and Bilingualism* (4th edn). Clevedon: Multilingual Matters Ltd.

Brooker, L. (2002) *Starting School – Young children learning cultures.* Buckingham: Open University Press.

Bourne, J. (2001) Doing what comes naturally: How the discourses and routines of teachers' practice constrain opportunities for bilingual support in UK primary schools, *Language and Education*, 15(4), 250–268.

Cable, C. (2004) 'I'm going to bring my sense of identity to this': the role and contribution of bilingual teaching assistants, *Westminster Studies in Education,* 27(2), 207–222.

Cable, C., Eyres, I. and Collins, J. (2006) Bilingualism and inclusion: more than just rhetoric?, *Support for Learning* 21(3), 129–134.

Cohen, L. Manion, L. and Morrison, K. (2000) *Research Methods in Education* (5th edn). London: RoutledgeFalmer.

Cummins, J. (2000) *Language, Power and Pedagogy: Bilingual Children in the Crossfire.* Clevedon: Multilingual Matters.

Cummins, J. (2001) *Negotiating Identities: Education for Empowerment in a Diverse Society.* Los Angeles: California Association for Bilingual Education.

Department for Children, Schools and Families (DCSF) (2007) *Supporting Children Learning English as an Additional Language. Guidance for practitioners in the Early Years Foundation Stage.* DCSF publications.

Department for Education and Skills (DES) (2003) *Every Child Matters.* Nottingham: DfES.

Department for Education and Skills (DfES) (2007) *Statutory Framework for the Early Years Foundation Stage.* Nottingham: DfES.

Department of Education and Science (1985) *Education for All, The Swann Report.* London: HMSO.

Drury, R. (2007) *Young Bilingual Learners at Home and School: Researching multilingual voices*. Stoke-on-Trent: Trentham Books.

Gonzales, N., Moll, L., Floyd Tenery, M., Rivera, A., Rendón, P., Gonzales, R. and Amanti, C. Funds of knowledge for teaching in Latino households, in Hall, K., Murphy, P. and Soler, J. (2008) (eds) *Pedagogy and Practice Cultures and Identities*. London: Sage/The Open University.

Harris, R. (1997) Romantic Bilingualism: time for a change?, in Leung, C. and Cable, C. (eds) *English as an Additional Language: Changing Perspectives*. Watford: NALDIC.

Lave, J. and Wenger, E. (1991) *Situated Learning: Legitimate Peripheral Participation*. Cambridge: Cambridge University Press.

Martin-Jones, M. and Saxena, M. (2003) Bilingual resources and 'Funds of Knowledge' for teaching and learning in multi-ethnic classrooms in Britain, in A. Creese and P. Martin (eds) *Multilingual Classroom Ecologies*. Clevedon: Multilingual Matters.

Moll, L. C., Amanti, C., Neff, D. and Gonzalez, N. (1992) Funds of Knowledge for Teaching: Using a qualitative approach to connect homes and classrooms, *Theory into Practice*, 31(2), 132–141.

Wenger, E. (1998) *Communities of Practice; Learning, Meaning and Identity*. Cambridge: Cambridge University Press.

Chapter 3

Developing professionalism in the early years
From policy to practice

Sue Owen and Gill Haynes

Sue Owen and Gill Haynes look briefly at the policy context of early years services over the past ten years before concentrating on the more recent policy and strategy developments linked to the *Every Child Matters* agenda (DfES 2003). This general survey then leads into a more specific focus on the policy related to workforce development in England as the context for the latest discussions of the development of professionalism in the early years workforce.

Background to early years services

Early years services in the UK have, until recently, lacked any form of national financial support or policy direction. Until 1996 when the Conservative Government introduced a voucher scheme to pay for part-time nursery education places for 4-year-olds, the extent of provision was determined by the commitment of individual local authorities or the purchasing power of parents. This led to patchy provision in which some areas had maintained neither nursery education nor any social services day nurseries at all, while others, such as Manchester, had a strong tradition of both. Equally, voluntary sector provision was dependent on the willingness of local councils to subsidise its costs and support training and advisory services for its staff. Both the voluntary sector and the growing full-time day care sector in child-minding and private day nurseries were dependent on demand and the ability of parents to pay. This structural diversity was always reflected in the profile of the various workforces, with the statutory services employing 'professional' teachers and nursery nurses (even if they were unequal in status) and the voluntary and independent sector developing their own training and qualifications to meet the needs and characteristics of their own practitioners.

When the National Childcare Strategy was brought in by the Labour Government in 1997–8, early years services gradually came under the jurisdiction of local education authorities and, at national level, the Department for Education (now the Department for Children, Schools and Families, DCSF) rather than their traditional home in health and social care (Jamieson and Owen 2000; Randall and Fisher 2001). This was a popular move with national early years' organisations which had fought for young children's services to be integrated under one department and for children's learning to be seen as the central element of universal services. The widespread adoption of the generic term 'early years services' was brought about by this long-standing campaign to eliminate the historic 'care/education'. Even though we have different professional profiles for practitioners it is still, it is argued, impossible to educate without caring, or care without promoting children's learning.

Early years services are also essential for working parents and, since 1997, children's day care has become a significant element in government economic policies designed to reduce social exclusion and child poverty. The National Childcare Strategy was based on extending free part-time nursery education to all 4-year-old and then 3-year-old children whose parents wanted to use it, but full day care is still the responsibility of parents. Although the government has put in place measures to help extend availability, most notably a system of tax credits which can be accessed by working parents using regulated day care, individual parents still have to pay for their own day care (Jamieson and Owen 2000; Randall and Fisher 2001).

The every child matters agenda

> ... we are proposing here a range of measures to reform and improve children's care – crucially, for the first time ever requiring local authorities to bring together in one place under one person services for children, and at the same time suggesting real changes in the way those we ask to do this work carry out their tasks on our and our children's behalf.
>
> (From the Prime Minister's Foreword to the Green Paper:
> *Every Child Matters*, HM Treasury 2003:1)

The Green Paper *Every Child Matters* was launched on 8 September 2003 by the Chief Secretary to the Treasury, thus showing that the Treasury as well as the service ministries of Education and Health, was behind this radical restructuring of services for children. The Foreword by the Prime Minister hinted at one of the programme's central features, the creation of structures which would ensure service integration; and it is this which is having one of the most transformative effects on the concept of professionalism for the workforce.

Although arising specifically from the case of an abused child (Victoria Climbié) *Every Child Matters* aims to do more than make recommendations to local authorities about how to improve their child protection systems. Instead it was designed to reform the entire system of children's services in England, placing them within an ethos based on children's rights and entitlements and on positive outcomes for children. These are to be planned and delivered by local authorities according to their knowledge of the needs in their areas, but assessed and inspected nationally through performance indicators. Although these outcomes are for all children, the focus of the strategy is very firmly on children who are at risk, and the contributing policies and guidance are designed to ensure that local authorities narrow the gap between such children and those who traditionally do well.

Every Child Matters: Next Steps (DfES 2004a) was published six months after the Green Paper and outlined the government's response to the consultation's findings. The wider strategy which it outlined included some key areas relating to early years services and it was supported by the 10 Year Childcare Strategy which was published six months later. The government stressed the important role which early years services have to play in *Every Child Matters* and that they should be a priority area within local authorities' Children and Young People's Plans. In this way the government's existing programme of expansion of early years services was brought into the fold of *Every Child Matters* and a new project was announced to create Sure Start Children's Centres in the most disadvantaged areas, combining health, family and parenting support and information services with integrated childcare and education for children from birth onwards. Doing well at school, avoiding social exclusion and contributing to the economy and society are all recognised here as being underpinned by the work done in a child's earliest years.

The final document, *Every Child Matters: Change for Children* (DfES 2004b), was published on 1 December 2004. It introduced the legislative changes in the Children Act 2004, and emphasised that the whole programme of reform was designed 'to shift the focus of services from dealing with the consequences of difficulties in children's lives to preventing things from going wrong in the first place' (DfES 2004b: 2). This transformation is to be effected by local authorities working in partnership with their communities and supported by the government through a programme of change management which includes Local Area Agreements negotiated between central and local government in order to 'achieve a balance between national and local priorities' (DfES 2004b: 22).

A policy 'umbrella' such as *Every Child Matters* will inevitably have something to say about the workforce which has to implement it, especially when, as this one does, it attempts to integrate a range of services which have arisen in very different circumstances and to meet different needs. Are the existing workforces trained and qualified in the skills and knowledge which they need to do this different task? Do they understand how to work effectively with the other professions they are expected to work alongside? Is there a direct relationship between training and education processes and the desired outcomes for children? Is there a core of 'professional' competence (i.e. knowledge twinned with skills) which an early years worker needs, and at what level should that be pitched?

Workforce reform has been an important element in the government's approach to services for young children since 1997. *Next Steps* announced a consultation document on a pay and workforce strategy which would begin to rationalise the existing, complicated situation of the children's workforce as a whole (DfES 2004a). The 'pay' element of the strategy was later dropped, although it was still being referred to in the 10 Years Strategy document published in December 2004. The document did, however, place a great deal of emphasis on the early years workforce as being key to the *Every Child Matters* reforms and as being particularly in need of change.

Interestingly, a very similar debate is taking place in the United States where the policy 'umbrella' of the *Good Start, Grow Smart* initiative in 2002 has instituted just such a review:

> There is increased public attention to the professional development of the early childhood workforce given the renewed policy focus on the early childhood years as laying the ground-work for school readiness and the specific emphasis in the Good Start, Grow Smart initiative on professional development of the early childhood workforce as a factor that can contribute to early learning and school readiness.

> (Zaslow and Martinez-Beck 2006: 9)

The 10 Year Childcare Strategy and its underpinning legislation, The Childcare Act 2006, is the key early years vehicle for taking forward *Every Child Matters*. It was published in December 2004 and its full title, *Choice for Parents: the Best Start for Children, a Ten Year Strategy for Childcare* (HM Treasury et al. 2004) clearly indicates the focus of the strategy which is on moving children out of poverty via the workforce participation of their parents. Having said this, the strategy also places an emphasis on the needs of vulnerable children, whether or not their parents are in the workforce, and on the needs of children from groups who have traditionally not fully benefited from early years services, such as disabled children and children from black and other minority ethnic groups. In essence, the 10 year childcare strategy is designed to rationalise, redesign and rebadge the existing early years initiatives so that they fit within the *Every Child Matters* framework.

The Childcare Act 2006 underpins the Strategy by giving certain duties to local authorities, including a duty to make sure that there is 'sufficient' childcare for children up to the September after they are 14 (18 for disabled children) which will be fulfilled if the local childcare market allows parents to make a choice about working. However, there is an emphasis on the needs of parents for whom the market is seen not to have provided for in the past: lower-income families and families with disabled children. The government stressed that making these responsibilities statutory would enshrine them within local authority performance assessment systems and ensure that they were taken seriously (McAuliffe, Linsey and Fowler 2006).

The Strategy does not just deal with expansion of places, but also with quality, and here there is to be a three-pronged approach. There will be the new single-quality framework for all children from birth: the Early Years Foundation Stage (DfES 2007), which will guide the approaches and activities within settings; the independent registration and inspection framework of Ofsted (Ofsted 2007); and, most importantly for this discussion, workforce reform designed to provide practitioners who are better trained and qualified to support young children and their families in reaching the desired outcomes of the policy.

A central aspect of the Strategy is that all full-day care settings will be 'professionally' led, i.e. by a graduate professional (DfES 2005) and this has been contentious for an early years workforce which, as we have seen above, is slowly being forged out of a very diverse range of practitioners with varied training, qualifications, service histories and career pathways. Some have argued, for example, that we need to maintain a non-graduate route into the profession for less academic workers who have strong skills in the care and education of young children and, moreover, that not all staff want to go on to obtain a degree. Others feel very strongly that higher education should be required for anyone who is charged with the learning of young children because this is such an important phase of education that requirements for it should be as high, if not higher, than for teachers of other phases.

It is the specific policy focus on the professionalisation of this workforce which we will turn to now.

Background to workforce reform

> With the emphasis firmly on professionalism in the workforce, it's good to see that opportunities for training are growing.
>
> (*Nursery World*, Summer 2007: 3)

Nursery World's annual training supplement, 'Training Today', captures the extent to which policy initiatives in the early years have transformed training and qualifications since the National Council for Vocational Qualifications (NCVQ) was set up in 1986 to develop a national system of vocational awards for both young people and adults. The supplement details the range of opportunities now available for people working in early years and integrated childcare settings, from new school-based awards, to full-time diploma and degree courses, sector-endorsed foundation degrees and accredited units to support the delivery of the Early Years Foundation Stage.

However, although the supplement tracks recent developments in the funding and availability of training and qualifications, it masks some crucial issues in the long-standing debate about what professionalism in the early years workforce really means, as debated in this book. Nor does it convey the scale of the task facing governments if the goal of 'creating a world class workforce' for the early years is to be realised in our lifetime (HM Treasury et al. 2004).

Although early years services lacked significant national financial support or policy direction before 1996, the importance of workforce development opportunities for practitioners had not been completely ignored. In 1990, the Rumbold Committee had noted:

> We welcome the work of NCVQ towards establishing agreed standards for childcare workers, including those in education settings. We believe that, given adequate resourcing, it could bring about significant rationalization of patterns of training. It should also improve the status of early years workers through recognition of the complex range and high level of the skills involved and by opening up prospects for further training.
>
> (DES 1990: 24)

But not everybody agreed that a 'complex range and high level of ... skills' were involved in caring for children and, at the beginning of the 1990s, workforce development barely figured as a priority on any political agenda. As Hevey and Curtis pointed out:

> One is forced to conclude that this lack of concern over training and qualifications for what are in reality highly responsible roles is underpinned by something more fundamental than free market philosophy. Rather it reflects confused and outmoded public attitudes that commonly

regard the care of young children as an extension of the mothering role and assume it all comes naturally to women. Such attitudes in turn reinforce the low status of early years work, helping to keep pay low and turnover high.

(Hevey and Curtis 1996: 213)

Although the 1989 Children Act had set out to improve quality in early years and childcare settings, its new minimum standards for training and qualifications were very low. At the time, the main providers of childcare for all age groups were registered childminders, where 'the threshold of entry' did not include any mandatory training. However, notwithstanding the lack of national interest, the Early Childhood Unit at the National Children's Bureau developed the highly influential concept of a 'climbing frame' of childcare qualifications, drawing on work that had taken place in 1991 as part of a project to develop national occupational standards for work with young children and their families (Hevey and Curtis 1996).

As a result of this work, National Vocational Qualifications (NVQs) in Childcare and Education at Levels 2 and 3 were launched in 1992. However, three years later, only 856 candidates had achieved Level 2; and 243 Level 3 (Hevey and Curtis 1996). Fifteen years on, over 83,000 NVQ certificates in Early Years and Childcare had been awarded (Local Government Analysis and Research 2007), together with tens of thousands of other related awards and qualifications.

This exponential growth in the availability and uptake of early years qualifications was the result of a number of factors, including demographic changes; the growing UK evidence base, which for the first time firmly linked improved outcomes for children to the higher qualification levels of people who work with them; and effective lobbying by the early years sector. Most important, however, was the incremental realisation by government that the wide spectrum of its policy goals could only be achieved through investment in raising the qualifications of the early years workforce.

The impact of demography

The National Childcare Strategy (DfEE 1998) was presented as a child-centred, educational initiative, to address the failure of the Conservative Government to implement its plans for universal nursery education. However, the strategy also reflected the changing needs of working families and the changing involvement of women with children under 5 in the workplace. In the early 1970s, less that a third of mothers with children under 5 were in paid work. By the late 1990s, this had doubled to nearly 60 per cent (Labour Market Trends 2002).

Sustained recruitment to the workforce to cater for working families was therefore a priority and it was estimated that 90,000 new recruits would be needed to deliver the strategy. But the economic changes of the 1980s, together with women's own rising educational achievements and improvements in service-sector job opportunities meant that recruitment to a career with traditionally low pay, poor training opportunities and no progression routes had very limited appeal (Cameron 2004). As a result, government became much more open to the proposition that more emphasis should be placed on developing the workforce and that new career routes should be opened up to recruit the workforce that was needed to achieve their policy goals.

Up to this date, there had been no industry training organisation for Early Years. With backing from the Department for Education and Employment, in November 1998, the first UK-wide Early Years National Training Organisation was launched to drive through these early steps to developing the workforce. These included new nationally accredited awards to meet the specific needs of parts of the sector, the development of Level 4 S/NVQs and the introduction of sector-endorsed early years foundation degrees.

The creation of the NTO was an important step because, although there had been a growing emphasis on 'quality' as a key aspiration of the government's national childcare strategy, there was very little national data about training and qualification levels to act as a lever for change. One of the NTO's first tasks was to deliver the first England-wide Children's Workforce Survey in 1998, which revealed the low levels of qualifications and training opportunities throughout the sector. However, when the national standards for childminding and day care were revised to coincide with the transfer of regulation from local authorities to Ofsted in September 2001, training and qualifications were still set at minimum levels.

This failure to use regulation as a lever to raise standards and professionalise the workforce characterised the government's approach to workforce reform in the early years for the whole of the last decade, in marked contrast to occupational models in countries like New Zealand and Denmark. Both these countries employ strategies which combine strong regulatory frameworks with public funding of *supply*, with New Zealand (in 2002) opting for a single three-year early years qualification for those working with children aged 0 to 6; and Denmark promoting a unified structure for all care professions (the pedagogue) via a single full-time three-and-a-half-year degree level course, with regulation which requires that all day care facilities have fully qualified managers and deputies.

The NTO was closed down in March 2002 as part of the government's strategy to develop a network of strategic Sector Skills Councils (SSCs). This coincided with a period of intense change linked to the 2002 Comprehensive Spending Review. The various strands of the national childcare strategy were gradually being drawn together into a programme of Children's Centres, initially focused on the most disadvantaged areas. At the same time, evidence from the Effective Provision of Pre-school Education (EPPE) project was beginning to feed through, including the finding that:

> Settings which have staff with higher qualifications, especially with good proportion of trained teachers on the staff, show higher quality and their children make more progress.
>
> (Sylva et al. 2004: 56)

However, the vacuum which had been created through the loss of the Early Years NTO meant that progress towards developing a coherent occupational model to address the fragmentation in the sector stalled. When progress resumed, it was in the context of a much broader strategy developed in response to Lord Lamming's report into the death of Victoria Climbié. From this point, developing professionalism in the early years became part of the much wider agenda of workforce reform for the *whole* of the children's workforce (DfES 2003).

Reforming the children's workforce

Building on ideas outlined in the Green Paper (DfES 2003) and the subsequent Ten Year Childcare Strategy (HM Treasury et al. 2004), in April 2005 the government consulted on a specific Children's Workforce Strategy to improve the skills of the workforce. At the same time, the Children's Workforce Development Council (CWDC) for England was set up to drive through the reforms. However, although the occupational groups represented by the CWDC (its 'footprint') includes all those practitioners formerly represented by the Early Years NTO, significant parts of the early years and children's workforce – teachers, teaching assistants, and play workers – were included in the footprint of other Sector Skills Councils (SSCs). To overcome these structural problems, government also set up a Children's Workforce Network (CWN) as a forum for joint working between the various sector skills councils.

The government's response to the consultation on the Children's Workforce Strategy was finally published in February 2006 (DfES 2006a). It confirmed their goal to have an 'integrated qualifications framework' in place by 2010 which would 'help with recruitment, retention and remodelling the workforce by supporting improved career pathways across [the sector] and better progression opportunities' (DfES 2006a: 22). However, it rejected the idea of a generic graduate worker for the children's workforce, based on the pedagogic approach (Boddy et al. 2005). Instead, it prioritised 'establishing a more professional workforce in the early years' in order to raise the status of working with pre-school children. Specifically, it charged the CWDC to develop a new Early Years Professional (EYP) role with graduate status for those leading practice in children's centres and full-day care settings; and allocated £250m over two years to a Transformation Fund to finance the EYP programme and to improve the qualification levels of the workforce as a whole. Arguably, an unintended consequence of these developments has been to marginalise both the long-established professional groups like nursery nurses and more recent roles and training pathways, such as Higher Level Teaching Assistants (HLTAs) and Senior Practitioners.

During 2006, the new EYP Status and training pathways were defined and developed and the first awards were made in early 2007. At the same time, work on developing an Integrated Qualifications Framework (IQF) forged ahead, based on a unit and credit framework, the Qualifications and Credit Framework (QCF), devised by the Qualifications and Curriculum Authority (QCA) in partnership with the regulatory authorities for Wales and Northern Ireland. The aim of this aspect of reform is to develop a simple and effective structure that allows for the accumulation and transfer of credit achievement over time, to meet the needs of individual learners and employers.

In early 2007, the CWDC also issued advice to government about the strategies and targets needed to raise the qualification levels in the early years workforce as a whole. It recommended that the early years career pathway should be built on Level 6 (the Early Years Professional) and Level 3; that the minimum qualification for the early years workforce should be Level 3; and that at least 70 per cent of the workforce should hold a relevant Level 3 qualification by 2010. It also recommended that the Transformation Fund should continue, and that regulation on workforce standards should be more robust.

Summary

Although considerable progress has been made since the Workforce Strategy response was published in 2006, the most recent Workforce Survey showed the scale of the task ahead. Only 4 per cent of early years practitioners not in schools held a qualification at Level 4 or above; and less than 60 per cent held a Level 3 qualification (DfES 2006b). Pay across the sector remains low and, although the take-up of the Early Years Professional route has proved popular (with the 1000th candidate awarded the new status in October 2007), there are concerns about how Early Years Professionals in Children's Centres will be able to achieve parity of pay and conditions with qualified teachers in schools. The early versions of the Every Child Matters workforce reform agenda talked of a strategy to:

> improve the skills and effectiveness of the children's workforce developed in partnership with local employers and staff . . . with the aim of moving towards a framework that fairly rewards skills and responsibilities.
>
> (DfES 2003:12)

However, as noted above, references to pay and rewards are absent in later documents, and it appears that government is moving away from a commitment to review pay, conditions and rewards, at least in the short term.

Recent government changes have created two new departments to focus on improving outcomes for children, the Department for Children, Schools and Families (DCSF) and the Department for Innovation, Universities and Skills (DIUS); and from April 2008, the Children's Workforce Development Council (CWDC) will become an Executive Non-Departmental Public Body (ENDPB). Working with local authorities and its stakeholders in the statutory, private and voluntary sector, it is to these bodies that the sector will now look, for delivering the next steps in professionalising the early years workforce.

References

Boddy, J., Cameron, C., Moss, P., Mooney, A., Petrie, P. and Statham, J. (2005) *Introducing Pedagogy into the Children's Workforce: Children's Workforce Strategy: A Response to the Consultation Document*. London: TCRU.

Cameron, C. (2004) *Building an Integrated Workforce for a Long-Term Vision of Universal Early Education and Care*. London: Daycare Trust.

Department for Education and Employment (1998) *Meeting the Childcare Challenge: A Framework and Consultation Document*. London: HMSO.

Department for Education and Skills (2003) *Every Child Matters – Summary*. London: DfES.

Department for Education and Skills (2004a) *Every Child Matters: Next Steps*. London: DfES. (www.everychildmatters.gov.uk – accessed 10/10/2005).

Department for Education and Skills (2004b) *Every Child Matters: Change for Children*. London: DfES. (www.everychildmatters.gov.uk – accessed 10/10/2005).

Department for Education and Skills (2005) *Children's Workforce Strategy, Consultation Paper*. London: DfES.

Department for Education and Skills (2006a) *Children's Workforce Strategy: Building a World-Class Workforce for Children, Young People and Families*. London: DfES.

Department for Education and Skills (2006b) *The 2005 Childcare and Early Years Providers Surveys Brief N: RB760–764*. London: DfES.

Department for Education and Skills (2007) *The Early Years Foundation Stage: Setting the Standards for Learning, Development and Care for Children from Birth to Five*. London: HMSO.

Department of Education and Science (1990) *Starting with Quality: Report of the Committee of Inquiry into the Educational Experiences Offered to Three-and-Four-Year-Olds* (the Rumbold report). London: HMSO.

Hevey, D. and Curtis, A. (1996) 'Training to work in the early years'. In G. Pugh (ed.), *Contemporary Issues in the Early Years* (2nd edn). London: Paul Chapman.

HM Treasury (2003) *Every Child Matters* (Cm 5860). London: TSO.

HM Treasury, DfES, DWP, DTI (2004) *Choice for Parents: The Best Start for Children* (Ten Year Strategy for Childcare). London: HMT, DfES, DWP and DTI.

Jamieson, A. and Owen, S. (2000) *Ambition for Change: Partnerships, Children and Work*. London: National Children's Bureau.

Labour Market Trends (2002) *Labour Market and Family Status of Women; United Kingdom, Autumn, 2001*. London: ONS.

Local Government Analysis and Research (2007) *Quarterly Monitoring of Care Sector NVQs (England) Report for Second Quarter 2006*. London: LGA.

McAuliffe, A., Linsey, A., and Fowler, J. (2006) *Childcare Act 2006: The Essential Guide*. London: National Children's Bureau.

Nursery World (2007) 'Training today' (Summer 2007).

Ofsted (2007) *Framework For the Regulation of Childminding and Day Care*. London: Ofsted.

Randall, V. and Fisher, K. (2001) 'Child day care provision: explaining local variation', *Children and Society, 15(3)*, 170–80.

Sylva, K., Melhuish, E., Sammons, P., Siraj-Blatchford, I., and Taggart, B. (2004) *The Effective Provision of Pre-School Education (EPPE) Project: Final report*. London: Institute of Education.

Zaslow, M. and Martinez-Beck, I. (2006) *Critical Issues in Early Childhood Professional Development*. Baltimore: Paul Brookes Publishing.

Chapter 4

Working in teams in early years settings

Mary Read and Mary Rees

Mary Read and Mary Rees provide theoretical and practical insights for early years practitioners into ways of working together. They highlight the importance of communication in forging and maintaining professional relationships and consider how to develop and manage strategies for dealing with conflict within teams. They conclude by discussing the personal and professional development of individual team members and pose helpful questions for leaders and managers of teams.

In all the many and varied early years settings there is perhaps one common charac-teristic: a number of adults work together to meet the needs of children. The likelihood of excellent early childhood provision is enhanced by the team's ability to work collaboratively, and being a member of an effective team is a source of satisfaction and support for many early years workers. The variable nature of settings and the range of people involved mean there is no guaranteed recipe for team success. An effective group of early years practitioners emerges as the result of an investment of time and energy by all concerned. If an effective team is valued as an essential part of quality early years provision, it is necessary to identify how this can be achieved. In many instances too little attention or status is given to either the skills of teamwork or to the process of working collaboratively. This chapter addresses these important areas. It encourages consideration of the role and skills of the early years practitioner and questions how these contribute to the efficiency of the whole team. It places the skills of teamwork in a leadership context, seeking to elevate the status of teamwork beyond a 'muddling through together' to a planned, professional activity.

In any early years setting there is probably a core team of adults who work together on an ongoing daily basis consisting of staff and volunteers, all with different roles and expertise. In a large organisation, early years practitioners may work in a small core team which is only part of the whole. In either case the core team may form part of a wider team encompassing, for example, speech and language therapists, physio-therapists or professionals from social services. In reading this chapter it may be helpful to identify specific teams in individual contexts and reflect on current practice and professional development.

The process of working collaboratively within early years settings calls for a new style of leadership not *of* but *within* teams. The ever-changing and evolving nature of early years settings means that practitioners can bring much more to a setting than simple compliance with professional practice guidelines. The demand for new collaborations for children and families is proliferating external interactions and influences for early years teams. This means that team structures and practitioners themselves have become more flexible and adaptive by nature.

So how can effective teamwork be developed? A number of features characterise successful teams.

Finding time for inter-professional dialogue

Finding time

Young children make continuous, challenging demands on the adults who work with them. Finding time to focus on staff needs can be difficult as there is a real danger of responding to children's immediate needs to the exclusion of all else. Looking at the daily or weekly programme to identify potential time availability for staff to meet is a vital step in team development. Finding an appropriate time which includes part-time and hourly paid staff can be problematic, therefore solutions have to be found through open discussion and negotiation. Perhaps a monthly rota of short meetings is more viable than a weekly set time.

The Cherry Tree case study (Figure 4.1) shows how one large centre faced the important issue of planning for children with special needs. The willingness to confront these problems and seek a workable situation provides a starting point for team commitment. Whalley (in Pugh 1996) documents an interesting approach to finding quality meeting time at Pen Green Centre for Under Fives and Families by freeing up Wednesday afternoons. Failure to secure an appropriate meeting programme involving

Wk beg 3rd Oct			
Activity	Focus	Specific children	Comments
Wet sand	tracing number for week	Kirsty – K Alan – say name as he traces	
Water	vocab: full empty	Gary – talk to other children	
Story	remember and repeat sequence	all	

Figure 4.1 Case study

everyone may lead to individuals feeling marginalised and devalued. The potential contribution of some team members is lost and the cohesion of the team is damaged as a result.

Cherry Tree is a large children's centre including several children with special educational needs. The specific needs of the children mean that the team felt it was important that all staff were familiar with the different programmes and targets necessary for their development. Many of the staff were paid on an hourly basis so meeting time was precious. This is how planning was coordinated.

- Monthly one-hour meeting for all staff defining main activities. All staff to attend, either paid or time off in lieu.
- Booklet for each session where all significant events are noted.
- Children's records open to all staff.
- Assessment meetings to discuss individual children weekly on a rota basis. Minutes written up and available for staff who cannot attend.

Planning recorded (see below) so that all staff are familiar with learning focus of activities.

Using time effectively

Valuable staff time needs to be used effectively. This is easy to say but rather more difficult to establish and maintain. A possible starting point is to keep a brief log of meetings taking place over a week or two (Figure 4.2). The resulting information can then be shared within the team or raised with the manager. A log of this type can show whether the meeting time is well used or that there are areas for significant improvement. Meeting B could be probed further – was the manager meeting with staff when the decision had in fact already been taken? If so, why? Could the relevant information

Meeting and purpose	No. of people	Contribution	Achievement	Comments
A. Weekly planning to establish outline of week's activities 1 hour	Total 8 4 teachers and 4TAs (Teaching assistants)	Teachers 85% TAs 15% Miss X and Mrs Y (both TAs) no contribution	Plan agreed mainly repeat of previous week 2 new activities	Lacked focus; some useful evaluation; dominated by teachers
B. Purchasing decision meeting – order for outdoor play equipment 1 hour	10 manager + full-time and part-time staff	Manager – majority others – questions	Order not agreed	Staff insufficient info. to reach decision. Lots of disagreement, staff raising alternatives – soft play, books etc.

Figure 4.2 Meeting log

have been provided as a written proposal? How was the original decision to purchase outdoor play equipment reached?

The use of logs to investigate the efficiency of meetings has potential to be extended by two or more people comparing perspectives. Figure 4.3 shows the manager's view of meeting B. Manager and staff were at cross-purposes, everyone was dissatisfied and the opportunity for agreement was lost. In this case the simple log would enable the team to focus on the real issues standing in the way of a team decision making approach, and make sensible changes rather than continue to set up frustrating experiences.

Meeting and purpose	No. of people	Contribution	Achievement	Comments
Purchasing decision meeting – order for outdoor play equipment identified by OFSTED as priority for upgrading 1 hour	10 manager + full time and part time staff	Little contribution from staff	Order not agreed	Staff reluctant to use outdoor play area – especially through winter. Suggesting alternatives based on personal preference.

Figure 4.3 Meeting log – manager's perspective

The log format can be adapted in a number of ways to access the desired information: the length of meetings; the cost (number of people × number of hours × hourly rate of pay) and the contribution of individual or particular categories of staff. The decision to investigate meeting efficiency through logs or other methods needs to be openly shared with all team members and the outcomes discussed. This ensures real use of the material and pre-empts any sense of seeking someone to blame.

Setting the agenda

A clear agenda is a key tool in ensuring that meeting time is well used. The list of items commonly provided has limited value. It gives only the area of discussion and provides no clue about key questions or issues, parameters for the discussion or desired outcomes. Meetings, particularly those where crucial decisions are necessary, have greater potential for success if everyone attending has the opportunity to consider the critical issues beforehand. Figure 4.4 illustrates an agenda which has this purpose. It allows participants to think about the items and be ready to offer a view. A meeting which is structured in this way helps to avoid the pitfalls of participants changing their mind afterwards or feeling that they have been pressured into a course of action without time for thought. Ideally, all team members should leave a meeting feeling satisfied with the decision making process, even if they have had to make some personal compromises.

The agenda should also give the timing for the meeting, perhaps for the individual items, but essentially for the start and finish. The quality of contributions deteriorates rapidly if staff are worrying about collecting children from the child minder or wondering how much longer they will have to sit there.

Staff meeting agenda
3.30   Tea available
3.45–5.00   Meeting in large staffroom
Minutes   Susan's turn

1. Update on calendar.
2. Use of equipment fund
   £500 available. Various possibilities
   (a) outdoor equipment (catalogue marked with possibilities on staffroom noticeboard – please
       look) Storage is an issue;
   (b) replacement sand/water equipment for Red Room;
   (c) new book stock;
   (d) other suggestions.
   NB: money has to be spent by end of this month so decision required at meeting.
3. Open Day
   Date? Needs to be Tuesday or Thursday in February. Please come with suggestions.
   Particular idea/events to be included? Foyer display – suggestions?
4. AOD
   Unless just brief announcement please notify to manager in advance.

Figure 4.4 Agenda

Minutes of meetings can be very useful in recording decisions made and action agreed, although it should not be assumed that they are always necessary. It is very rarely useful to record the detail of discussion, particularly as this is a time consuming and tedious task. A rotating responsibility with a standard proforma provided can be a simple solution. The proforma need be nothing more than a version of the agenda with a column for decisions, dates and responsibilities.

Forging and maintaining professional relationships

Building the team

Successful teamwork requires a group of individuals to share the daily working experience in a positive and proactive manner. Over time the members of a team develop ways of working with each other, responding to the needs and idiosyncrasies of colleagues, recognising strengths and weaknesses, and valuing the complementary contributions that each makes to the team effort. Handy (1990, p. 128) summarises teams as a:

> collection of individuals gathered together because their talents are needed to perform a task or to solve a problem. If the team wins, all those in it win. If the team loses they all lose. There is a common purpose, and the sense of camaraderie that should go with a common purpose.

The challenge for the team is to have a shared understanding of the common purpose so that team members can act confidently and with a clear understanding of their individual role. Handy (1990) also puts forward an analysis of the stages of team growth, using the headings 'forming, storming, norming and performing'. He suggests that all teams have a period in which they are finding their own identity – the forming stage. Then comes a period of challenge (storming) when individuals begin to assert themselves, moving into the norming phase as they settle to new ways of working. The final phase comes when the team is mature and able to perform at high levels of efficiency. Part of this process in Handy's view is about the establishing of the trust which has to build over time to allow a team to work efficiently.

Trust and shared understanding cannot be merely agreed upon in a meeting or laid down in a set of policies. They grow through the daily occurrences in the workplace, the discussion between individuals and the decisions that are made. Teams that have been working together over time develop their own forms of verbal short-hand to share ideas and suggestions, and are able to ground their discussion in an understanding formed through day-to-day communication and awareness of each other's views. This can be an unnerving experience for a new team member who may feel shut out or de-skilled by exchanges which he or she cannot follow. For example, in planning an event an established team draws upon the knowledge and experience of all the previous events of this type; making tacit assumptions and using abbreviated references to occasions, incidents, successes and disasters. Individuals who have collaborated with one another in an ongoing situation are able to rely upon each other's skills, making allowances for personal preference or dislike for particular tasks.

Positive communication

As the days and weeks pass the early years team members will communicate with each other on a myriad of subjects and with thousands of interactions. The key feature for success is the quality of this communication, rather than the quantity. The notion of positive communication is a helpful one in that it contains several strands. Being positive, in the sense of ensuring our communication includes plenty of praise and affirmation, is an important aspect of working successfully with others. It is important to reflect honestly and ask questions such as . . . how often do I communicate praise to my colleagues? . . . to a volunteer or part time worker? . . . to a parent? . . . to my boss? The expectation that the manager will praise the subordinates sometimes leads to disappointment and frustration if workers feel their manager does not give sufficient recognition to their efforts. The successful team member looks for opportunities to communicate positively with support, praise and even delight throughout the daily interaction with colleagues. Honest and sincere positive feedback oils the wheels of the daily task and enables all team members to benefit from both giving and receiving affirmation. The valuing of the contribution is key to team success.

Another strand of positive communication is that of the locking together of team thinking. To operate effectively the various individuals need to mesh ideas and actions. Where two or more colleagues are working together there should be clear communication with specific instructions as necessary. This requires time for individuals to check their understanding with one another and perhaps even to have written clarification. The key issue is that team members need to understand the importance of appropriate communication and the need for others to question and seek clarification. A team which is able to communicate openly and clearly avoids wasting time on frustration and misunderstanding. Look at this example and see whether it could happen in your setting.

> The other day the teacher said: 'I want them to paint rainbows. Paint rainbows using as few colours as possible.' So we mixed colours and talked about it and painted rainbows. And then she said, 'Oh, you could have done it this way.' And I thought 'Oh knickers, she didn't say that, she wasn't that specific.' That's happened a few times and I feel I haven't just got the wrong end of the stick, I've got the wrong stick!
>
> (Teaching assistant talking about her experiences)

Managing conflict

It is important not to have an over-optimistic picture of the effective team. An established ability to work together does not deny the possibility of conflict or disagreement. A good team will also develop strategies for dealing with those occasions on which agreement is not easily reached. In fact some teams may thrive and operate extremely efficiently with an element of argument or challenge which pushes the team forward. Continual agreement may indicate a team that is complacent or bored. Teams tend to have a productive period and then need to be challenged or changed (Handy 1990) to reinvigorate and remotivate them.

One of the vital aspects in managing conflict is the separation of the disagreement and the person. It is possible to disagree completely with a colleague's view of how to manage a child's difficult behaviour and yet continue to work with them in a professional and appropriate manner. Goleman (1998, p. 220) summarises the paradox: 'On one hand, the wisdom holds that the more freewheeling and intense the debate, the better the final decision; on the other hand, open conflict can corrode the ability of a team to work together'. The ability to listen to colleagues is a key feature in avoiding conflict. There is a significant difference between merely listening to the words used and trying to actively understand meaning and feelings. The team that values listening to one another and devotes precious time to exploring feelings and concerns is likely to avoid the potential descent into disagreement and acrimony. Pedler and Boydell (1994) put forward the useful notion of 'supportive listening' and give some strategies for practising this skill with a 'speaking partner' in order to help your development. If this is an area which is relevant, some of these ideas could be tried by the early years team.

A clear understanding of roles and responsibilities

We have established that there is a great diversity of expertise within the early years team. This is a strength of the team, as children need to mix with a variety of adults who relate to them in different ways. The different skills of individuals all add to the strength of the team if recognised and deployed sensitively. It is also important to take careful account of the current employment legislation, legal requirements and best practice in the appointment and management of staff; these are dealt with comprehensively by Reason (1998) elsewhere.

Establishing roles

In order to operate effectively within a team, each member needs to know where they fit in, how their own role relates to that of others, their particular responsibilities and, equally important, what tasks should be referred to others in the team. Each team member needs the confidence of understanding where the pieces of the jigsaw fit in. However in any setting which is flexible and responsive enough to meet the changing needs of children, there are bound to be grey areas where responsibilities are not always clear or there is a degree of overlap.

Roles and responsibilities are often implicit in an established team. Staff seem to instinctively work with each other. However, when there is a new member, it becomes more difficult to explicitly describe current working practice. There are occasions when a team can become too stagnant, when the different roles become too rigid to allow for personal and professional growth. Thus it would seem to be part of an effective team's responsibility to make roles and responsibilities more explicit, understood by everyone and regularly reviewed, perhaps as part of the staff development or appraisal process. Although there may be one manager who has overall responsibility, each member of the team should regard themselves as having responsibility for both their own role and also the team as a whole (Raelin 2003).

Role definitions

Roles and responsibilities often operate on two levels, the formal and the informal. For example, it may be a particular team member's responsibility to organise the mid morning drink for children. This is a routine task which is understood by all. However, there may be different aspects of the role which are less explicit but nonetheless important to the efficiency of the team, for example who takes responsibility for dealing with lost property. The shared understanding of the parameters of individual responsibility is crucial; we all need to know that our individual contributions are important and valued.

Job descriptions provide a formal definition of roles and responsibilities and need to be as clear and precise as possible. In Figure 4.5 the working relationships section describes how the member of staff relates to others in the team, for example who works with whom at different times. The duties and responsibilities clarify in as much detail as possible the boundaries of the post and provide a clear starting point for the formal role and responsibility of staff. However, the remit of the early years setting is so wide that such descriptions cannot entirely capture the reality. Job descriptions are sometimes couched in very general terms and try to encompass every eventuality. They do not always relate directly to the day to day pattern of work. Informal allocation of duties is an important function and needs to recognise the different strengths of individuals. Members of the team may have particular strengths in the following areas:

- relating to parents
- dealing with children's tantrums
- diffusing potentially problematical situations
- having new ideas for art and craft activities

Job description		
Post title		
Department	Post grade	
Location	Post hours	
Purposes and objectives of post		
Accountable to		
Immediate responsibility		
Working relationships		

Duties and responsibilities		
Support for children		
Support for staff		
Support for unit/setting		
Other duties		
Agreed by the post holder		
Agreed by the supervisor		Date

Figure 4.5 Job description
Source: Adapted from Lorenz (1998).

- displaying children's work
- observing children
- settling new children in
- remembering key dates
- working together.

It is important to consider how these skills may be exploited within the team. Members tend to grow into these roles rather than be allocated to them. In deploying staff, individual strengths should be recognised and valued.

Opportunities for change

There are of course occasions when acquired roles, formal or informal, seem impossible to amend or to shed. For example, does a particular member always clear up, look after the sick children or tend to work with those children who need extra help? The more roles are reinforced by continuing to perform duties that fit with it, expectations to adhere to those roles will be placed upon particular members of the team. This may be perfectly acceptable or it may limit the skills of individuals who are unable to extend and develop their practice beyond certain parameters. A skilled manager will give the team opportunities to develop by varying the tasks that they perform. Confident team members will be flexible enough to extend their practice through new challenges. The balance between using individual strengths and extending personal and professional development is important.

Team skills: personal and professional development

How does this relate to individual team members in a specific context? How can everyone in the team be encouraged to take responsibility for the development of their personal skills? Is there shared ownership of team building and working together to achieve goals? The questions below may be used to analyse current practice and identify ways forward.

- Are all staff active team members? Do they accept and act upon their own responsibilities when working with others? How often do they put forward ideas or actively respond to other people's suggestions? Small improvements can be equally as important as major innovations. Are staff at all levels encouraged to put forward good ideas, and are there positive opportunities for these to be shared and acted upon?
- Does everyone in the team take an active part in meetings? Are there main contributors? A meeting log is a useful way to find out. Can everyone contribute to the agenda for meetings? Is it possible for staff to suggest items that they consider to be important?
- Are all contributions (including your own) valued? How is this demonstrated? Do all staff take responsibility for praising and supporting others? Put yourself in another team member's position and think about whether they feel valued.

- Do all staff communicate directly and sensitively with others in the early years team? Do they actively listen to everyone's contribution? Is communication always clear and unambiguous? Often people think they are clear but give quite another signal to the listener. One way of checking communication skills is for colleagues to pair up and give each other feedback.

Our final message is that working with other adults should be an enjoyable aspect of being in an early years team. Using some of the strategies suggested in this chapter may enhance team skills and foster real professional benefits from interaction with colleagues.

References

Goleman, D. (1998) *Working with Emotional Intelligence*. London: Bloomsbury.

Handy, C. (1990) *Inside Organisations*. London: BBC Books.

Lorenz, S. (1998) *Effective In-class Support: The Management of Support Staff in Mainstream and Special Schools*. London: David Fulton Publishers.

Pedler, M. and Boydell, T. (1994) *Managing Yourself*. Aldershot: Gower.

Raelin J. A. (2003) *Creating Leaderful Organizations: How to Bring Out Leadership in Everyone* San Francisco: Berrett-Koehler Publishers.

Reason, J. (1998) *Good to Work For*. London: National Early Years Network.

Whalley, M. 'Working as a team', in Pugh, G. (ed.) (1996) *Contemporary Issues in the Early Years: Working Collaboratively for Children*. London: Paul Chapman/National Children's Bureau.

Chapter 5

Professional roles in the early years
Linda Miller

In this chapter, Linda Miller explores the nature of professionalism for early years practitioners. She discusses reforms in the children's workforce across the UK and considers the developments in each nation for raising the standards and qualifications of the early years workforce. She considers training and professional development routes and examines the discussions and debates surrounding the requisite knowledge and skills of practitioners. She argues that the challenge for practitioners undertaking further professional development is to develop a critical and analytical perspective towards their practice in order to uncover new professional insights.

Introduction

Professionalism can be difficult to define. Some people might claim to know it when they see it, but ideas vary about what it is. Dictionary definitions suggest that it involves belonging to or being connected with a particular profession or demonstrating the skills relating to a profession. It is likely that early years practitioners will be at various points along a continuum of professional development depending upon their age, stage in their career and level of training and qualifications. As Abbott and Pugh (1998, p. 156) said 'The ways in which early years workers become competent, knowledgeable and skilful will continue to be many and varied.' This chapter addresses some of the issues which have been a barrier to professionalism in the early years in the past. The chapter also looks to the future and considers the changing role of the early years professional, through a consideration of training and professional development routes, qualifications, and the developing and increasingly diverse role of the early years practitioner and the importance of all early years professionals working together towards common outcomes.

Background

Traditionally, in the United Kingdom (UK), there has been a philosophical and structural divide between early years care and education provision, which evolved as a result of administration by two different government departments (David 1995), although as Owen and Haynes (2008) state, it is impossible to educate without caring, nor care without promoting children's learning. The diversity of early years provision, which was traditionally split across the statutory, voluntary and independent sectors, has resulted in inequalities within the early years workforce in relation to pay, working conditions and opportunities for undertaking qualifications and professional development (Owen and Haynes 2008).

In 1998 Penn noted that 99 per cent of those working in early childhood services were women. In a review of early years training Hevey and Curtis (1996) found that the majority of day care and pre-school services were staffed by 200,000 unqualified early years workers. It would seem that little has changed in the last decade or so. The early years workforce is still under qualified, poorly paid and predominantly female; 40% of the workforce are not qualified to level 2 (a basic level of training) and just 12% are qualified to level 4 or above (related to managerial level) (DfES 2005a). In the 20 countries surveyed in the OECD report men represent less than 1% of the workforce in Early Childhood Education and Care (ECEC) (OECD 2006). The English Government has set a target of increasing male childcare and education workers to 6%. Thus working within the early years is viewed as 'women's work', and this, some would argue is the reason for it not being recognised as of sufficient importance to be properly remunerated and valued. One outcome of this history is that differences in training routes, status, pay and conditions for those working with young children have evolved and, despite recent policy developments, these issues remain unresolved (Miller 2008).

Qualifying the early years workforce

We know from research studies such as *The Effective Provision of Pre-School Education (EPPE) Project* (Sylva et al. 2003) that the quality of provision in early years settings is linked to the quality of staff that work in them. Reforming the workforce through a programme of training and qualifications is therefore seen by governments as crucial in raising the quality of services for children and parents. In the UK, we are seeing the emergence of new professional roles which relate to the different ways in which the development of early years practitioners are being viewed and how training and qualification routes are being developed and regulated in each of the four countries. If the future emphasis is to be on integrated education and care and increasingly on work in multi-agency teams, it is likely that different practitioners will form part of these new professional teams. Such a development will require a commitment on the part of practitioners to achieving graduate level qualifications and to undertake further and continuing professional development. It will also require appropriate recognition within the early years sector, and preferably at government level, through status, pay and equitable conditions.

Developments in England

The government's response in England to the consultation on the *Children's Workforce Strategy* (DfES 2006) confirmed the goal to have an integrated qualifications framework in place by 2010 which is intended to aid recruitment, retention and remodelling of the workforce, by supporting better opportunities for progression and improved career pathways (DfES 2006). The framework will embrace four inclusion principles: qualifications will be: fit for purpose; meet regulatory requirements where appropriate; be shared across the workforce and will reflect the common core (http://www.iqf.org.uk/ accessed 5/12/2008).

The vision of the Ten Year Strategy is to ensure quality through reforming the children's workforce. *The Common Core* (DfES 2005b) of skills and knowledge for the entire children workforce sets out six key areas:

Communication
Children and young persons development
Safeguarding and promoting the welfare of children
Supporting transitions
Multi agency working
Sharing information.

The English government's consultation on the future of the children's workforce resulted in a new lead graduate professional role the Early Years Professional (EYP) (DfES 2005a). Prior to this consultation, *The Effective Provision of Pre-School Education (EPPE) Project* (Sylva et al. 2003) recommended there should be a good proportion of trained teachers, *or equivalent* (my italics) leading in early years settings in order to achieve good outcomes. The OECD (2001) report said:

> Staff working with children in the ECEC programmes have a major impact on children's early learning and development. Research shows the link between strong training and support of staff – including appropriate pay and conditions – and the quality of ECEC services. In particular, staff that have more formal education and more specialised early childhood training provide more stimulating, warm and supportive interactions with children.
>
> (OECD 2001: 158)

EYPs are required to be graduates and to demonstrate that they can meet a set of national standards covering the areas: knowledge and understanding; effective practice; relationships with children; communicating and working in partnership with families and carers; teamwork and collaboration and professional development. This is achieved through a choice of four pathways to enable access for practitioners at different stages in their professional development.

It is proposed that the EYP role will have equivalence to Qualified Teacher Status; however, 'equivalence' has not yet been defined. Government intends that there will be an EYP in all children's centres by 2010, and in every full day care setting by 2015. The government plan is that the Early Years Professional will be a 'change agent' who will raise standards in early years settings, and will lead practice in the Early Years Foundation Stage (EYFS) and support and mentor other practitioners.

Developments in Northern Ireland

In 1999 the Northern Ireland National Childcare Strategy highlighted the need for early years practitioners to be appropriately educated. Walsh (2007) estimates that 30% of staff have no qualifications and there is a wide variety of qualifications within the childcare/ pre-school sector. Teacher education focuses on primary age children, yet nursery schools and classes are required to have a qualified teacher, and providers in the private and voluntary sector are required to arrange support from a qualified teacher. As in the English study, the 'Effective Provision of Preschool Education Project in Northern Ireland' (Melhuish et al. 1999) emphasised the importance of a *suitably* (my italics) trained teacher or equivalent.

As part of the Early Years expansion programme, the need to support funded pre-school centres in the voluntary and private sector to raise standards was recognised and helped to 'prepare children for school'. This support could come from a qualified teacher or an early years specialist with a National Vocational Qualification (NVQ) Level 4, a specified Early Childhood Studies Degree or a Higher National Diploma. A scoping of the Childcare and Early Years workforce led by the Northern Ireland Social Care Council (NISCC) (http://www.niscc.info/intro.htm) will inform developments. The Northern Ireland Social Care Council (NISCC) has a Workforce Development Committee which is responsible for identifying and addressing the skills needed for the working with children part of the sector. A sector skills agreement will outline how employers, training providers and stakeholders work together to provide training for the children's workforce. The accompanying Sector Qualification Strategy will detail the qualifications for the whole social service workforce, including those early years workers in the voluntary and private sectors. Induction standards for social care and children's services workers are being implemented from Spring 2008 (The Open University 2008).

Developments in Scotland

In 2006, the Scottish Executive published a *National Review of the Early Years and Childcare Workforce* (Scottish Executive 2006a) and a response (Scottish Executive 2006b), setting out the key points for action. The Scottish Social Services Council (SSSC) requires a trained workforce by 2009 as part of the drive to raise standards and increase professionalism with the social services workforce. There is a focus on three key themes: Leadership, Worker Development, and Flexibility.

A major consultation, the National Review of the Early Years and Childcare Workforce undertaken by the Scottish Executive, recommends both work-based and academic routes towards a qualified workforce: http://www.cwdcouncil.org.uk/eyps (accessed 14/10/2008).

Leadership in the early years sector will be through a degree or a work-based equivalent. As in England there is a new professional role, that of manager/lead practitioner and standards for lead practitioners/managers (QAA Scotland 2007). Also, as in England, there will be an Integrated Qualifications Framework. The Standard for Childhood

Practice, developed by the SSSC, set the standards for a new award. In the longer term, all early years and child care managers will be required to gain new awards of 360 credits at SCQF Level 9 for registration with the SSSC (Scottish Government 2007). From September 2009, nursery and childcare workers will be able to access programmes offering new qualifications on the integrated qualifications framework (The Open University 2008).

Developments in Wales

In 2007, the Welsh Assembly Government reported that the mechanisms for delivering high quality training to the early years sector needed urgent review. The stated aim is to have one adult in each early years setting who has studied child development to degree level. The Welsh Childcare Strategy includes a commitment to create a workforce development plan through the Welsh Assembly and the Sector Skills Council for Care and Development. The Care Council has set up a Wales-wide Children and Young People's Workforce Development Network, which aims to improve the skills of the children's workforce. Its remit includes the development of core knowledge and skills, a qualifications framework and a career framework for the sector (http://www.ccwales. org.uk accessed 5/12/2008). The Children's Workforce Strategy includes research into the capacity to deliver Level 4 and higher qualifications for the early years sector (The Open University 2008).

A review of Initial Teacher Training (Furlong et al. 2006) proposes a move to graduate entry and the development of 'Pre-professional' degrees offering specialist routes such as Early Years, as previously the teacher training curriculum has been weighted towards the National Curriculum (Wynn Siencyn and Thomas, 2007). The Flying Start programme for birth to three year olds will be delivered from integrated centres or community focused schools by 'trained professionals'. The Foundation Phase has high-lighted the need for recruitment, education and skills development amongst the early years workforce, as the 26,000 staff in Wales working in a range of early years settings is deemed not to be sufficient (The Open University, 2008).

There is a clear commitment across the UK to develop the Early Years workforce and new graduate roles, but in contexts which vary in terms of degrees of regulation and the specification of standards and outcomes. As the OECD (2006) report points out, the choice for the lead role in early childhood is a complex one.

Working with young children: the adult's role

Adults working with young children need to be skilled and knowledgeable. A willing-ness to reflect upon practice and to learn from this is an important dimension of the role of the early years practitioner. Tiziana Filippini (1997), the pedagogue who accom-panied The Hundred Languages of Children exhibition, featuring the work of nurseries in the Reggio Emilia region of Italy, has said 'a nice lady is not enough' to ensure that this happens. Lilian Katz (1995) has also argued that children need to be around thinking adults. These statements underline the need for professional training and qualifications in the early years.

What does the early years professional need to know?

> Adults have the power to make a major difference to children's lives and their development by what they offer children and by how they behave towards them.
>
> (Lindon 1993, p. 75)

Early years practitioner can make a difference, not only in their direct contact with young children but in their support for other adults such as parents, carers and colleagues. The importance of the adult in the development of children's learning and their well-being has been well documented (Bruner 1963, Vygotsky 1978) and the ways in which adults can use this potential power positively. Vygotsky (1978) was particularly interested in the ways in which knowledge is passed from one human to another and much of his research on child development and communication focused on the effects of our social interactions on learning. He suggested that although we can all learn new skills and knowledge as individuals, it is through our interaction with others that our early experiences are extended.

The debate about the content of, and the knowledge base for, training and qualifications for early years practitioners is both long standing (Thompson and Calder 1998) and ongoing (Miller and Cable 2008). As discussed above, as part of the reform process in England, a common core of skills, knowledge and competence has been developed for all those who work with children, young people and families, to be met through training and qualifications (DfES 2005b) and also standards for the Early Years Professional Role (http://www.cwdcouncil.org.uk/eyps accessed 14/10/2008). In Scotland the Standard for Childhood Practice is in place (QAA, 2007). In both England and Scotland an Integrated Qualifications Framework (IQF) will attempt to provide a common baseline of skills acquisition and knowledge to enable career progression and work across professional boundaries.

Whilst supporting moves towards a better qualified and appropriately remunerated workforce, Moss (1998, 2008) has been a long standing critic of moves which reduce the autonomy of early years workers through external standards and regulation of practice, which prescribe 'from above' what they should know, understand and do. He describes such moves as a 'factory model' of learning, with a centrally controlled curriculum emphasising learning goals, targets and outcomes. He questions whether the early childhood worker is a 'technician' and reproducer of knowledge to young children or a pedagogue, researcher and co-constructor of knowledge (Moss 1998). Also, such externally defined standards and specified outcomes can define what is valued by a certain group of people (i.e. government agencies), for example meeting educational targets and outcomes, but not necessarily by others, such as practitioners in the workplace.

Miller (2008) has considered an alternative to Moss' view; that externally regulated standards offer an opportunity for practitioners to demonstrate a specialist body of knowledge and skills and can contribute to a sense of professional identity. However, practitioners will need to consider whether such standards and outcomes match their own values and beliefs, and so will need to take a critical and reflective stance in relation to both theory and their practice. The challenge for practitioners who undertake further professional development, often after years of valuable practical experience, is to acknowledge and draw upon that experience, and more importantly to analyse it. To develop a critical perspective in relation to their practice in order to see familiar practice with a new, professional eye. Schön (1983) refers to this process as 'reflection in action'.

Lally (1995) has said that practitioners who cannot give confident answers to 'why' questions about their practice will be weak on rationale and therefore vulnerable to outside pressures. Gibbs (1988) argues that to have an experience is not sufficient for learning to take place; there also has to be reflection on the experience or the learning potential may be lost and cannot then be used to inform new situations. The learner must make the link between theory and practice, as illustrated by Tracey below, a student on an Early Childhood Studies Degree Course.

Tracey is the parent of two children and is a very experienced practitioner. The following is an extract from her address to incoming students at the Open Day for her course, in which she reflects upon her experience of the previous year.

> As the course progressed, I began to look at myself in a different light. I looked much more closely at the way I worked, putting into practice a lot of the learning, but with the realisation that I needed to question myself a great deal more about the 'why' of doing things. I also began to come to the conclusion that much of what I learned came from what I was prepared to put in. Maybe the most poignant moment for me, were some words said to us by one of the tutors during a teaching session on creative expression. She said that we needed to look deeper at our own learning, under the surface of what was being taught. From that day these words stayed with me and I looked at the teaching and learning assignments in a different light, not just taking the modules for what they were, but questioning, thinking, reading and researching more about the subject concerned.

Summary

The development of a more professional workforce is an evolving process and considerable progress has been made in the last decade as discussed above. Cable and Miller (2008) argue that as a workforce which is gaining increasing recognition and access to professional development opportunities, early years practitioners have a unique opportunity to influence outcomes for children and their families. Wherever early years practitioners are on this journey to professionalism, and whether they are working mainly alone, with colleagues, or within a more formal multidisciplinary team, the development, learning and well-being of children must be at the heart of what they do (Elfer 2006).

The author would like to thank Tracey Alexander for her contribution to this chapter.

References

Abbott, L. and Pugh, G. (eds) (1998) *Training to Work in the Early Years*. Buckingham: Open University Press.

Bruner, J. (1963) *The Process of Education*. New York: Vintage.

Cable, C. and Miller, L (2008) Looking to the future', in Miller, L. and Cable, C. (eds) (2008) *Professionalism in the Early Years*, London: Hodder Education.

Children's Workforce Development Council – England (http://www.iqf.org.uk accessed 5/12/2008).

Children's Workforce Development Council – England (www.cwdcouncil.org.uk accessed 4/12/2008).

Children and Young People's Workforce Development Network Wales (http://www.ccwales.org.uk accessed 5/12/2008).

David, T. (1990) *Under Five – Under Educated?* Buckingham: Open University Press.

Department for Education and Skills (DfES) (2005a) *Children's Workforce Strategy: A Strategy to Build a Word-Class Workforce for Children and Young People*. Nottingham: DfES Publications.

Department for Education and Skills (DfES) (2005b) *Common Core of Skills and Knowledge for the Children's Workforce*. Nottingham: DfES Publications.

Department for Education and Skills (DfES) (2006) *Children's Workforce Strategy: Building a Word-Class Workforce for Children, Young People and Families. The Government's Response to the Consultation*. Nottingham: DfES Publications.

Elfer, P. (2006) Exploring Children's Expression of Attachment in Nursery, *European Early Childhood Education Research Journal*, 14, (2), 81–195.

Filippini, T. (1997) 'The Reggio Approach'. Paper delivered at *The Hundred Languages of Children Exhibition Conference*, The Picture Gallery, Thomas Coram Foundation for Children, London, 11 July.

Furlong, J., Hagger, H., and Butcher, C. (2006) *Review of Initial Teacher Training Provision in Wales*. Oxford: Oxford University, Department of Educational Studies.

Gibbs, G. (1988) *Learning by Doing: A Guide to Teaching and Learning Methods*. London: Further Education Unit.

Hevey, D. and Curtis, A. (1996) 'Training to work in the early years', in Pugh, G. (ed.) *Contemporary Issues in the Early Years: Working Collaboratively for Children*, pp. 211–231. London: National Children's Bureau/Paul Chapman.

Katz, L. (1995) 'Multiple perspectives on the right start'. Paper delivered at *The Start Right Conference*, Barbican, London, 20–22 September.

Lally, M. (1995) 'Principles to practice in early years education', in Campbell, R. et al. (eds) *Supporting Children in the Early Years*, pp. 9–27. Stoke-on-Trent: Trentham Books.

Lindon, J. (1993) *Child Development from Birth to Eight*. London: National Children's Bureau.

Melhuish, E., Quinn, L., McSherry, K., Sylva, K., Sammons, P., Siraj-Blatchford, I., Taggart, B., and Gümmares, S. (1999) *Effective Pre-School Provision in Northern Ireland*. Belfast: Stranmillis University College.

Miller (2008) Developing new professional roles in the early years, in Miller, L and Cable, C. (eds) (2008) *Professionalism in the Early Years*, London: Hodder Education

Miller, L and Cable, C. (eds) (2008) *Professionalism in the Early Years*, London: Hodder Education.

Moss, P. (1998) 'Young children and early childhood institutions: who and what do we think they are?' Paper delivered at the *Child at the Centre Conference*. NES Arnold/ National Children's Bureau Conference, East Midland Conference Centre, 16–17 July.

Moss, P. (2008) 'The democratic and reflective professional: rethinking and reforming the early years workforce', in Miller, L. and Cable, C. (eds) (2008) *Professionalism in the Early Years*, London: Hodder Education.

OECD (2001) *Starting Strong. Early Childhood Education and Care*, Paris: Organisation for Economic Co-operation and Development.

OECD (2006) *Starting Strong 11. Early Childhood Education and Care*, Paris: Organisation for Economic Co-operation and Development.

Owen, S. and Haynes, G. (2008) 'Developing professionalism in the early years: from policy to practice', in Miller, L. and Cable, C. (eds) (2008) *Professionalism in the Early Years*, London: Hodder Education

Penn, H. (1998) 'Facing some difficulties', in Abbott, L. et al. (eds) *Training to Work in the Early Years*, 26–38. Buckingham: Open University Press.

QAA Scotland (2007) *Scottish Subject Benchmark Statement: The Standard for Early Childhood Practice*. Glasgow: QAA Scotland

Schön, D. (1983) *The Reflective Practitioner*. New York: Basic Books.

Scottish Executive (2006a) *National Review of the Early Years and Childcare Workforce, Report and Consultation*. Edinburgh, Scottish Executive.

Scottish Executive (2006b) *National Review of the Early Years and Childcare Workforce, Scottish Executive Response*. Edinburgh: Scottish Executive.

Scottish Government (2007) *Update on National Review of Early Years and Childcare Workforce*, http://www.cwdcouncil.org.uk/eyps (accessed 14/10/2008).

Sylva, K., Melhuish, E., Sammons, P., Siraj-Blatchford, I., Taggart, B. and Elliot, K. (2003) *The Effective Provision of Pre-School Education (EPPE) Project: Findings from the Pre-School Period: Summary of Finding*. London: Institute of Education/Sure Start.

The Open University (2008) *Thinking About Change*, Milton Keynes, The Open University; also available online in the Course Resources folder on the E100 website.

Thompson, B. and Calder, P. (1998) 'Early years educators: skills, knowledge and understanding', in Abbott, L. et al. (eds) *Training to Work in the Early Years*, pp. 38–55. Buckingham: Open University Press.

Vygotsky, L. S. (1978) *Mind in Society*. Edited by Cole, M. et al. Cambridge, MA: Harvard University Press.

Walsh, G (2007) 'Northern Ireland', in Clark, M. and Waller, T. (eds) *Early Childhood Education and Care: Policy and Practice*. London: Sage Publications.

Wynn Siencyn, S. and Thomas, S. (2007) 'Wales', in Clark, M. and Waller, T. (eds) *Early Childhood Education and Care: Policy and Practice*, London: Sage Publications

Chapter 6

Leadership in a multi-agency context
Caroline Jones and Linda Pound

The theme of this chapter is teamwork within multi-agency contexts within early years provision. Caroline Jones and Linda Pound outline the challenges and emphasise the role of negotiation in establishing and maintaining good working relationships across what were previously seen as professional boundaries. The Common Assessment Framework is also considered in some detail. A case is made for an inclusive approach to collaboration which cuts across professional boundaries and embraces different perspectives.

Does the involvement of a range of professional agencies, parents and the voluntary sector make complicated decisions easier or easy decisions more complicated?

(Riddell and Tett 2001: 1)

Introduction

[. . .] This chapter extends the theme of teamwork by focusing on the notion of the 'wider' team in the context of multi-agency working. As a setting manager you will have worked with professionals from outside the setting in order to meet specific children's needs. In this chapter, we highlight the challenges and benefits for early years settings of working with 'outside' agencies. We suggest that effective implementation of multi-agency working is largely dependent on the co-operation of practitioners working with children in their settings. As a leader, it is part of your role to share information and skills as well as to develop positive working relationships with other professionals.

The chapter explores links between multi-agency working and improving outcomes for children. [. . .] We move on to discuss issues relating the CAF, a generic tool to assess children's actual and potential 'additional needs' which relies on information sharing. The chapter concludes by looking at ways in which multi-agency working is being evaluated.

What is multi-agency working?

The drive towards 'partnership' working has gradually been replaced by the terms 'integrated' services, or 'integrated' working, encompassed in the notions of 'multi-agency' working and 'inter-agency' co-operation, used interchangeably in policy documents. There have been a number of attempts to define what is meant by multi-agency working and a variety of terms used, such as inter-agency, trans-disciplinary, inter-professional, multi-professional, multi-disciplinary and so on (Sanders 2004; Lumsden 2005). For the purposes of this chapter, we look at those professionals who, for whatever reason, come into contact with children in their settings and who should be working together and sharing information with each other, within the bounds of confidentiality.

The political basis for 'joined up' working and 'seamless' thinking is that it has inherent benefits for everyone involved. Common sense as well as more official channels dictate that members of different professions should share their knowledge and expertise. The commitment to the principle of working together stems from the belief that children's needs are not easily boxed into health, social or educational compartments and that children should be seen holistically within the context of a setting, a family and a community. As Wall (2006: 161) notes:

> We must work together in a collaborative manner sharing expertise, information and skills which need to be managed in a way that addresses the needs of families. Parents should not be responsible for passing on information from one professional to another. It is the responsibility of professionals.

Professionals should be working together to provide integrated, high quality support focused on the needs of the child. According to the DfES *Statutory Guidance on Inter-agency Co-operation* (2005: 13) such provision should be based on a shared perspective, effective communication systems and mutual understanding:

> Multi-agency working has a valuable role to play in improving outcomes for children and young people. Collaboration between people working in universal, targeted and specialist services strengthens inter-professional relationships, stimulates trust, promotes shared vision and values, increases knowledge of local services, provides alternative and creative intervention strategies, and addresses a wide range of risk factors. This, in turn, facilitates early identification, early intervention and preventative work.

The intention is that sectors should be working together at all levels, not only at ground level but at local and national levels. The Children Act 2004 requires each local authority to make clear arrangements for multi-agency working through establishing a Children's Trust (see Figure 6.1).

The Children Act 2004 also requires local authorities to establish a system of co-operation between 'relevant partners' in order to improve the well-being of children and young people and to safeguard and promote their welfare. Relevant partners include health and police authorities, and district councils. Children's well-being in the early years is defined as the mutually reinforcing *Every Child Matters* outcomes; [. . .] for childcare and nursery education these are:

- helping children to be healthy;
- protecting children from harm or neglect and helping them to stay safe;
- helping children enjoy and achieve;
- helping children make a positive contribution to the provision and the wider community;
- organization.

Section 10(1)(c) of the *Statutory Guidance* (DfES 2005) states that other agencies engaged in activities for or with children and young people should be working co-operatively, including the children and families themselves, voluntary, private and community sector bodies, childcare and play organizations. The *Statutory Guidance* also suggests that multi-agency working arrangements should take place in and around places where children spend much of their time, such as schools or children's centres. Alternative settings might include village halls, sports centres, libraries and health centres.

Although few would disagree that there are potential benefits in working together to improve outcomes for children, it is important not to underestimate the complexity of creating multi-agency structures. It can present a number of challenges to delegated leaders, practitioners and parents. As Powell (2005: 81) notes, 'multi-professional

Figure 6.1 A Children's Trust in action
Source: DfES (2005: 7).

practices can be viewed as a comparatively uncomplicated, shared practitioner construction of children and their families'. The reality for many families is that different professionals only see bits of the child and do not see them holistically. This results in frustration for families as they struggle to find their way through a whole host of professionals, often having to repeat the same information over and over again.

According to Lumsden (2005) the embracing of other professionals, children, young people and their families is essential in developing shared meanings and working in collaboration. This implies that it is relationships between individual practitioners that will ultimately determine the reality of multi-agency working. It has been noted that the recent focus on the integration and co-ordination of early years settings and other professionals requires 'something more than benign co-operation across existing professions' (Abbott and Hevey 2001: 80). It seems that practitioners can no longer afford to stay within the 'comfort zone' of their own setting but must be prepared to listen to, and be listened to by, other professionals.

Harrison *et al.* (2003) consider the potential benefits of multi-agency working. They suggest that it centres energy and resources on a common problem, enabling a coherent and holistic approach to services for children. It can also lead to increased access to funding, and to greater credibility and authority. They list the characteristics of successful multi-agency working as:

- involving more than two agencies or groups, sometimes from more than one sector, for example, community health and education, and including key stakeholders;
- having common aims, acknowledging the existence of a common problem and having a shared vision of what the outcome should be;
- having an agreed plan of action;
- consulting with others including parents, children and the community;
- having agreed decision-making structures which are clearly articulated;
- striving to accommodate the different values and cultures and participating agencies;
- sharing resources and skills;
- the taking of risks;
- exchanging information using agreed communication systems;
- acknowledging and respecting the contribution that each agency can bring;
- establishing agreed roles and responsibilities, for example, through agreed sub-groups with terms of reference.

On the surface, some progress appears to have been made, notably the establishment of inter-agency early years centres, such as jointly funded Sure Start Centres, Integrated Children's Centres and Early Excellence Centres. However, there still appear to be some unresolved issues. Sloper (2004) concluded that there was little evidence of the effectiveness of multi-agency working in achieving improved outcomes for children and families. In a review of the work of Early Excellence Centres, Anning (2001) notes that teams of professionals from different agencies have been appointed with the brief to work in 'joined up' ways, although scant attention has been given to the challenge this creates for workers. The challenge is for practitioners to articulate and share their personal and professional knowledge of new ways of working. Other challenges include false perceptions of collaboration, commitment of time and resources, the need for positive personal relationships and clashes of beliefs between agencies.

A process of negotiation

Multi-agency working is a practical and evolving process of negotiation and communication between groups of professionals, occupations, sectors, agencies and disciplines. The term suggests that the children's workforce should work in a team context, forging and sustaining relationships across agencies and respecting the contribution of others working with children, young people and families. The implication is that all practitioners should actively seek and respect the knowledge and input of others. In the early years context there has been increasing intervention from 'outsiders' in recent years (e.g. advisory teachers, area SENCOs and development workers), each with their own message and each taking up precious time. In order to take full advantage of the knowledge, expertise and skills of each agency it is essential for practitioners to understand the roles and responsibilities of those working within each agency. This in turn requires a willingness of those working in schools or early years settings to accept the 'expertise' of others as an asset rather than a threat. However, forging shared perspectives with 'outside agencies' can be difficult to achieve when at best they may only visit from time to time and at worst may appear to see themselves as the 'professionals' on the basis of their experience, specific expertise and qualifications. A leader has to anticipate and manage possible sources of tension relating to differences in professional cultures including attitudes, values, beliefs and working practices. Positive relationships need to be encouraged if these visiting professionals are to be viewed as part of the wider team.

At the level of an individual early years setting, it is everyone's responsibility to ensure that the provision meets the needs of children and that each child reaches their full potential. For some children, this can only be achieved by input from several professionals. The most common reason for statutory or voluntary agencies to work with individual schools or early years settings is to support and advise practitioners in working with children who have been identified as needing extra support due to SEN.

The following scenario illustrates how easily tension may arise.

Case Study

Isabel, a 4-year-old, diagnosed with autistic tendencies, has some behavioural and communication difficulties. She has spent over a year in a private nursery where the staff are experienced and trained in this field. With the support of a keyworker, she had been fully included in the life of the nursery, with few adaptations. The visiting SEN teacher suggested that Isabel would benefit from the use of a timeline and the staff were willing to try this strategy. However, on reflection after a period of time staff realized that Isabel was not benefiting from the timeline, and it was making her stand out as different to all the other children. The position of the timeline was also seen as exclusive as it highlighted to the other children and the parents that Isabel was a 'problem' and was special. The nursery manager telephoned the visiting SEN teacher and explained that she was going to remove the timeline from the wall. There was a rather heated discussion. When the visiting SEN teacher returned the situation was again discussed. The manager pointed out that they worked with Isabel every day and knew best, but the SEN teacher felt affronted that her idea had been rejected. After that point, no other children with SEN were referred to that nursery and the nursery manager lost confidence in the local SEN support services.

This case shows that multi-agency working involves a complex process of negotiation between individuals of which communication is an essential ingredient. By contrast, where there are positive relationships, the situation can be very productive. Support services can provide invaluable advice, in clarifying problems, in suggesting strategies for promoting learning and behaviour management and in liaising with parents. Outside specialists can help in the early identification of SEN and act as consultants, although it is still the SENCO who still has prime responsibility for co-ordinating the provision made for the child.
[. . .]

The CAF

Since the publication of the Green Paper *Every Child Matters* (DfES 2003) and the Children Act 2004, managers of early years settings have been inundated with non-statutory guidance and policy documents. One initiative, the CAF, was specifically intended to 'drive multi-agency working by embedding a shared process, developing a shared language of need and improving the information flow between agencies' (DfES 2005: 15). It sets out to help practitioners develop a shared understanding of children's needs and forms a basis for early intervention before problems reach crisis point. It can be used by practitioners who have been on training to assess the needs of unborn babies, infants, children and young people.

A common assessment is generic rather than specific. It is not concerned with measuring progress towards specific milestones or targets and can be used earlier than specialist assessments. It may also feed into other types of assessment, for example, the SEN *Code of Practice*. Common assessments are intended to be an easy and accessible process for all practitioners: holistic and voluntary, solution- and action-focused. They are transferable between services and areas based on developing a culture of understanding and trust. The common assessment process is based on the idea of a continuum of needs and services (see Figure 6.2), although the majority of children should not need a common assessment. A common assessment is not appropriate, for example, in situations where a child has obvious needs and a specialist or statutory assessment is required. Practitioners need to decide which children are at potential risk of poor outcomes without extra services, although this does not guarantee the provision of those services.

As Figure 6.2 shows, children said to have 'additional' needs may require targeted support either from a single practitioner or a range of integrated services. However, children with complex needs (who are still part of the broad group with additional needs), require statutory or specialist services. These children may or may not have 'SEN' which are 'educational'.

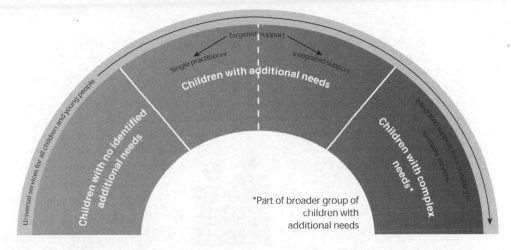

Figure 6.2 Continuum of needs and services (DfES 2006a: 7)

How to do a common assessment

The CAF process consists of three steps, officially referred to as preparation, discussion and delivery (see Figure 6.3). First the practitioner needs to check if anyone else is working with the child as a common assessment may already be in place, by asking the parent or carer, or there may be a local system for logging common assessments. Discussion with a line manager and colleagues could also help decide if a common assessment is needed. If the practitioner is not sure whether an assessment is needed the CAF pre-assessment checklist can be used (DfES 2006b). It is intended to lead to better understanding as to whether an assessment is needed, a decision to be made jointly with the child and the child's parents or carers.

The information is recorded during the discussion with the child and family onto the CAF form. It is essential to ensure that parents understand what information is being recorded, what will be done with it and when. The CAF form is an instrument for recording the discussion, which has eight stages with discussion prompts provided for each. The practitioner is required to record the child's strengths as well as needs. The discussion prompts are listed below.

1   Explain the purpose of the assessment.
2   Complete the basic identifying details.
3   Assessment information.
4   Details of the parents/carers.
5   Current home and family situation.
6   Details of services working with the child.
7   Assessment summary
    (a) development of the child
    (b) parents and carers
    (c) family and environment.
8   Conclusions, solutions and actions.

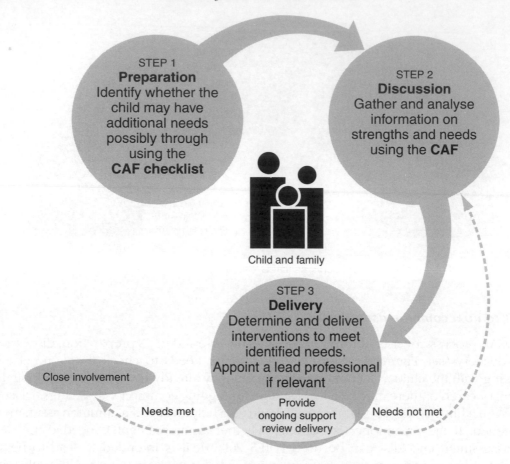

Figure 6.3 The three steps in the common assessment process (DfES 2006a: 17)

Stage 7 is the basis of the discussion which is intended to be collaborative and based around the three domains of children, parents and environment. First, the development of the child, including areas such as health, behaviour, learning and self-esteem is discussed. The second element relates to parents and carers and is concerned with basic safety and care, emotional stability, guidance, boundaries and stimulation. Third, family and environmental factors form part of the assessment. This area covers aspects such as housing, finance and family well-being.

It may be that the child's needs are such that no additional action is required. If action is needed it could be by the family, within the service or setting carrying out the assessment, or there may be a need to try and access support from other agencies. Where it is agreed that the child has complex needs and integrated services are required, the practitioner will need to contact the relevant person in the local area.

Where appropriate, it is the lead professional who assumes responsibility for co-ordinating the provision of services. The lead professional stems from the CAF process where a child's needs are such that they require support from more than just one practitioner. One practitioner assumes the role of lead professional in co-ordinating the action identified as a result of the assessment process. In some cases, where the child's needs are more complex and they receive a specialist assessment, there may already be a single point of contact who will assume the role of lead professional (e.g. named social worker, keyworker).

Information-sharing

The non-statutory guidance on information-sharing intended for everyone working with children or young people, in the public, private and voluntary sectors, including volunteers, suggests that improving information-sharing is a 'cornerstone' of the government strategy to improve outcomes for children (DfES 2006c).

It is claimed that sharing information is essential to enable early intervention to help those who need additional services, thus reducing inequalities between disadvantaged children and others. The guidance sets out six key points (DfES 2006c: 5):

1 Practitioners should explain to children, young people and families from the beginning of the process which information will be shared, the reasons why and how it will be shared. The exception being that if an open explanation would put the child or others at risk of significant harm.
2 The safety and welfare of the child is paramount and must be an overriding consideration.
3 Whenever possible, if the child or family do not consent to have information shared, their wishes should be respected.
4 You should seek advice especially if you have concerns about a child's safety or welfare.
5 It is essential to check that information is accurate, up to date, necessary for the purpose, and shared securely with only those who need to see it.
6 Record decisions whether you decide to share information or not.

Although information should be shared on a 'need to know' basis the potential for sharing information is enormous, with implications not only for workload and time management but primarily in relation to consent and confidentiality. One daunting factor is the sheer number of professionals with whom practitioners may have to work in education, health and social services as well as the many voluntary organizations. Figure 6.4 shows the key agencies working with children or young people.

The hub shown has 13 sectors and each has its own internal communication network. Although maintained schools have been required for some time to publish information about their arrangements for working with health, social services, local authority support services and any relevant local and national voluntary organizations, it is a huge task for non-maintained early years settings to find out who the support services and agencies are and how to contact them. The list below is a typical non-exhaustive example:

- Speech and language therapist.
- Area SENCO.
- Development worker.

- Advisory teachers.
- Community nurse/health workers.
- Educational psychologist.
- Child Development Centre.
- General practitioner.
- Physiotherapist.
- Social workers.
- Education welfare officer.
- Family support worker.
- Specialist teachers (e.g. of sensory impairments).
- Parent Partnership Service.

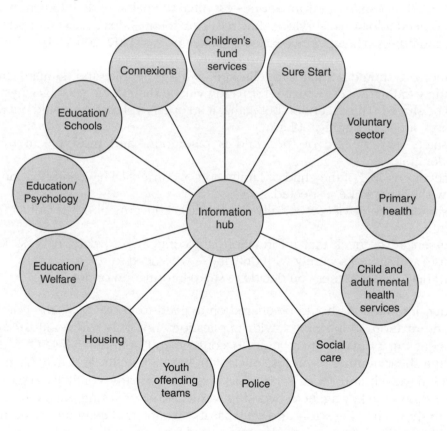

Figure 6.4 The information hub
Source: DfES (2003: 54).

Case Study

A practitioner had been concerned for some time regarding 2-year-old David's health and nutrition. She had observed that the contents of his lunchbox were sparse and nearly always the same. When she tried to speak to his mother informally, she commented that all he ate at home was dog food (there were several dogs in the family flat) and how cheap it was. The practitioner reported her concerns to the manager. The manager contacted the social services. Discussions followed involving the health visitor and housing department, social services and the local Sure Start centre. Through information-sharing the professionals worked together with the parents to improve the child's living conditions and diet.

The Data Protection Act 1998 does not prevent the sharing of information but sets parameters for sharing information lawfully. Professionals need to record and update parental consent to share information with others, preferably in writing. Professionals need to be made aware of the nature of confidentiality, and when and why it is sometimes possible to pass on information *without* consent. This is a complex area and there are significant training implications.

Evaluation of multi-agency working

The success of multi-agency working will be continually evaluated at various levels. Statutory arrangements are in place for joint inspection of all children's services in a local authority. Ofsted and the Commission for Social Care Inspection are beginning to assess performance annually and give an overall rating of a council's children's services in improving the lives of children. Joint Area Reviews report on how well services are working together to secure positive outcomes for children and young people. They involve nine inspectorates and commissions in assessing how social, health, education and criminal justice services and systems combine to contribute to improved outcomes. Progress is monitored against priority national targets and other indicators. In primary schools, Ofsted inspectors judge the extent to which the education in the school meets the needs of the range of pupils and the contribution made by the school to the well-being of those pupils. Inspectors assess the overall effectiveness of the school, including how far the curriculum is responsive to external requirements and local circumstances. This would include any extended services, the effectiveness of links with other providers, services, employers and other organizations to promote the integration of care and education so as to enhance learning and promote well-being. In early years settings Ofsted inspectors also judge whether the childminding, day care and/or nursery education meet the needs of the range of children for whom it is provided and how well the organization promotes children's well-being. The clear message is that the entire children's workforce should be working together at every level – with each other and with parents and families to improve the lives of children.

For multi-agency working to be effective in practice, there needs to be a clear and explicit rationale as there may be deep-rooted cultural differences between professional groups, vested interests in maintaining boundaries and statutory restrictions undermining efforts. A number of key issues such as lack of time, lack of understanding of the purpose of multi-agency practice, professional rivalry and ownership of resources still need to be addressed. Challenges remain in the areas of planning, implementation and ongoing management. These include promoting an increased understanding and awareness of the roles and responsibilities of other professionals, joint funding, joint training, joint policies, rationalization of professional differences and joint planning (Wall 2006).

[. . .]

References

Abbott, L. and Hevey, D. (2001) Training to work in the early years: developing the climbing frame, in G. Pugh (ed.) *Contemporary Issues in the Early Years*, 3rd edn. London: Paul Chapman Publishing.

Anning, A. (2001) Knowing who I am and what I know: developing new versions of professional knowledge in integrated service settings. Paper presented to the BERA Annual Conference, University of Leeds, 13–15 September.

DfES (Department for Education and Skills) (2003) *Every Child Matters*, Cm 5860. London: The Stationery Office.

DfES (Department for Education and Skills) (2005) *Statutory Guidance on Interagency Co-operation to Improve the Wellbeing of Children: Children's Trusts*. Nottingham: DfES.

DfES (Department for Education and Skills) (2006a) *The Common Assessment Framework for Children and Young People: Manager's Guide*, available at: www.every child.matters.gov.uk/caf/?cidm=booklet, accessed 9 January 2007.

DfES (Department for Education and Skills) (2006b) *Common Assessment Form and Pre-assessment Checklist*, available at: www.everychildmatters.gov.uk/resources, accessed 9 January 2007.

DfES (Department for Education and Skills) (2006c) *Information Sharing: Practitioners Guide*, available at: www.everychildmatters.gov.uk/information, accessed 10 January 2007.

Harrison R., Mann, G., Murphy, M., Taylor, A. and Thompson, N. (2003) *Partnership Made Painless: A Joined Up Guide to Working Together*. Dorset: Russell House Publishing.

Lumsden, E. (2005) Joined-up thinking in practice: an exploration of professional collaboration, in T. Waller (ed.) *An Introduction to Early Childhood*. London: Paul Chapman Publishing.

Powell, J. (2005) Multiprofessional perspectives, in L. Jones, R. Holmes and J. Powell (eds) *Early Childhood Studies: A Multiprofessional Perspective*. Maidenhead: Open University Press.

Riddell, S. and Tett, L. (2001) Education, social justice and inter-agency working: joined-up or fractured policy? in S. Riddell and L. Tett (eds) (2001) *Education, Social Justice and Inter-agency Working: Joined-up or fractured policy?* London: Routledge.

Sanders, B. (2004) Interagency and multidisciplinary working, in T. Maynard and N. Thomas (eds) *An Introduction to Early Childhood Studies*. London: Sage.

Sloper, P. (2004) Facilitators and barriers for co-ordinated multi-agency services, *Child Care, Health and Development*, 30(6): 571–80.

Wall, K. (2006) *Special Needs and Early Years*, 2nd edn. London: Paul Chapman Publishing.

Chapter 7

Approaches to curricula in the early years

Linda Miller, Jane Devereux, Alice Paige-Smith and Janet Soler

---

This chapter considers five approaches to early years curricula. Two of these examples consider what we have to learn from taking an historical perspective (Steiner and Montessori). More recent approaches (Schema, Te Whaariki and Reggio Emilia) offer a contrasting perspective on the more centralised models which are being developed in a number of countries, including England. The chapter argues that a consideration of alternative approaches enables us to look at the work of others and have insights into our own practice.

Introduction

In this chapter we explore five examples of curricula, which have influenced practice in early childhood education and care. They have been chosen to illustrate both recent and historical influences on early years curricula in the UK. Curricular guidance for the early years has become increasingly centralised in a number of countries, which has extended debates about what and how young children learn (Bennett 2001). However, alongside the development of this more centralised system practitioners have retained and woven influences from other approaches and models into their practice. These other approaches to curricula stem from research, from a particular set of beliefs or from a distinctive vision attributable to one influential figure.

Developing early childhood curricula involves making decisions and choices about what children should learn. Making these choices involves different groups such as early childhood practitioners, teachers, educational experts and policy makers. The early childhood curricula discussed in this chapter are based on official guidance issued by government and ministers, or are generated more locally for different early childhood settings, or have their origins in the distinctive vision of one educator – or they may embrace more than one of these influences. We have chosen these particular examples in order to illustrate the rich variety of approaches that early years practitioners bring to their work.

Two of the approaches discussed have been influenced by the work of great educators of the past, Rudolph Steiner (House 2000) and Maria Montessori (Montessori 1912). More recently the work of Chris Athey (1990) on Schema, has influenced early years practice in some settings. One example of curricula we focus on is 'Te Whaariki' developed in New Zealand (Ministry of Education 1996). This is a centrally generated national curriculum for early childhood, but is distinctive because it addresses both cultural and language issues in English and Maori and because of the involvement of stakeholders in its conception and development. In Italy, central government has traditionally been much less prescriptive about what children should learn at any stage of education. The Reggio Emilia approach is an example of a localised system that offers a distinctive approach to teaching and learning in early childhood, and which has been extremely influential on professional thinking in countries throughout the world.

The influence of Steiner education

Rudolph Steiner (1861–1925) established his first school in 1919 in Stuttgart for the children of the Waldorf Astoria cigarette factory workers. Steiner was approached by the factory owner to set up the school, as he was known as the founder of the Anthroposophy movement and a leading figure in the movement for social renewal and was concerned about the spiritual background of human evolution (Chalibi 2001). There are currently more than 770 Rudolph Steiner Waldorf schools and 1,200 kindergartens worldwide as well as many teacher training courses. Steiner viewed education as appropriate when it: 'allows the pupil's body to develop healthily and according to its needs, because the soul (of which this body is the expression) is allowed to grow in a way consistent with the forces of its development' (Steiner 1919: 3). He emphasised the nature of the whole human being, how the teacher should have insight into children, and that education was not just about knowledge but also about encouraging human beings to change existing social conditions. The approach is based on the principles of Steiner education as well as the individual creativity of the teacher (Stedall 1992).

Curriculum

The young child is seen as having a close relationship to nature and to the world about him or her. Early years educators' greatest tools are considered to be 'example and love' (Schweizer 2000: 23) and the young child is considered to be defenceless and trusting. Formal schooling does not begin until the child is aged six to seven. Until children are seven they are considered to need to develop their senses which may be over stimulated through urban living, and there is an emphasis on creative play, imagination and rhythm: 'What is right to offer the child under seven to learn when he absorbs so much so fast? The delicate senses are all embracing; the child absorbs willy-nilly the world around, recreating it through the divine gift of imitation in play, speech and behaviour' (Schweizer 2000: 23).

Hence Steiner education attempts to provide children with opportunities to explore nature and their senses and the world around them through the curriculum they experience in the early years. According to Schweizer, working with festivals brings children in touch with the seasons and develops a sense of rhythm in their lives. Rhythm is considered to be important for children and is brought into the curriculum through an awareness of the seasons, through a nature table for instance or through the rhythm of children's songs and rhymes, which are considered to stimulate the child's language beyond daily usage (Britz-Crecelius 1972). The importance of rhythm and repetition is established through the daily, weekly and termly curriculum. Different days will be for special activities such as drawing, painting or cooking and the daily timetable will be routinely followed, punctuated by songs to indicate any changes in activity. The same songs or poems during ring time would be repeated every day for one month. The sharing of food prepared with the children begins with a grace and ends with thanks: 'They help of their own accord with the cooking or spreading, baking or chopping, serving, laying tables and washing up. It is a social occasion as well as nourishing' (Schweizer 2000: 25). Steiner proposed that children should learn to read and write after the age of seven, that writing should develop from drawing, that alphabet letters emerge from children's artistic sense and also that reading is considered to arise from writing. Alongside a curriculum based on the Arts such as music and painting, eurhythmic movement, or movement with meaning, is considered to be a way of encouraging children's development.

Play

Play is considered to develop children's ability to persevere and concentrate; it also allows the child to fill in time without being bored (Britz-Crecelius 1972). Within a Steiner perspective, games like hide and seek and peek a boo 'reflect the transition from there to here, the transition from the spiritual to the physical world, which takes place every morning on waking up' (Britz-Crecelius 1972: 18). Exploring the four elements is a part of the early years curriculum and children are encouraged to play with earth and water through digging in mud and sand and having access to a tap or buckets of water. Games with an element of air would include using kites, which create the opportunity for children to measure their own strength against the force of the wind. Children are also encouraged to join in with adult tasks such as cleaning and cooking as they are considered to learn through imitation. Pretend and imaginary play are encouraged as a way of developing the child's imagination and of conquering their surroundings. Some of the permanent play activities which would be available in a playgroup or kinder-garten would include: a play house with rag dolls, doll clothes, covers, baskets to carry dolls (using soft colours such as pink and light purple), a table with wooden and natural cups, pans, spoons, fir cones, water play, wooden bricks, natural wooden objects, wooden train set, knitted dolls which can be used as puppets, and wooden strollers.

The role of the adult

Steiner wrote about the ways in which teachers should educate children within the context of setting up the Waldorf school in the early twentieth century. At that time

Steiner was concerned with the impact of the development of modern industry and what could be considered to be appropriate education, especially as the first Steiner school was set up for the children of factory workers. From birth to six or seven the child's soul is considered to go through a transformation when 'the human being naturally gives himself up to everything immediately surrounding him in the human environment' (Steiner 1919: 2). The role of the teacher who is entrusted with the education of the child is considered to be very influential: 'the child's soul becomes open to take in consciously what the educator and teacher gives, which affects the child as a result of the teacher's natural authority . . . whatever the teacher does should be sufficiently alive' (Steiner 1919: 2). Within Steiner playgroups and kindergartens there is a concern that the educator should nurture the child's individuality and creativity, and to also be a type of 'mentor' or supportive adult for the child. Rather than lead or control the children, the role of the adult is to guide young children through ritual activities that take place during the day. The adult would not instruct the children directly but would lead the child or children into activities through song – for instance 'Let's all tidy up now' would be chanted at clearing up time. The children are considered to learn through imitation and repetition of activities, songs, rhymes and story. During painting sessions the adult may sit and paint rather than instruct and when children play creatively they will allow the children to develop their own fantasy play situation only intervening to support the children's fantasy. House (2000) suggests that the importance of a Steiner approach in the early years is that it provides a central role to the importance of play which is unstructured by adults. He suggests that the Steiner approach to early years education should be publicised more widely as it is an 'effective alternative to the assessment-obsessed, anxiety-driven fare on offer in the state sector' (House 2000: 10) and this may be one of the reasons why parents choose Steiner playgroups or kindergartens for their children.

The Montessori approach

Dr Maria Montessori was born in 1870 in Italy where she studied engineering, before training as a doctor. In 1896 she was the first woman to graduate from the University of Rome Medical School where she worked in the psychiatric clinic developing an interest in the treatment of children. Gradually, she became interested in the education of all children and in 1907 opened her first 'children's house' in a poor area of Rome, San Lorenzo. Because of her medical training she initially approached the education of children from a scientific, rather than a philosophic or educational perspective; this significantly affected the way she worked and the structured materials that she developed. Throughout her life she travelled all over the world spreading her ideas and developing her philosophy until her death in 1952.

Underpinning philosophy

Montessori began by observing children and used the classroom as a laboratory to develop and test out her materials. She had a great love and respect for children and believed that each child is unique with a potential that needs releasing. Montessori saw the dignity of the child, along with freedom and independence, as cornerstones of practice. She believed that children had an inner and outer self and that the inner rhythm of the child's soul was crucial in helping children to grow and understand their world. She advocated that if the adult guided the child's outer self, the inner self would take care of itself (Montessori 1912). In Montessori's view this inner self helps the child towards independence, which she viewed as the ultimate goal for children. Montessori did not believe the child was an empty vessel that the parent or teacher had to fill up and felt that neither a nursery school nor the home offered children the kind of environment they needed. She set out to create 'a *natural* environment for the child' (that is, one suited to their nature) (Standing 1966: 4). Another way of describing the Montessori method is to say it is a 'method based on the principle of freedom in a prepared environment' (Standing 1966: 8).

Montessori based her work on the idea that children were very different from adults and used the term metamorphosis (meaning change of shape) to describe how children's minds and bodies were constantly changing. She developed a series of different didactic materials that she saw as leading to order, understanding and independence. According to Montessori, if children were inducted into this ordered environment and systematic ways of working, then 'active discipline' would be internalised by the child. Montessori practitioners do not discipline children in the traditional sense yet the environment is very controlled. Children are not free to wander but are encouraged to work with the materials, which for many practitioners may seem antagonistic to ideas of freedom.

The role of the adult

In Montessori settings the adult is seen as a guide rather than a teacher, with great emphasis placed on not intervening unnecessarily in what the child is doing. The child as the learner leads, the guide follows, thus respecting the child's inner life. Montessori believed that all children have a natural desire to find out and understand by doing, thus the guide inducts the child into the required way of working with each new piece of equipment, as appropriate to their age and stage of development. Each piece of equipment is designed to incorporate a specific learning purpose and must be used in a particular way. Children may repeat and play with the materials as much as they wish but the ways in which they can use the materials are clearly prescribed.

In training guidance is given to teachers on how to instruct children and model particular behaviours and ways of working; every teacher practises using each piece of apparatus in the correct way many times. As a child becomes more familiar with the material then the teacher steps back and observes.

Approach to practice

Within a Montessori setting children are placed in multi-age groups in three to six year spans, usually: 0–3, 3–6, 6–12, 12–15 and 15–18. Montessori viewed these mixed age groups as important for social development and for learning from peers. The environment is organised into subject areas and children are free to move around the room and work with a particular piece of apparatus without time restriction. Children work individually, with practitioners supporting one child at a time; group work is not a common feature of Montessori settings. Teachers or guides do not correct children as they work, but use observation to plan individual projects to support their needs.

The materials

The Montessori intellectual materials include the practical life curriculum, sensorial education, language and maths. Overlaying this is the cultural curriculum that includes geography, history, biology, music and arts. Within these areas Montessori devised structured activities and designed specific apparatus to develop children's knowledge, skills and awareness of the world. Equipment for all activities is child sized and children are expected to do most things for themselves. For example, practical life exercises such as pouring peas enable them to practise the skills needed to eventually get a drink independently. They are also expected to clear up after an activity. A typical piece of apparatus is number rods of different lengths, designed to introduce children to ideas of number. The first activity is to lay them out in order and if 'done properly, they form a sort of stair' (Standing 1966: 146). A series of set activities then follow as the guide observes the child's development. Using the apparatus in ways other than those prescribed is not encouraged.

This prescribed approach to practice highlights tensions for many practitioners between the espoused notion of freedom and the prescribed nature of the materials. Today there are many Montessori nurseries, but not all are staffed by Montessori trained practitioners and therefore may not follow the approach advocated by Montessori.

Schema

Chris Athey's work on Schema has its origins in the Froebel Educational Institute Project (1990), which aimed to provide information about the ways in which young children acquire knowledge. Athey was strongly influenced by the writings of Piaget. A key task of the project was to document the developmental sequence of behaviour in a group of young children, ranging from early motor behaviours through to thought and forms of representation. The project also aimed to provide an enrichment programme based on new kinds of collaboration between parents and practitioners.

What are Schema?

Athey worked with practitioners, observing children alone and interacting with others such as parents, to try to establish commonalities and continuities in their learning. Through her research (1973–1978) she showed how children's 'forms of thought' are fed by experiences provided in the home and in early years settings. According to Athey, children find their own match between the curriculum offered and their current cognitive concerns, which she describes as a series of patterns that children show in their learning and play. These patterns she called 'schema' and described each as 'a pattern of repeatable behaviour into which experiences are assimilated and gradually co-ordinated. Co-ordination leads to higher-level and more powerful schemas' (Athey 1990: 37). So for Athey, schema are repeatable patterns of action that help children to make early categorisations and from that, to develop more logical and general classifications about the world around them. For example when babies apply a particular action or schema, such as sucking, to a variety of objects they gradually become more able to generalise about objects, which can be sucked. They may also, according to Foss (1974), use a series of schema with objects to explore such ideas as throwing, sucking and banging; from this behaviour they begin to generalise about which objects belong to which categories. As a child develops it then becomes the role of the adult to provide experiences that enable the child to use their existing schema. Further experiences are then assimilated into the child's cognitive structures and their breadth and depth extended. Athey (1990: 37) claims therefore 'increase experiences and schemas will be enriched'.

Athey's research (1990) found that schema manifested themselves in children's play. Examples of identified schema are:

- Trajectory – interest in up and down and along and back
- Rotation – interest in things that rotate
- Enclosure – interest in boundaries
- Enveloping and containing – covering and putting objects in containers
- Connecting – interest in joining things together in various ways and forms
- Transporting – moving things about in different ways.

Athey also identified three developmental stages relating to schema:

- Motor level – where the behaviours shown by the child do not appear to have any representational significance
- Symbolic representation – the child is able to represent events symbolically through their actions, play or in other forms such as drawing, modelling and painting
- Thought level – the child is able to give a description about an event or action after it has occurred.

These three different levels of functioning were found to relate to increasing chronological age – motor level was found in the youngest children and thought level in the older children.

Implications for practice and the role of the adult

The case study below illustrates Hannah's emerging patterns of behaviour over a six week period.

CASE STUDY

Hannah (4yrs 3mths)

Hannah played with lots of small equipment. She had her own bag in which she brought her teddy, wrapped in his special blanket, to nursery where he stayed until home time. Teddy was taken out of the bag when her mother came to collect her, then Hannah would wrap herself and Teddy together in the blanket before leaving. Hannah was frequently observed in the home corner playing with the dolls, wrapping them up and putting them in prams or cots and covering them with blankets. In the outside play area she was often seen hiding in the bushes setting up homes or dens; she always made a door that could shut. She collected and stored 'treasures' wrapped in tissue inside matchboxes. She would bring different wrapped objects to nursery and often covered her work or things she made. Her drawings of people were usually contained inside some kind of building. When she finished a painting, she often covered it over with a dark colour saying that it was 'night' or 'finished'.

These observations collected by the adults working with Hannah, show predominant patterns of play, which were driven by her interest in enveloping, covering and containing objects. Adults working with young children and using schema as a framework for their practice, seek to look beyond what children are playing with, to observe what they are doing with materials and objects. In Hannah's case the practitioners provided a range of 'enveloping' activities that extended her experiences. For example, they developed a wormery, which involved Hannah in digging for worms, putting them into the soil and wrapping the container with black paper. Thus she added to her knowledge of enveloping and adapted and modified her understanding through different experiences.

Within the schema framework, children's play patterns change and develop and they may show more than one dominating pattern. Sharing observations and understandings allows adults to be aware of children's predominant schema and to plan for these to be supported and extended by both parents and practitioners.

Athey suggests that 'where schemas have been well nourished by wide experiences, consistently accompanied by articulate speech, development has been accelerated' (Athey 1990: 204).

Te Whaariki

New Zealand has developed a national curriculum framework for early childhood, 'Te Whaariki' (Ministry of Education 1996). The developers of the New Zealand early childhood curriculum were working in similar contexts to those involved in the development of the early childhood curriculum in England (Miller 2000) in that the curriculum was linked to the National Curriculum in primary schools. Despite this constraint, the developers of Te Whaariki developed a framework, which has implemented a bicultural perspective, an anti-racist approach and reciprocal relationships with the Maori community in New Zealand (Smith 2002).

The development of Te Whaariki

Margaret Carr and Helen May, who were responsible for co-coordinating the development of the New Zealand early childhood curriculum, wished to incorporate 'equitable educational opportunities and quality early childhood policies and practices' into the framework (Carr and May 2000: 53). Diverse groups of practitioners and representatives from different types of early childhood services were involved in consultations, as were people with nationally recognised expertise. Maori perspectives were a separate, but integrally related framework and the document is written in both English and Maori (Smith 2002). During consultations early childhood practitioners expressed a 'local, situated and often personal view of the early childhood curriculum' (Carr and May 2000: 53). This view did not necessarily fit with the government objective of establishing a national curriculum framework and many early childhood practitioners had difficulties with applying the word 'curriculum' to practice in early childhood settings. Nevertheless, Smith (2002) says that 'The introduction of holistic, open ended inclusive curriculum guidelines in New Zealand has been a success' (p. 17).

The curriculum

The New Zealand early childhood curriculum is usually referred to by its shortened title of 'Te Whaariki' (Ministry of Education 1996), which means a woven mat on which everyone can stand; this reflects the philosophy of the curriculum. It interweaves central principles, strands and goals into different patterns or programmes which each centre is expected to weave into its own curriculum. It is designed to cover the age range 0 to 5 years and is divided into three age groups, i.e. 'infants', 'toddlers' and the 'young child'.

The four broad principles which provide the framework are:

1. Empowerment – the curriculum empowers the child to grow and learn.
2. Holistic development – the curriculum reflects the way children learn and grow.
3. Family and community – the wider world of the family and community are an integral part of the curriculum.
4. Relationships – children learn through responsive relationships with people, places and things.

The five strands, which are underpinned by goals are:

- Well being – involving goals relating to health and safety.
- Belonging – involving goals relating to links to family and community, a sense of place, routines and customs and acceptable behaviour.
- Contribution – involving goals relating to opportunities for learning and a sense of self.

- Communication – involving goals relating to protection of the language symbols of their own and other cultures.
- Exploration – involving goals relating to play and active exploration of the environment.

'Te Whaariki' is mandatory in all government-funded early childhood programmes in New Zealand (Ministry of Education 1996, Smith 2002).

As with the Reggio Emilia approach in Italy, discussed later in this chapter, Carr and May argue that this curriculum cannot be imported as it stands into other countries, as it embodies bicultural and community values that are specific to New Zealand. The weaving metaphor of the mat embodies their bicultural vision of the New Zealand child which underpins this curriculum (see Carr and May 2000: 61).

The role of the adult

As in the 'emergent curriculum' of Reggio Emilia centres described below. Te Whaariki draws on Vygotskian sociocultural theory. Within this theoretical framework knowledge and understanding are socially constructed between the child and a more able 'other', rather than passively received. Teachers and practitioners have an interactive role and help to 'scaffold' the child's learning; hence relationships are highly important and children take an active role in their own learning (Smith 2002).

Reggio Emilia

Reggio Emilia is a community supported system of early childhood education and care situated in a small town in northern Italy. During the last two decades it has become internationally known for its provision for children under 6, through 'The Hundred Languages of Children' touring exhibition (Malaguzzi 1996) and through visits to the region from practitioners and authorities concerned with early childhood education. The wider influence of Reggio Emilia on early years practitioners throughout the world has been immense. The Municipality of Reggio Emilia operates the network of early childhood educational services; it co-exists alongside a publicly funded system of pre-schools for all three to six year olds.

Loris Malaguzzi founded the Reggio Emilia system of early childhood education after his experiences in the Second World War; he strongly believed that a new society should nurture a vision of children who could act and think for themselves (Malaguzzi 1995). This led to an early childhood education system founded on the perspective of the child. Carlina Rinaldi, who has worked alongside Malaguzzi for many years, says that the cornerstone of the Reggio Emilia experience is based on the image of children as rich, strong, and powerful. Children are seen as unique subjects with rights rather than simply needs (Rinaldi 1995).

Approaches to practice

Malaguzzi drew on Vygotsky's theory briefly described above. Within this approach, knowledge is not 'transmitted' by the adult, but is co-constructed by the child and adult as they find meanings together. The nature of the relationship between the child and adult is central, as is listening to the child's views and ideas. A key feature of the work of Reggio Emilia centres is an ongoing dialogue which questions and challenges existing educational viewpoints and accepted teaching practices and approaches. This dialogue is shared with the children, parents, teachers, administrators, politicians and educators from other countries. Through this professional dialogue practitioners in Reggio Emilia centres have challenged the dominating ideas and accepted practices of early childhood teaching by 'deconstructing' (i.e. taking apart existing ideas and theories), to look at how they have shaped our ideas and beliefs about children and the ways in which we work (Dahlberg 2000). Time for this discussion and for planning and preparation is built into the working week. Time is also given to children to discuss ideas, develop co-operative projects, to research and problem solve and to revisit work and ideas already undertaken (Abbott and Nutbrown 2001).

The emergent curriculum

Within Reggio Emilia centres there is no written curriculum with prescribed goals and methods, the child is seen as a starting point for an 'emergent curriculum' (Rinaldi 1995: 102). This is a localised approach to teaching and learning that cannot be readily transferred and applied to another culture or context. The approach has evolved because the centres have not been constrained by external factors stemming from government objectives, the pressures of external assessment or the need to implement prescribed curriculum content. Malaguzzi refers to the 'hundred ways' in which he believes children learn and practitioners and other adults are urged to 'listen' to the many languages through which children communicate. Long and short term projects, which stem from the children's ideas, experiences and interests, serve as the main framework for the emergent curriculum. A criticism of the approach is that because there is no written curriculum there is a lack of accountability to the wider society. Advocates of the approach argue that there is a detailed recording of the curriculum process, which opens practice to criticism and scrutiny. This is achieved through documenting the children's work through photographs, slides and film and in the form of publications and the travelling exhibition.

The role of adults

In Reggio Emilia centres parents are seen as central to the programme and are closely involved from an early stage. The information they offer about their child is fed back into the children's activities and experiences, thus keeping the child as a learner at the centre. Adults working within Reggio Emilia view group work as an important form of social learning. Groups of children stay with the same teachers over a three-year period in order to create a stable and secure environment and to provide for continuity of learning experiences for the children. The adult is seen as a facilitator of children's learning, helping the children to explore ideas and to determine problems that arouse their interest. The 'pedagogista' works with parents and teachers towards educational aims and goals and has a co-ordinating role with many facets, including administration and training (Fillipini 1995). The artelier (artist in residence) is closely involved in project work and in the visual documentation of the children's work (Vecchi 1995).

The environment

A focal point of Reggio Emilia centres is the piazza, a central meeting place where children play and talk together. The visually appealing and stimulating environment of Reggio centres has had an influence on some early years settings in the United Kingdom; in particular the use of light, mirrors and reflective surfaces. Reggio Emilia centres have large windows and white walls and use mirrored surfaces, particularly the tetrahedron with a mirrored interior, where children can sit and see themselves from many angles. The work of the children is displayed and portrays the ongoing projects and research, which document the emergent curriculum (Abbott and Nutbrown 2001).

Conclusion: gaining insights into practice

Moss (1999: 8) has discussed how looking at other approaches to working with young children 'provides us with a sort of lens for looking at our own situations . . . a lens which helps to make the invisible visible and to see what is visible in a different light'. In other words, looking at the work of others allows us insights into our own practice and helps us to see this in a new light.

References

Abbott, L. and Nutbrown, C. (2001) 'Experiencing Reggio Emilia', in Abbott, L. and Nutbrown, C. (eds) *Experiencing Reggio Emilia: implications for preschool provision*. Buckingham: Open University Press.

Athey, C. (1990) *Extending Thought in Young Children*. London: Paul Chapman Publishing.

Bennett, J. (2001) 'Goals and curricula in early childhood', in Kamerman, S. (ed.) *Early Childhood Education and Care: International Perspectives*. New York: The Institute for Child and Family Policy at Columbia University.

Britz-Crecelius, H. (1972) *Children at Play: Preparation for Life*. Edinburgh: Floris Books.

Carr, M. and May, H. (2000). 'Te Whaariki: Curriculum Voices', in Penn, H. (ed.) *Early Childhood Services: Theory, Policy and Practice*. Buckingham: Open University Press.

Chalibi, M. (2001) *Waldorf, Awakening to Tomorrow*. Berlin: Freunde der Erziehungskunst.

Dahlberg, G. (2000) 'Everything is a beginning and everything is dangerous: some reflections of the Reggio Emilia experience', in Penn, H. (ed.) *Early Childhood Services: Theory, Policy and Practice*. Buckingham: Open University Press.

Fillipini, T. (1995) 'The role of the pedagogista: an interview with Lella Gandini', in Edwards, C., Gandini, L. and Forman, G. (eds) *The Hundred Languages of Children: The Reggio Emilia Approach to Early Childhood Education*. United States: Ablex Publishing Corporation.

Foss, B. (ed.) (1974) *New Perspectives in Child Development*. Harmondsworth: Penguin Books.

House, R. (2000) 'Psychology and Early Years Learning: Affirming the Wisdom of Waldorf', *Steiner Education* 32 (2), 10–16.

Malaguzzi, L. (1995) 'History, Ideas and Basic Philosophy: An Interview with Lella Gandini', in Edwards, C., Gandini, L. and Forman, G. (eds) *The Hundred Languages of Children: The Reggio Emilia Approach to Early Childhood Education*. United States: Ablex Publishing Corporation.

Malaguzzi, L. (1996) *The Hundred Languages of Children: A Narrative of the Possible* (catalogue of the exhibit), Reggio Emilia, Italy: Reggio Children.

Miller, L. (2000) 'Play as a foundation for learning', in Drury *et al. Looking at Early Years Education and Care*. London: David Fulton Publishers.

Ministry of Education (1996) *Te Whaariki. He Whaariki Matauranga mo nga Mokopuna o Aotearoa: Early Childhood Curriculum*. Wellington: Learning Media.

Montessori, M. (1912) *The Montessori Method*. New York: Frederick Stokes Company.

Moss, P. (1999) *Difference, Dissensus and Debate: some possibilities of learning from Reggio*. Stockholm: Reggio Emilia Institutet.

Rinaldi, C. (1995) 'The emergent curriculum and social constructivism: an interview with Lella Gandini', in Edwards, C., Gandini, L. and Forman, G. (eds) *The Hundred Languages of Children: The Reggio Emilia Approach to Early Childhood Education*. United States: Ablex Publishing Corporation.

Schweizer, S. (2000) 'Creating a meadow for childhood, education for a new millennium, what do young children need today?' *Steiner Education* 32 (2), 23–8.

Smith, A.B. (2002) 'Promoting diversity rather than uniformity: theoretical and practical perspectives', in Ffthenakis, W.E. and Oberhuemer, P. (eds) *Early Childhood Curricular Issues: International Perspectives*. Germany: Leske and Budrich.

Standing, E. M. (1966) *The Montessori Revolution in Education*. New York: Schocken Books.

Stedall, J. (1992) *Time to Learn, A film about Rudolf Steiner Waldorf Education*, A Hermes Films Production, Forest Row, Sussex.

Steiner, R. (1919) *An Introduction to Waldorf Education*, The Anthroposophic Press, www.elib.com/Steiner/Articles/IntroWald.phtml.

Vecchi, V. (1995) 'The role of the atelierista': an interview with Lella Gandini, in Edwards, C., Gandini, L. and Forman, G. (eds) *The Hundred Languages of Children: The Reggio Emilia Approach to Early Childhood Education*. United States: Ablex Publishing Corporation.

Part 2
Children's lives

Gill Goodliff

Introduction

In the second part of this book we consider different aspects of childhood and children's lives. Each chapter invites you to contemplate ways of understanding young children and their play, and the importance of the everyday experiences and encounters you provide to support their learning, development and well-being. As you read we encourage you to reflect on your own values and beliefs about what children can and should do and how you support them. Themes that are considered in these chapters include: the significance of children's active participation in their own development and learning; children's health and well-being, healthy eating and health promotion; heuristic play; access to outdoor spaces and the potential for creativity across the curriculum; the importance of working with parents; the development of language and literacy and the teaching of initial reading; children's spontaneous song play and the potential of ICT and new technologies.

In Chapter 8 Tim Waller explores and critically discusses contemporary theories and perspectives on children and childhoods. Drawing on international literature and research, he examines key features of a contemporary view of the child that questions and challenges traditional theories of child development. He argues that a holistic view of childhood takes account of the differing contexts of children's lives, recognises their agency and the significance of children's active participation in co-constructing knowledge and meaning. This chapter also acknowledges the potential impact of new technologies on children's lives and research methods.

The background to more recent policy initiatives contained within the *Every Child Matters* agenda (DfES 2003) is illustrated by Angela Underdown in Chapter 9, through a case study of Jason and his mother. We see that issues such as child poverty and the links with health and well-being continue to pose challenges in the present day. This is despite past interventions and attempts to address such inequalities discussed by the author.

The play of babies and toddlers is the focus of Chapter 10. Ruth Holland discusses the impact that the heuristic play sessions introduced in her nursery had on the observed play behaviours of children aged 13 to 24 months old. Drawing on research into children's different kinds of play behaviours, the author discusses the findings from her own observations. She considers the involvement of practitioners in fostering, facilitating and observing exploratory play sessions with children under the age of three.

The theme of Chapter 11 concerns the opportunities and potential learning value of outdoor spaces to young children. Ian Shirley discusses practical ways in which practitioners might offer children access to outside locations, where they can experience the wonders waiting to be discovered through exploring with all their senses. He argues that encouraging direct personal exploration and considering children's emotional responses to familiar and unfamiliar places, can foster children's creativity and stimulate learning.

In Chapter 12 Marian Whitehead provides a brief overview of the complex issues and challenges surrounding the development of language and literacy in the early years of childhood. The teaching of initial reading and the controversies and dilemmas arising from compulsory synthetic phonics instruction in early years settings is the main focus of the chapter. However, guidance on good practice permeates the chapter. The concluding discussion prompts practitioners to review their own knowledge and practices.

We know that the creative and imaginative experiences offered to young children can too often be limited and superficial. In Chapter 13 Bernadette Duffy argues that creativity is part of every area of the curriculum and that all areas of learning have the potential to be creative experiences. In order to ensure that *all* children have access to a broad range of creative and imaginative experiences, she contends that practitioners must be aware of the importance of all children feeling valued and their voices heard. The author stresses the importance of working with parents and carers in encouraging creativity. The chapter concludes with examples of creativity in action across the curriculum.

Children's well-being is a central tenet of the *Every Child Matters* agenda (DfES 2003). Chapters 14 and 15 relate directly to children's health and well-being. Patti Owens considers the interpersonal world of the child through three key themes which inform developmental theory. She then examines in some detail Stern's model of infant development, in particular attachment theory. She considers the implications of Stern's work for early years practitioners in the context of a climate where 'success' may be measured in terms of achievement rather than children's emotional well-being. The *Early Years Foundation Stage* in England (DCSF 2008) is concerned with promoting young children's health. In Chapter 15 Deborah Albon and Penny Mukherji focus on healthy eating as an important aspect of health promotion and the early years curriculum. The authors offer strategies to early years practitioners for developing, monitoring and evaluating a health promotion programme.

Susan Young, in Chapter 16, reveals how young children 'play with song' as they engage in play alone or together. Discussing the observations she made of two and three, and three and four year olds in different settings, the author draws practitioners' attention to the ways young children spontaneously play with 'song' in their everyday activities. She describes the inventive way one observed practitioner fostered 'song play' with the children in her nursery. The chapter concludes by encouraging all early years practitioners to re-think and reflect on the potentially rich learning experiences they can provide by engaging children in and fostering 'playing with song'.

ICT has become an integral part of learning and teaching in many primary schools; however provision in the early years is much more variable. In Chapter 17, the final chapter of this part of the book, Mark O'Hara draws on research in four early years classrooms to explore how, when and for what purposes ICT is used. He suggests that ICT has the potential to support young children's learning, but that changes in the way it is used and opportunities for it to be used to support children's learning are necessary, if all children are to engage with and learn through new technologies.

References

Department for Children, Schools and Families (DCSF 2008) *The Early Years Foundation Stage*, http//www.standards.dfes.gov.uk/eyfs/.

Department for Education and Skills (DfES) (2003) *Every Child Matters*. Nottingham: DfES.

Chapter 8

Modern childhood
Contemporary theories and children's lives

Tim Waller

In this chapter Tim Waller explores and critically discusses contemporary theories and perspectives on children and childhoods. Drawing on international literature and research, he examines key features of a contemporary view of the child that questions and challenges traditional theories of child development. He argues that a holistic view of childhood takes account of the differing contexts of children's lives, recognises their agency and the significance of children's active participation in co-constructing knowledge and meaning. The chapter also acknowledges the potential impact of new technologies on children's lives and research methods.

Childhood may be defined as the life period during which a human being is regarded as a child, and the cultural, social and economic characteristics of that period.

(Frones, 1994: 148)

[. . .]
This chapter identifies five features of contemporary theories about children's 'development' and discusses their relevance to modern childhood. These are:

1 There are multiple and diverse childhoods
2 There are multiple perspectives of childhood
3 Children are involved in co-constructing their own childhood
4 Children's participation in family, community and culture makes a particular contribution to their life
5 We are still learning about childhood.

The explicit purpose of the chapter is therefore to explore alternative, contemporary views and not to repeat traditional texts (of which there are many) that consider children and childhood mainly from a psychological point of view.

Brown (1998), Moss (2001) and MacNaughton (2003), for example, remind us of the importance of equity and the need to examine and question our own assumptions about children and childhood. It is common for adults to underestimate children. It is generally acknowledged that children are unique individuals, live in a social world, and that there is no such thing as 'normal' development (Donaldson, 1978; Dunn, 1988; Rose, 1989).

Moving towards a contemporary view of the child, the terms 'child' and 'child development' and, the whole concept of childhood have been questioned. Drawing on a range of perspectives, including the emerging sociology of childhood, the concept of childhood and the social history of children are examined and discussed and a holistic view is promoted. The chapter considers issues of equality and how they affect children and also focuses on children's participation in the family and community. Insights offered by recent research into early brain development are also evaluated.

There are multiple and diverse childhoods

A contemporary view acknowledges that childhood is not fixed and it is not universal, it is 'mobile and shifting' (Walkerdine, 2004). This means that children experience many different and varied childhoods. There are local variations and global forms, depending on class, 'race', gender, geography, time, etc. (see Penn, 2005 for a detailed discussion of alternative childhoods). Until recently, most of the published research and writing about children, childhood and child development has focused on individual development as a natural progress towards adulthood. This natural progress is conceived as the same for all children regardless of class, gender or 'race' (see MacNaughton, 2003: 73). Much of this considerable body of work, written from the perspective of psychology and developmental psychology, has promoted what Walkerdine (2004: 107) suggests is an 'essential childhood'. This is a traditional, western developmental view of the child, which is used to categorize all children throughout the world (Dahlberg, 1985; Walkerdine, 1993). Penn (2005), cites Rose (1989), who makes the point that a 'normal' child is a:

> curious mix of statistical averages and historically specific value judgements. The most striking aspect of the 'normal' child is how abnormal he or she is, since there is no such person in reality and never has been. The advantage of defining normality is that it is a device that enables those in control or in charge to define, classify and treat those who do not seem to fit in.

> (Penn, 2005: 7)

Over 95 per cent of this literature originates from the USA (Fawcett, 2000) and much of it has been written by men, or from a male perspective. Walkerdine (1993: 451) argues that so-called 'scientific' psychological 'truths' about child development 'have to be understood in terms of the historical circumstances in which the knowledge was generated'. For Walkerdine therefore, this knowledge has been generated in a patriarchal society and the story of child development is one that has been dominated by a male view. She argues strongly that relying on psychology to explain child development 'universalizes the masculine and European' (1993: 452).

Recently, due to the growing influence of a new sociology of childhood, cultural and anthropological studies, an alternative view which argues that childhood is an adult construction that changes over time and place has been put forward (see, for example,

Gittins, 2004; Prout and James, 1990; James et al., 1998; Mayall, 2002). For MacNaughton (2003: 71) the development of the child is not a fact but a cultural construction. When we describe a child's development we are describing our cultural understandings and biases, not what exists in fact (Dahlberg et al., 1999).

As Penn (2005: 97) reminds us, 'the situation of most of the world's children is very different from those we study in North America and Europe'. The circumstances of the 80 per cent of the children who live in other parts of the world is significantly different in terms of wealth, health and culture (see Penn, 2005: 98–108).

1 in 6 children is severely hungry
1 in 7 no health care at all
1 in 5 has no safe water and 1 in 3 has no toilet or sanitation facilities at home
Over 640 million children live in dwellings with mud floors or extreme overcrowding
Over 120 million children are shut out of primary schools, the majority of them girls
180 million children work in the worst forms of child labour
1.2 million children are trafficked each year
2 million children, mostly girls, are exploited in the sex industry
Nearly half the 3.6 million people killed in conflict during the 1990s (45 per cent) were children
15 million children orphaned by AIDS, 80 per cent are African
(UNICEF: The State of the World's Children, 2004)

Further, the whole idea and usefulness of actually categorizing and studying something called 'child development' has recently been questioned. [. . .] Clearly change and transformation happen throughout human life, but the argument is about how that change is understood and constituted. Dahlberg (1985) asserts that due to the central and dominant influence of developmental psychology our view of the child has been constrained to a scientific model of natural growth. Typically, this model of the child defines development in terms of a relatively narrow range of psychological aspects such as social, emotional and cognitive or intellectual and physical development. However, as Riley (2003: 13) points out, these inter-related aspects are complex and developmentalism does not fully account for the complexity nor explain how they operate together in a holistic way. Zuckerman (1993: 239) also, argues that theories which suggest regular and predictable patterns of development oversimplify the reality of children's lives and actually hinder our understanding of childhood.

Dahlberg et al. (1999) also argue that development itself is a problematic term to apply to childhood because it produces oppressive practices. Walkerdine (1993) and Silin (1995) argue that our perspectives on the child have contributed to their oppression and exploitation in different ways because we are in a process of judging their differences to us as inadequacies or weaknesses rather than alternative ways of knowing (Silin, 1995: 49). MacNaughton (2003: 75) discusses this point and cites Cannella (1997: 64) who asserts that, 'child development is an imperialist notion that justifies categorising children and diverse cultures as backward and needing help from those who are more advanced'.

However, while there is an argument for the recognition of the social construction of childhood and the emerging sociology of childhood, as articulated above and in the section below, this is only one of multiple perspectives of childhood. Walkerdine (2004), for example, rightly questions the place of modern accounts of childhood that replace psychological understandings of individual development with sociological interpretations that focus on 'how child subjects are produced' (2004: 96). She argues that this 'dualism' replaces internal views of the child with external and that child development has a place. Considering childhood as a simple progression through defined stages is, however, too simplistic. There are multiple and diverse childhoods and in order to study childhood one has to consider a range of perspectives.

There are multiple perspectives of childhood

A number of alternative and multiple perspectives can be drawn on to explain contemporary childhood (Walkerdine, 2004). These perspectives are culturally influenced and change over time. As Kehily (2004: 1) points out, different disciplines have for a long time developed different ways of approaching the study of children. Recently, however, a growing body of international work from the perspective of sociology (James and Prout, 1997; Mayall, 2002), early childhood education (MacNaughton, 2003), critical theory and feminism (Walkerdine, 1993) and cultural studies (Cole, 1996) has been critical of the place of developmental psychology in producing explanations of children as potential subjects, whose presence is only understood in terms of their place on a path towards becoming an adult (Walkerdine, 2004: 96). A current understanding of children's development is, therefore, that it can be approached from a variety of perspectives and that these perspectives are culturally influenced and change over time.

James and Prout (1997: 8) identified the following key features of the 'new sociology of childhood':

- childhood is understood as a social construction
- childhood is a variable of social analysis
- children's relationships and cultures are worthy of study in their own right
- children are active social agents
- studying childhood involves engagement with the process of reconstructing childhood in society.

They suggest that 'the immaturity of children is a biological fact of life but the ways in which this immaturity is understood and made meaningful is a fact of culture'. For Cunningham (1995: 3), 'childhood cannot be studied in isolation from society as a whole'. In contemporary culture childhood has become a formal category with a social status, and is seen as an important stage in development. This status has been given boundaries by our society's institutions; families, clinics, early years settings and schools, etc. Jenks (1982) and Hoyles and Evans (1989) infer that this analysis places 'childhood' within a social construct, rather than a natural phenomenon.

The idea of childhood as a separate state to adulthood is a modern one. Aries (1962: 152) argues that very little distinction between children and adults was made until sometime around the fifteenth century: 'in mediaeval society childhood did not exist'. From the fifteenth century onwards children began to appear as children, reflecting their gradual removal from everyday adult society. Then, following the advent of compulsory schooling in the late nineteenth century (in Europe), the specific category of 'childhood' was produced, constructed (Aries, 1962) and institutionalized (Walkerdine, 1993).

Alternatively, Pollock (1983) suggests that it is mistaken to believe that because a past society did not possess the contemporary western view of childhood, that society had no such concept. Even if children were regarded differently in the past this does not mean that they were not regarded as children. However, he does acknowledge that the particular form of modern childhood is historically specific. Historical studies of childhood suggest that, in the UK, childhood was re-conceptualized between the end of the nineteenth century and the start of World War I (Gittins, 1998). These studies demonstrate a significant shift in the economic and sentimental value of children. Over a fairly short period the role of working-class children changed from one of supplementing the family income to that of a relatively inactive member of the household in economic terms to be protected from the adult world of hardship (Cunningham, 1995). Zelitzer (1985) argues that children's contributions to the family in western contexts is economically worthless but emotionally 'priceless'. Children's value lies in their ability to give meaning and fulfilment to their parents' lives.

Alwin (1990) points out that the distinct category of childhood arose out of attitudinal shifts that placed children in the centre of the family and encouraged an affectionate bond between parents and their children. Thus, for Alwin, childhood is defined by four criteria: protection, segregation, dependence and delayed responsibility. Further, Gittins (2004) argues that the development of childhood as a concept was class-specific, reflecting the values and practices of a rising European middle-class that increasingly differentiated adults and children, girls and boys.

Views of childhood, therefore, *have changed* and *are changing*. The main factors impacting childhood are; economic, demographic, cultural and political. Since 1945, as a result of economic conditions in the West and the increase of compulsory schooling to the age of sixteen, a 'teenage' culture involving clothes, music, media and films has been constructed. Teenagers are defined by their potential spending power and targeted by advertising in the same way as adults. More recently, a further group of 'tweenagers' or 'tweenies' have been distinguished (*The Guardian*, 2001). These are defined as seven to twelve-year-olds who already show teenage tendencies. For example, seven to twelve-year-old girls who currently shop for 'designer' clothes wear make up and own mobile phones.

There is also a growing recognition of the impact of digital technology on children's lives (see, for example Buckingham, 2000; Facer et al., 2002; Labbo et al., 2000; Luke, 1999; Yelland, 1999). They argue that it is important to consider how the development of the personal computer, computer games and access to digital communications technology such as email and the internet has affected children's experiences and relationships between children and adults. While Postman (1983) predicted that computer use would lead to greater divisions between children and adults, this has not appeared to be the case. Many children have become experts in using technology and are able to access and use information in different ways as a result (see Heppell, 2000; Luke, 1999). Yelland (1999), also, argues that we need to take account of the child's perspective of electronic media.

Children are involved in co-constructing their own childhood

While a child is clearly biologically determined as a young person, a 'child' is also socially determined in time, place, economics and culture. There is debate about the role of adults in this social construction of childhood and the agency of children in their own lives. Mayall (1996: 1), for example, has argued that, 'children's lives are lived through childhoods constructed for them by adults' understanding of childhood and what children are and should be'. Currently there is an acknowledgement of the significance of the dimension of power in relations between children and adults, and the impact of this relationship on our concept of and study and understanding of children and childhood (Riley, 2003). As Connell (1987) points out, power sometimes involves the direct use of force but it is always also accompanied by the development of ideas (ideologies) which justify the actions of the powerful. Canella (2001) argues that adult/child categories create an ageism that privileges adult's meanings over those of children.

Alderson (2005: 129) draws on gender studies to identify and emphasize the significance of these adult definitions and ideas in the lives of all children. The columns in Table 8.1 relate to what women and men were assumed to be like and Column 1 can also be applied to how children are perceived and presented in traditional child development literature and adult constructs of the child.

Alderson (2005: 131) argues that:

- children often seem weak and ignorant because they are kept in helpless dependence
- children who try to move to Column 2 may be punished
- they are not allowed to gain knowledge and experience
- it suits adults to keep Column 2 for themselves.

While there are many recent examples of literature that promote positive views of competent children, Alderson argues that there is a problem, especially with older

Table 8.1 'Half people'

Column 1 – women	Column 2 – men
Ignorant	Knowing
Inexperienced	Experienced
Volatile	Stable
Foolish	Wise
Dependent	Protective
Unreliable	Reliable
Weak	Strong
Immature	Mature
Irrational	Rational
Incompetent	Competent

Source: Alderson, 2005: 129

approaches, that emphasize negative stereotypes of children (based on Column 1) because of their age.

A modern view of the child acknowledges agency, that is, children's capacity to understand and act upon their world. It acknowledges that children demonstrate extra-ordinary competence from birth. It is informed by Malaguzzi's (1993: 10) concept of the 'rich child'. The child who is 'rich in potential, strong, powerful and competent'. This perspective sees the child as actively participating in her own childhood (Riley, 2003: 15). This view also asserts that while adults have power, children have power to resist that power. Hendrick (1997: 59) makes a significant point about the agency of the child. He argues that changes in the conception of childhood did not just happen, they were contested and not least important among the contestants were the children themselves.

Mayall (2002: 21) suggests that children are best regarded as a minority social group and she locates children's agency within the restriction of this minority status. Mayall (1994, 2002) does, however, acknowledge the significant role that children play in providing support and making and maintaining relationships in families. She recognizes children 'as agents, with specific views on the institutions and adults they interact with' (1996: 2). A number of recent writers (for example Corsaro, 1997; Qvortrup et al., 1994) go further and have argued that children are active agents who construct their own cultures. Children have their own activities, their own time and their own space (Qvortrup et al., 1994: 4). For example, Pollard's (2000) study on the agency of children at primary school in England showed how children learn to survive and cope with school through their own culture and the support of their peer group. 'Breaktime' is seen as a particularly significant site, providing the time and location for children's culture (see Blatchford, 1998). Children's views of their own childhood are therefore particularly significant. As Lloyd-Smith and Tarr (2000: 66) point out, the Children Act (1989) in the UK established the right of the child to be listened to. An important aspect is children's own views of their daily experience. Qvortrup et al. (1994: 2) argue that 'children are often denied the right to speak for themselves either because they are held incompetent in making judgements or because they are thought of as unreliable witnesses about their own lives'. Thomas (2001: 104) suggests that listening to children is important because:

- they have the right to be heard
- it can enhance their welfare
- it leads to better decisions.

Thomas argues that if there is presumption of competence, rather than incompetence, children often turn out to be more capable and sophisticated than they are given credit for. He suggests that the advantages of working with a presumption of competence and respect for children and what they wish to communicate are apparent in both childcare work and social research (2001: 110). However, Hill (1999) cited in Stainton-Rogers (2004: 140), makes the point that attempts to discover the views of parents as service users is only a recent trend and, in social care, it is even more unusual for children to be consulted.

Stainton-Rogers (2004) discusses the different perspectives of parents and children. It is clear from interviews with children (Pollard, 2000; Mayall, 2002, etc.) that parents' priorities are quite different to those of children. Stainton-Rogers (2004: 140) gives the example of parents' views of schools being concerned with performance and appearance ('league tables' and the physical environment), whereas children are concerned about social interaction and self-esteem (being treated with respect and not bullied). Parents expressed concern about their children facing external threats from traffic, being abducted by strangers and violence on the street – but children are most concerned about tension and conflict with peers. Research and literature by Carr (2001, *Children's Learning Stories*) and Clark and Moss (2001, *The Mosaic Approach*) for example, demonstrates the value and potency of listening to children. MacNaughton (2004: 46) suggests that 'children make their own meanings, but not under conditions of their own choosing'. MacNaughton (2004: 47) identifies four 'conditions of power' that impact on children:

1 The power of pre-existing cultural imagery and cultural meanings.
2 The power of expectations.
3 The power of positions.
4 The power of the marketplace.

MacNaughton argues that children enter a pre-existing world in which each of these conditions of power is already accomplished. As an example she discusses the children's entertainment and toy industry to show how global capital produces the material culture through which children construct their meanings. However, as Riley (2003: 14) points out, children are powerful consumers in the multi-million dollar industry of childhood that is focused around clothes, toys, books and electronic and digital media (see Luke, 1999; Buckingham, 2004).

Thus, while there is some debate in contemporary literature about the effect of adult power on childhood, children are seen as actively involved in the co-construction of their own lives. A modern explanation of childhood therefore seeks to understand the definitions and meaning children give to their own lives and recognizes children's competence and capacity to understand and act upon their world.

Children's participation in family, community and culture makes a particular contribution to their own life

Much of the recent literature in the field of early childhood argues that there is a need to consider the wider political, social and cultural context of childhood. Bronfenbrenner (1977) acknowledged a range of contextual factors that impact directly and indirectly on the development of a child in his concept of ecological systems. [. . .] Ecological systems theory represents the child's development as multilayered and the benefit of this model is that it places the child and the child's experience at the heart of the process of development. While it is a useful framework, it can be used to imply that context is something that impacts *on* the child, rather than *with* and *through* the child's participation. It does not fully articulate agency and co-construction. The recent influential work of proponents of the socio-cultural or 'situative perspective' such as Rogoff (1998, 2003), will now be briefly considered. [. . .] The socio-cultural perspective has adapted and enhanced the ideas of Vygotsky (1978, 1986) and provided valuable new insights into the collaborative nature of learning and the social construction of knowledge. It has been particularly influential in the field of early childhood. This perspective takes into account not just the child but the social, historical, institutional and cultural factors in which the child participates and co-constructs. It recognizes that human activity is heavily influenced by *context*, which includes artefacts, and other people. The socio-cultural approach also emphasizes the shared construction and distribution of knowledge leading to the development of shared understanding and common knowledge (Greeno, 1997; Lave, 1988; Edwards and Mercer, 1987; Rogoff, 1990; Pea, 1993). As a result, the child is not seen as an individual learner but as a participant in a range of meaningful and instructional social practices. Learning and development are inseparable from the concerns of families and interpersonal and community processes. This is a dynamic and evolving cultural context, in which it is meaningless to study the child apart from other people. Participation, as contrasted with acquisition, is therefore a key concept here.

We are still learning about children and childhood

If children are active participants in dynamic and evolving cultural contexts, as argued above, it follows that we will always be learning about children and childhood. In addition, changes in technology and new methods of investigation and research can also generate new areas of knowledge and understanding. One aspect of young children's progress that has received considerable attention over the last 10 years is early brain development (BERA SIG 2003: 18). Following recent advances in computer technology leading to the development of brain imaging techniques, such as Functional Magnetic Resonance Imaging (fMRI) and Positron Emission Tomography (PET) scans, neuroscientists have been able to measure activity in the brain and map the growth of the brain (Blakemore, 2000). However, there has been a debate surrounding the implications of this neuroscientific research for education and care in the early years (BERA SIG 2003: 18).

What the research has usefully shown is that there is a very rapid increase in the development of the brain for young children, especially those under three years of age Riley (2003: 3). The brain appears as early as the third week after conception (27 days) and develops rapidly, so that by end of the seventh month of pregnancy the baby's brain has all the neurons of the adult brain and many to spare (Catherwood, 1999). Crucial are the synapses – the connections between cells (neurons) where information is exchanged. Most development of synapses occurs after birth, however, at birth the neonate has approximately half the number of synapses of the adult brain. Very rapid growth then occurs from 2–4 months, so that by 6 months a baby has more synapses than an adult. Stimulation from the environment causes 'learning' either by stabilizing existing networks in the brain or by forging new ones. The ability of the brain to develop connections (or synapses) is known as plasticity. Recent brain research (Blakemore,

2000) has revealed that, after the age of three, plasticity continues at a slower rate until the age of ten.

Debate has focused on the possibility of 'critical periods' for learning, when plasticity is greatest. The argument is that if children do not have certain experiences during these critical periods, they will forever miss the opportunity to benefit from the experience. For this reason some writers (such as, Brierley, 1994; Sylwester, 1995) advocate 'hot-housing'. For example, starting to teach music to children under three, because the brain is so receptive to learning early on (see Blakemore, 2000). Bruer (1997), however, argues that making links between cognitive neuroscience and education is 'a bridge too far' and Blakemore and Frith (2000: 2) point out that brain research does not necessarily suggest the need to rush to start teaching earlier – indeed late starts may be considered to be in tune with the research.

A major assertion as a result of new information on early brain activity and growth was the acknowledgement of the extent to which the quality of early experience influences a child's later development. Because the vast majority of synapses are formed during the first three years of life and reduce after the age of 10, these first three years are seen as critical. However, it is now argued that while there are optimal 'windows of opportunity' for the development of synapses in the first three years, the brain is extremely flexible. An individual's capacities are therefore not fixed at birth, or in the first three years of life (Bransford et al., 2000). Bransford et al. (2000) review the work of 16 leading researchers in cognitive science in the USA. Key conclusions from this evidence suggest, according to BERA SIG (2003: 18), that learning changes the structure of the brain; learning organizes and reorganizes the brain and different parts of the brain may be ready to learn at different times. Thus, although there are prime times for certain types of learning, the brain also has a remarkable capacity to change.

BERA SIG (2003: 19) also usefully summarizes evidence from brain research that matches with psychological research as follows:

1 Experience – everything that goes on around the young child changes the brain.
2 Everything the baby sees, hears, touches and smells influences the developing network of connections among the brain cells.
3 Other people play a critical role.
4 Babies and young children have powerful learning capacities.
5 They actually participate in building their own brain.
6 Radically deprived environments may influence development.

Summary

This chapter has identified and discussed five key tenets of contemporary childhood. The tenets have articulated a complex model of childhood which is fundamentally different from a narrow 'developmental' approach. This model acknowledges that there are multiple and diverse childhoods. There are local variations and global forms, depending on class, 'race', gender, geography and time. This model also acknowledges that while there are multiple perspectives of childhood, it would be wrong to ignore or disregard developmental insights. Views of childhood have changed and are changing. Students of early childhood need to understand how and why child development theory is a product of certain historical, cultural and economic conditions. Some theoretical perspectives are particularly suited to explaining certain aspects of growth and change over time but the complex and interlinked nature of children's 'development' needs to be recognized. Developmental psychology should be studied alongside sociological, historical and anthropological accounts of childhood.

However, a critical difference between contemporary and traditional views of childhood is that the former recognizes the differing contexts of children's lives, children's agency and the significance of children's involvement in co-constructing their own childhood through participation in family, community and culture.

After 150 years of recognized child study we are still learning about children and childhood, the power of adults and the ability of children to determine their own future. Greater recognition of children's perspectives, the impact of new technology on children's lives and research methods will lead to further insights that will strengthen understanding and articulate new theories of early childhood.

References

Alderson, P. (2005) 'Children's rights: a new approach to studying childhood', in H. Penn, *Understanding Early Childhood: Issues and Controversies*. Maidenhead: Open University Press and McGraw-Hill Education.

Alwin, D.F. (1990) 'Historical changes in parental orientations to children', *Sociological Studies of Child Development*, 3: 65–86.

Aries, P. (1962) *Centuries of Childhood*. London: Cape.

Blakemore, S.J. (2000) *Early Years Learning*. (Post Report 140) London: Parliamentary Office of Science and Technology.

Blakemore, S.J. and Frith, U. (2000) 'The implications of recent developments in neuroscience for research on teaching and learning'. ESRC-TLRP [available: *www.ex.ac.uk/ESRC-TLRP*].

Blatchford, P. (1998) *Social Life in School*. London: Falmer Press.

Bransford, J.D., Brown, A.L. and Cocking R.R. (2000) *How People Learn: Brain, Mind, Experience and School*. Washington, DC: Academy Press.

Brierley, J. (1994) *Give me a Child Until he is Seven: Brain Studies and Early Education* (2nd edn). London: The Falmer Press.

British Educational Research Association Early Years Special Interest Group (BERA SIG) (2003) *Early Years Research: Pedagogy, Curriculum and Adult Roles, Training and Professionalism*. Southwell, Notts: BERA.

Bronfenbrenner, U. (1977) 'Toward an experimental ecology of human development', *American Psychologist*, 32: 513–531.

Brown, B. (1998) *Unlearning Discrimination in the Early Years*. Stoke on Trent: Trentham Books.

Bruer, J.T. (1997) 'Education and the brain: a bridge too far', *Educational Researcher*, 26(8): 4–16.

Buckingham, D. (2004) 'New media, new childhoods? Children's changing cultural environment in the age of technology', in M.J. Kehily (ed.) *An Introduction to Childhood Studies*. Maidenhead: Open University Press and McGraw-Hill Education.

Burr, R. (2002) 'Global and local approaches to children's rights in Vietnam', *Childhood*, 9(1): 49–61.

Canella, G.S. (1997) *Deconstructing Early Childhood Education: Social Justice and Revolution*. New York: Peter Lang.

Canella, G.S. and Greishaber, S. (2001) 'Identities and possibilities', in S. Greishaber and G. Canella (eds) *Embracing Identities in Early Childhood Education: 'Diversity and Possibilities'*. New York: Teachers College Press.

Carr, M. (2001) *Assessment in Early Childhood Settings*. London: Paul Chapman Publishing.

Catherwood, D. (1999) 'New views on the young brain: offerings from developmental psychology to early childhood education', *Contemporary Issues in Early Childhood*, 1(1): 23–35.

Clark, A. and Moss, P. (2001). *Listening to Young Children: The Mosaic Approach*. London: National Children's Bureau.

Cole, M. (1996) *Cultural Psychology: A Once and Future Discipline*. Cambridge, MA: The Belknap Press of Harvard University Press.

Connell, R. (1987) *Gender and Power*. Sydney: Allen and Unwin.

Corsaro, W.A. (1997) *The Sociology of Childhood*. London: Pine Forge Press.

Cunningham, H. (1995) *Children and Childhood in Western Society Since 1500*. London: Longman Group Ltd.

Dahlberg, G. (1985) *Context and the Child's Orientation to Meaning: A Study of the Child's Way of Organising the Surrounding World in Relation to Public Institutionalised Socialisation*. Stockholm: Almqvist and Wiskell.

Dahlberg, G., Moss, P. and Pence, A. (1999) *Beyond Quality in Early Childhood Education and Care: Postmodern Perspectives*. London and New York: RoutledgeFalmer.

Department of Health (1989) *Children Act 1989*. London: HMSO.

Donaldson, M. (1978) *Children's Minds*. Harmondsworth: Penguin.

Dunn, J. (1988) *The Beginnings of Social Understanding*. Oxford: Basil Blackwell.

Edwards, D. and Mercer, N. (1987) *Common Knowledge: The Development of Understanding in the Classroom*. London: Methuen.

Facer, K., Furlong, J., Furlong, R. and Sutherland, R. (2002) *ScreenPlay: Children and Computing in the Home*. London: RoutledgeFalmer.

Frones, I. (1994) 'Dimensions of childhood', in J. Quortrup, G. Sgritta and H. Wintersberger (eds) *Childhood Matters: Social Theory, Practice and Politics*. Aldershot: Avebury.

Gittins, D. (1998) *The Child in Question*. Basingstoke: MacMillan.

Gittins, D. (2004) 'The historical construction of childhood', in M.J. Kehily (ed.) *An Introduction to Childhood Studies*. Maidenhead: Open University Press and McGraw-Hill Education.

Greeno, J. (1997) 'On claims that answer the wrong questions', *Educational Researcher*, 26(1):5–17.

Hendrick, H. (1997) 'Constructions and reconstructions of British childhood: an interpretative survey, 1800 to the present', in A. James and A. Prout (eds) *Constructing and Reconstructing Childhood: Contemporary Issues in the Sociological Study of Childhood*. London: RoutledgeFalmer.

Heppell, S. (2000) 'Foreword', in N. Gamble and N. Easingwood (eds), *ICT and Literacy*. London: Continuum.

Hill, M. (1999) 'What's the problem? Who can help? The perspectives of children and young people on their well-being and on helping professionals', *Journal of Social Work Practice*, 13(2): 17–21.

Hoyles, M. and Evans, P. (1989) *The Politics of Childhood*. London: Journeyman Press.

James, A. and Prout, A. (eds) (1997) *Constructing and Reconstructing Childhood: Contemporary Issues in the Sociological Study of Childhood*. London: RoutledgeFalmer.

Jenks, C. (1982) *The Sociology of Childhood*. London: Batsford.

Kehily, M.J. (ed.) (2004) *An Introduction to Childhood Studies*. Maidenhead: Open University Press and McGraw-Hill Education.

Labbo, L.D., Sprague, L., Montero, M.K. and Font, G. (2000) 'Connecting a computer center to themes, literature, and kindergartners' literacy needs', *Reading Online*, 4(1). Available online at: http://www.readingonline.org/electronic/labbo/ [Accessed 6/8/00].

Lave, J. (1988) *Cognition in Practice*. Cambridge: Cambridge University Press.

Lloyd-Smith, M. and Tarr, J. (2000) 'Researching children's perspectives: a sociological dimension', in A. Lewis, and G. Lindsay (eds), *Researching Children's Perspectives*. Buckingham: Open University Press.

Luke, C. (1999) 'What next? Toddler Netizens, playstation thumb, techno-literacies', *Contemporary Issues in Early Childhood*, 1(1): 95–100.

MacNaughton, G. (2003) *Shaping Early Childhood*. Maidenhead: Open University Press.

MacNaughton, G. (2004) 'Exploring critical constructivist perspectives on children's learning', in A. Anning, J. Cullen and M. Fleer (eds) *Early Childhood Education*. London: Sage.

Malaguzzi, L. (1993) 'For an education based on relationships', *Young Children*, 11/93:9–13.

Mayall, B. (1996) *Children, Health and the Social Order*. Buckingham: Open University Press.

Mayall, B. (2002) *Towards a Sociology of Childhood: Thinking From Children's Lives*. Buckingham: Open University Press.

Mayall, B. (ed.) (1994) *Children's Childhoods: Observed and Experienced*. London: Falmer Press.

Moss, P. (2001) *Beyond Early Childhood Education and Care*. Report to OECD Conference, Stockholm 13–15 June.

Pea, R. D. (1993) 'Practices of distributed intelligence and designs for education', in G. Salomon (ed.) *Distributed Cognitions: Psychological and Educational Considerations*. Cambridge: Cambridge University Press.

Penn, H. (2005) *Understanding Early Childhood: Issues and Controversies*. Maidenhead: Open University Press and McGraw-Hill Education.

Pollard, A. (2000) 'Child agency and primary schooling', in M. Boushel, M. Fawcett and J. Selwyn (eds) *Focus on Early Childhood: Principles and Realities*. Oxford: Blackwell.

Pollock, L. (1983) *Forgotten Children – Parent: Child Relations from 1500–1900*. Cambridge: Cambridge University Press.

Postman, N. (1983) *The Disappearance of Childhood*. New York: W.H. Allen.

Qvortrup, J., Bardy, M., Sgritta, G. and Wintersberger, H. (eds) (1994) *Childhood Matters: Social Theory, Practice and Politics*. Aldershot: Avebury.

Riley, J., (ed.) (2003) *Learning in the Early Years: A Guide for Teachers of 3–7*. London: Paul Chapman Publishing.

Rogoff, B. (1990) *Apprenticeship in Thinking: Cognitive Development in Social Context*. New York: Plenum Press.

Rogoff, B. (2003) *The Cultural Nature of Human Development*. New York: Oxford University Press.

Rose. S. (1989) *From Brains to Consciousness? Essays on the New Sciences of the Mind*. London: Penguin.

Silin, J. (1995) *Sex, Death and the Education of Children: Our Passion for Ignorance in the Age of Aids*. New York: Teachers College Press.

Stainton-Rogers, W. (2004) 'Promoting better childhoods: constructions of child concern', in M.J. Kehily (ed.) *An Introduction to Childhood Studies*. Maidenhead: Open University Press and McGraw-Hill Education.

Sylwester, R. (1995) *A Celebration of Neurones: An Educator's Guide to the Brain*. Alexandra, VA: ASCD.

The Editor (2001) 'Welcome to the tween age', *The Guardian*, 30 March, pp. 15.

Thomas, N. (2001) 'Listening to children', in P. Foley, J. Roche, and S. Tucker (eds) *Children in Society: Contemporary Theory, Policy and Practice*. Basingstoke: Palgrave.

UNICEF (2004) *The State of the World's Children*. New York: UNICEF.

Vygotsky, L.S. (1978) *Mind in Society*. Cambridge, MA: Harvard University Press.

Vygotsky, L.S. (1986) *Thought and Language*. New York: MIT Press.

Walkerdine, V. (1993) 'Beyond developmentalism', *Theory & Psychology*, 3(4): 451–469.

Walkerdine, V. (2004) 'Developmental psychology and the study of childhood', in M.J. Kehily (ed.) *An Introduction to Childhood Studies*. Maidenhead: Open University Press and McGraw-Hill Education.

Yelland, N.J. (1999) 'Technology as play', *Early Childhood Education Journal*, 26(4): 217–225.

Zelitzer, V. (1985) *Pricing the Priceless Child*. New York: Basic Books.

Zuckerman, M. (1993) 'History and developmental psychology: a dangerous liaison', in G. Elder, J. Modell and R. Parke (eds) *Children in Time and Space: Developmental and Historical Insights*. Hillsdale, NJ: Lawrence Erlbaum Associates.

Chapter 9

Health inequalities in early childhood
Angela Underdown

The background to more recent policy initiatives contained within the *Every Child Matters* agenda (DfES 2003) are illustrated in this chapter through a case study of Jason and his mother. Issues such as child poverty and the links with health and well-being continue to pose challenges in the present day. This is despite past interventions and attempts to address such inequalities described by Angela Underdown.

Case Study

Jason and his mother, Jacky, have recently moved into a women's refuge to get away from Jason's father, Ned, who has become increasingly violent. Jacky has always been short of money and lately Ned has been spending most of his wages on alcohol. Jacky's depression started when she was pregnant and, although she loves Jason, she found it difficult to form a close emotional bond with him. Jason has frequent temper tantrums and has become very aggressive with other children. Jacky is finding it hard to get Jason to the new nursery since they moved and he has missed even more sessions because of chest infections. The health visitor thinks that Jason's cough would improve if he wasn't always in a smoky atmosphere and if he lost some weight. Jacky has been trying hard to cook healthy food but Jason will only eat burgers and chips.

The effect of poverty on children's health

Jason is not experiencing the emotional, social or physical health that we might expect for a young child living in the United Kingdom (UK) in the 21st century. The fact that Jacky has little money and is living in temporary accommodation, causes added stress and impacts on all the family's health. There has been a sharp increase in the number of young children living in poverty in the UK over the past twenty years. In 1979, 1 in 10 children lived in a household with below half the average income, but by 1999 this had risen to 1 in 3 children (DSS 1999). This dramatic increase in children living in families with insufficient income has had a devastating effect on children's health, with the gap between health experienced by those in highest and lowest income groups becoming ever wider. Issues such as disability often put added financial pressures on a family. Parker (cited in BMA 1999) concluded in his study that 55% of families with a disabled child were living in or on the margins of poverty. The BMA report (1999: 103) also highlights the severe disadvantages of ethnic minority families with disabled children:

> The barrier of inadequate information and lack of interpreters, the reluctance to offer some services, such as respite care, because of misunderstandings about the role of the extended family and the poor housing and poverty exacerbate any problems of care.

Many children face situations where their health is compromised, but living in a family with insufficient income frequently compounds these difficulties, as can be seen in the following overview.

Children who live in families experiencing relative poverty are:

- Less likely to eat a healthy diet.

People in lower socio-economic groups shop more carefully to obtain more food for their money but they are more likely to buy foods with high levels of fat and sugar because they are richer in energy and cheaper than fruit and vegetables (Acheson 1998, Leather 1996).

> Why do children from poor families consume such a lot of fizzy drinks, milk and white bread? Penny for penny, a chocolate bar provides more calories than carrots, even from a market stall. If the child refuses what is offered there may be no money in the budget for an alternative.
>
> (Thurlbeck 2000: 809)

While poor families are understandably concerned with ensuring that children's stomachs feel full and that they have sufficient calories for energy, repeated studies have shown that coronary heart disease, certain cancers and obesity are linked to nutritionally poor diets in childhood. For children like Jason, adult ill health may well be the legacy from his poor childhood diet. Lack of money for iron-rich food such as red meat and green leafy vegetables has also led to outcomes such as iron deficiency anaemia, leading to reduced immunity and greater susceptibility to infection (BMA 1999).

- More likely to have a childhood accident.

Child accidents are the major cause of death for children aged over 1 year in the UK and children from the lowest social classes are four times more likely to die from an accident and nine times more likely to die from a house fire than a child from a more affluent home (OPCS 1994, Roberts 2000). Children in poorer neighbourhoods are also likely to have less safe places to play and often face increased danger from traffic. The reasons for such a wide differential in morbidity from accidents between the socio-economic groups has been the cause of much speculation. It is most likely that a wide combination of contributory factors interplay in these outcomes. For example, a smoke alarm may seem an unnecessary expense when struggling financially to provide food for the family and perhaps factors, such as depression or lack of awareness of child development, may mean that risks to children are evaluated differently from one family to another.

- Less likely to be breast fed for any length of time.

Despite the benefits of being breast fed being clearly shown by numerous research studies, there is a dramatic contrast in the incidence of breast feeding, with women in higher socio-economic groups being twice as likely to breast feed as women in lower social groups (BMA 1999). Research indicates that the physical, cognitive and emotional benefits of breast feeding are many, including fewer allergies, fewer infections, less diabetes and the promotion of brain and intestinal development (Jenner 1988, James et al. 1997).

- More likely to have parents who smoke.

Women from social class 5 are four times more likely to smoke in pregnancy than women in social class 1 (Foster et al. 1997), resulting in lower birth weight, and an increased risk of sudden infant death syndrome (Leather 1996). In addition, other research has linked parental smoking, in low income families, to less balanced diets. In families where both parents smoked, 26% reported that they were unable to afford essential dietary items such as vegetables and fruit compared with 9% in low income families where the parents did not smoke (Marsh and McKay 1994). In addition the prevalence of asthma and chest infections is higher where children passively inhale cigarette smoke (Upton et al. 1998). In the case study, Jason's health visitor was clearly concerned about his repeated chest infections and the possible links with passive smoking.

- Are more likely to have a parent suffering from depression.

Although at least 10% of all mothers suffer post natal depression (Cooper 1991 cited in Roberts 2000), studies indicate that the long-term effects of maternal depression on the cognitive and emotional development of children are more marked where there is socio-economic disadvantage (Murray and Cooper 1997; Petterson and Burke Albers 2001). Some children, like Jason, may find themselves living in a family where a combination of problems such as lack of money, domestic violence and maternal depression constantly interact to negatively influence health.

- Less likely to achieve well at school.

Children from disadvantaged backgrounds tend to have lower educational attainments and research studies (Duncan et al. 1994) have shown clear, deleterious links between poverty and children's cognitive abilities, from as early as two years of age (Smith et al.

1997). Acheson (1998: 40–1) recommends that more high quality pre-school education should be developed:

> . . . so that it meets, in particular, the needs of disadvantaged families. We also recommend that the benefits of pre-school education to disadvantaged families are evaluated and, if necessary, additional resources are made available to support further development.

The effects of domestic violence on children's health

Domestic violence is prevalent in all socio-economic groups. Studies have indicated that in homes where there is violence towards women, there is also violence towards one or more children in 40–60% of cases (Hughes et al. 1989). Between 75% and 90% of violent incidents in the home are thought to be witnessed by children, in itself constituting emotional abuse. Pre-school children living in violent situations may present with behavioural problems or physical responses such as headaches, stomach aches or diarrhoea as well as erratic nursery attendance and poor concentration (Hilberman and Munson 1977). Abrahams (1994) also found a range of emotional health problems, from being frightened and withdrawn to being angry and aggressive. However, the results of trying to leave a violent home often lead to health consequences for children. Living in a refuge or bed and breakfast may well expose children to a change in economic resources, they may have to leave their friends and neighbourhood, and some children, especially from ethnic minority groups, may face bullying (Mullender and Morley 1994).

How can these health inequalities be addressed?

The government commissioned an 'Independent Inquiry into Inequalities in Health' and the committee chaired by Sir Donald Acheson produced their report in 1999, highlighting three key areas for health improvement:

- all policies likely to have an impact on health should be evaluated with regard to their impact on health inequalities;
- a high priority should be given to the health of families with children;
- further steps should be taken to improve the living standards of poor families.

The government has pledged to tackle health inequalities and to end child poverty within a generation and raise the threshold for defining poverty from 50% to 60% of median income (DSS 1999, Howarth et al. 1999). The government policy agenda includes a whole range of initiatives to improve the health of children. The plan is to ensure that a combination of national policy and local action encourages new and innovative partnerships to tackle inequalities. The policy agenda includes:

- reducing child poverty by reforming benefits and tax systems;
- raising awareness of healthy behaviour through the Healthy Schools Programme;

- setting up The National Family and Parenting Institute to value and support family wellbeing;
- introducing a National Service Framework (NSF) for children's health to ensure consistency of health services for children in all areas and that children and families are consulted about services;
- strengthening the support available to families in disadvantaged areas through Sure Start for families with children under four years of age;
- setting up the Children's Fund to allow local projects to provide preventative services for 5–13 year-olds and their families;
- improving the health of children in care through the Quality Protects Scheme;
- improving access to healthy food through school breakfast clubs in disadvantaged areas and the National School Fruit Scheme (see example below).

Examples of three interventions to improve children's health

The national school fruit scheme – a national government scheme

During 2001 the Department of Health piloted a National School Fruit Scheme in a cross-section of 500 primary, infant, special and nursery schools. The scheme aims to ensure that every child between four and six years of age is offered a piece of fresh fruit every day. The scheme has been evaluated positively recording comments from teachers like the following:

> It has challenged our misconceptions that children won't eat fruit.

> An excellent filler between breakfast and lunch, especially as certain children have little or no breakfast.

Following early evaluations the Government plans to ensure that by 2004 every child will be entitled to a piece of fruit every day at infant school.

Bright beginnings – a voluntary sector project

The Children and Young People's Participation Project Warrington aims to promote healthy eating and child safety. This Children's Society group meets once a week and is open to anyone in the area who cares for a child of under 5 years. The group has a rolling programme of activities and carers decide which session they would like. Sessions include:

- healthy eating;
- eating ideas for children;
- cookery on a budget;
- fun with food.

This project is a partner to Warrington Child Accident Group, who recently carried out a campaign called 'Careful that's Hot' in response to statistics from Warrington Accident and Emergency Department in 2000 showing the extremely high number of injuries to children due to hot drinks and hot fat. The project supports this safety campaign by offering a 'SAFE (Safe Affordable Family Equipment) Buy' outlet, selling safety equipment and offering advice on safety to families. This scheme aims to offer families the knowledge and skills to make their own informed decisions about child safety.

Development of home zones – a local authority safety intervention

Some local authorities are launching 'Home Zone' schemes aimed at ensuring that the local neighbourhood is for people rather than transport. The Northmoor inner city estate in Manchester based their home zone on a consultation with local people. The area is now planted out with trees, there are safe play areas and an improved road layout with traffic calming measures.

A partnership approach

The schemes described above are innovative attempts to try to improve the health and safety of children, but they can only have a real impact on health if they are part of an integrated range of measures aimed at meeting individual and community needs. Jacky, for example, may need more support with parenting Jason, help with finding suitable accommodation and help for her depression. Every initiative can add another part to the puzzle of meeting health needs in a holistic way. So, to use the example of developing home zones: this not only provides for safe play in a pleasant environment, it also involves consulting with children, young people and adults to find out what they think will work. By actually participating, people can 'own' the changes and develop personally through meaningful contributions. By actively contributing, children and adults feel valued and competent, whereas those living in deprived situations often feel powerless and unable to influence. Sure Start projects are attempting to redress this power imbalance by actively listening and consulting with the community so that services are flexible to fit what parents and children want and need.

References

Abrahams, C. (1994) *The Hidden Victims: Children and Domestic Violence*. London: NCH Action for Children.

Acheson, Sir Donald. (1998) *Independent Inquiry into Inequalities in Health Report*. London: HMSO.

BMA (British Medical Association) (1999) *Growing up in Britain: Ensuring a healthy future for our children*. A study of 0–5-year-olds. London: BMA.

Department for Education and Skills (DfES) (2003) *Every Child Matters*. Nottingham: DfES.

DSS (Department of Social Security) (1999) *Opportunity For All: Tackling Poverty and Social Exclusion, The First Annual Report*. London: HMSO.

Duncan, G., Brooks-Gunn, J. and Klebanov, P. (1994) 'Economic deprivation and early childhood development', *Child Development* 65(2), 296–318.

Foster, K., Lader, D. and Cheesborough, S. (1997) *Infant Feeding*. London: HMSO.

Hilberman, E. and Munson, K. (1977) 'Sixty battered women', *Victimology: An International Journal* 2(3–4), 460–70.

Howarth, C., Kenway, P., Palmer, R. and Miorellie, R. (1999) *Monitoring Poverty and Social Exclusion*. York: Joseph Rowntree Foundation. London: New Policy Institute.

Hughes, H., Parkinson, D. and Vargo, M. (1989) 'Witnessing spouse abuse and experiencing physical abuse: a double whammy?', *Journal of Family Violence* 4, 197–209.

James, W., Nelson, M. and Ralph, A. (1997) 'Socio-economic determinants of health. The contribution of nutrition to inequalities in health', *British Medical Journal* 314, 1545–9.

Jenner, S. (1988) 'The influence of additional information, advice and support on the success of breast feeding in working class primiparas', *Child Care Health and Development* 14, 319–28.

Leather, S. (1996) *The Making of Modern Malnutrition: An Overview of Food Poverty in the UK*. London: The Caroline Walker Trust.

Marsh, A. and McKay, S. (1994) *Poor Smokers*. London: Policy Studies Institute.

Mullender, A. and Morley, R. (1994) *Children Living with Domestic Violence: Putting Men's Abuse of Women on the Child Care Agenda*. London: Whiting and Birch.

Murray, L. and Cooper, P. (1997) (eds) *Postpartum Depression and Child Development*. New York: Guilford Press.

Office of Population Censuses and Surveys (OPCS) (1994) *Child Accident Statistics 1993*. London: HMSO.

Petterson, S. and Burke Albers, A. (2001) 'Effects of poverty and maternal depression on early child development', *Child Development* 72(6), 1794–1813.

Roberts, H. (2000) *What Works in Reducing Inequalities in Child Health?* London: Barnardo's.

Smith, J., Brooks-Gunn, J. and Klebanov, P. (1997) 'The consequences of living in poverty for young children's cognitive and verbal ability and early school achievement', in Duncan, G. and Brooks-Gunn, J. *Consequences of Growing Up Poor*, 132–89. New York: Sage.

Thurlbeck, S. (2000) '*Growing Up in Britain*' (Review), *British Medical Journal* 320, 809.

Upton, M., Watt, G., Davy Smith, G. *et al.* (1998) 'Permanent effects of maternal smoking on offsprings' lung function', *Lancet* 352, 453.

Chapter 10

'What's it all about?' – how introducing heuristic play has affected provision for the under-threes in one day nursery
Ruth Holland

This chapter focuses on the impact of heuristic play sessions on the observed play behaviours of children aged 13 to 24 months old. Drawing on research into children's different kinds of play behaviours, nursery manager Ruth Holland discusses the findings from her observations. The author considers the involvement of practitioners in fostering, facilitating and observing exploratory play sessions with under-threes.

Introduction

> Too many books and training materials bunch the needs of under fives together but we must take care to perceive the needs of each child as unique, and to acknowledge that they each have special learning needs at different stages in their development.
>
> (Rouse and Griffin 1992:149)

The above statement describes a situation of which I have become increasingly aware. As co-owner/manager of a 60-place day nursery where over half the children are under 3, and approximately one third of children are under 2, part of my role is to oversee the planning of play and activities. Much of the material written about play is produced with 3 to 5 year-olds in mind, and does not specifically address the needs of younger children, with the result that play for children under 3 is often a watered down version of play aimed at 3 to 5 year-olds. For example a leaf printing activity may be carried out with a group of 3 to 5 year-olds with the aim of increasing the children's awareness of leaf shape or autumn colours and/or extending the children's painting skills, as well as many other possibilities. When this same activity is offered to a group of 18 to 24 month-old children who may be more interested in putting their hands in the paint, dripping paint from the brush or floating the leaves off the table, adults are often guilty of expecting the same response as they do from older children. We need to be careful that we are not guilty of fitting the child to the activity rather than the activity to the child.

One specific factor which should be considered when planning play provision for children under 3 is the tremendous rate at which development takes place. Two of the major milestones affecting children's play are mobility and speech acquisition; i.e. the needs of a small baby lying on a mat are going to be very different from the child who has just learned to walk, and again different from the child whose speech has become fluent. [. . .]

Heuristic play

In my quest to discover more about play for children under 3 I have found work around the concept of heuristic play particularly fruitful.

'Heuristic play' is a term used by the trainer and educator Elinor Goldschmied to describe the early stages of play in which children's absorption is predominantly for putting in and out, filling and emptying containers and receptacles of all kinds. Here there is no question of success or failure. It is all new discovery and there is no 'right' or 'wrong'. The child learns from observing directly what these objects will 'do' or 'not do', in sharp contrast to much of the 'educational' equipment which has a result predetermined by the design which has been devised by the adult maker.

Part of the adults' role is to collect, buy or make a good quantity of objects such as empty tins and metal jar caps, woollen pom-poms, wooden clothes pegs, wooden and metal curtain rings and ping pong balls. The underlying idea is that these objects should offer the widest variety of materials and that they should be available to the children in large quantities.

Hair curlers of differing diameter; large and small corks; rubber door stops; varied lengths of chain, fine- to medium-sized links, not large chains; and large bone buttons can also be added to the collection (Goldschmied 1987).

The role of the adult

The role of the adult is partly that of organiser in collecting, caring for and thinking up new types of interesting items. They unobtrusively reorder objects and initiate the collecting by the children and the putting away of the materials in bags. They are essentially a facilitator, and as such they remain quiet, attentive and observant. They may study a particular child and note down all that he or she does with the materials, recording the quality of the child's concentration. The children are fully aware of their presence, though they do not encourage or suggest, praise or direct what the children do. (Only if a child begins to throw things about and disturb the others is it a wise plan to offer a receptacle and encourage her to place the things into it.)

It is important for the adult, during this heuristic play period, to sit on a chair. In this way she can be available to all the children and watch carefully what is going on. When the children are active in a group adults are likely to miss a great deal of what is significant in their behaviour if they are not seated. A child left free to choose what she wants to do in this secure atmosphere will tell a sensitive observer a lot about herself and so increase our understanding of her as an individual.

Staff who have experienced conducting this kind of play session have noted that:

- an atmosphere of tranquil concentration develops;
- children become absorbed in pursuing their own exploration of the material for periods of half an hour and more, without direct reference to the adult;
- conflicts between the children are very infrequent because there are abundant materials, but at the same time there are many friendly interchanges between them, with gestures and early verbal comments;
- during the long nursery day this activity brings calm enjoyment both for them and for the adults. The staff have an opportunity to observe the children in a way which is not easy at other times in the busy day;
- where there are children under the age of 2 in a mixed age group, it is possible, when there is a staff member available, for her to give some special attention to a very small group. It offers a great advantage since often the younger children find they have to compete for attention with the older ones;
- as soon as a child begins to have some command of language the nature of her use of the material changes and items are put to an imaginative use as another, more complex, type of play emerges. Instead of 'What can I do with it?', the question moves to 'What can this object become?' For example, a wooden cylinder, instead of being popped through a hole, may be used as a feeding bottle for a doll. To link this to the treasure basket phase, the same cylinder has been used, by the seated baby, to grasp, suck and bang with.

[. . .]

Play and the under-twos

Some observations

Goldschmied (1987) recommends heuristic play for children 10 to 20 months old. As staff we made a conscientious decision to include this type of play in our curriculum. We decided that the most appropriate place to introduce this sort of play in our nursery was the Toybox room, where the children are 13 to 24 months old. One of my first observations involved two children, Richard and Harry (both 24 months), using the bobbins as trumpets, thus progressing along the continuum of learning from *What can they do with the objects?* to *What are they really for?* The use of the bobbins engaged the children's imagination and enabled them to make an attempt at deciding what the objects were really for, although at this stage it was quite clear that the former question was the more important.

[. . .]

I believe that Hutt *et al.* (1989) have made an immense contribution to our view of play, moving us from the simplistic notion of 'it is what all young children do' to a recognition that it is a complex, high level activity which, like all learning, is developmental. She argues that under the umbrella term 'play' there are many different behaviours, and only through close observation of, and involvement in, young children's play can the adult really understand what is going on and begin to help children move on to the next stage. The terms 'ludic' and 'epistemic' play are used to distinguish two very different kinds of play behaviours; they require different responses from adults.

Epistemic play behaviour
- is concerned with acquisition of knowledge and skill problem solving
- gathers information
- is exploratory
- is productive
- discovers
- is invention, task or work orientated
- is relatively independently of mood state
- has constraints which stem from the nature of the focus of attention
- needs adults to:
  – support
  – encourage
  – answer questions
  – supply information
  – be involved.

Ludic play behaviour
- is playful
- is fun
- is lacking in specific focus
- is highly mood dependent
- has constraints which (when they exist) are imposed by the child
- does not need to involve adults
- requires that adults should be sensitive to children's needs
- can be changed by insensitive intervention
- has the key features of enjoyment and fantasy
- is unconstrained
- is idiosyncratic
- is repetitive
- is innovative
- is symbolic.

Smilansky (1968) added a further category to Piaget's work, 'constructive play', in which objects are manipulated to construct or create something. I observed examples of such play during the session when Brittany (aged 23 months) stacked the bobbins, Lucy stacked the tins together, and Theo (13 months) placed the coat pegs all round the perimeter of the tin.

[. . . I also observed] the epistemic behaviour as described by Hutt *et al.* (1989), which is play that is exploratory, intent, attentive and assimilatory. This has important implications for adult involvement or at least, adult availability, if (as Hutt argues) the presence of the adult in epistemic, as distinct from ludic play, is crucial.

Important issues

I was so impressed with the quantity and quality of epistemic behaviour, as described above, that I turned my thoughts to two questions: how can we extend the opportunities for these children to gain learning experiences through exploratory play? Does this pattern of mainly exploratory play with some constructive and some symbolic play repeat itself if different toys are provided?

Taking my first question, I know the answer cannot just be 'more heuristic play', as we have found that if this play is offered more than two or three times a week to each child they begin to lose interest. I believe that this could be overcome if we had access to limitless new materials to add and swap with the existing materials but, as we don't, then other answers need to be sought.

In an attempt to answer the question I set up a water play session following the guidelines for heuristic play. Other toys and possible distractions were removed as far as possible and there was enough equipment to avoid conflict over sharing. Staff took on the role of observers and did not intervene.

The resources for the activity comprised ten shallow trays set out on tables. Each tray contained either warm, cold, clear or coloured water, with either ice cubes, corks or stones. After a while tea strainers and small beakers were added.

As I observed this activity I found, as with the heuristic play, that the behaviour was predominantly epistemic.

Another instance was when I observed this same group of children taking part in a gluing activity. As with the previous two activities all other toys were removed, each child had their own paper, glue, spreader and cut pieces of tissue paper, and staff intervened as little as possible.

The epistemic behaviour was repeated. The object of the children's intent was the glue. A great deal of time was spent stirring, dipping, spreading and making marks, with the glue and spreader on the paper. Sticking the tissue paper on was mainly ignored, unless suggested by staff, and then very often it was done quickly so the child could get back to exploring the glue. The children spent an average of 30 minutes gluing – Louisa (aged 24 months) spent 40 minutes at this activity and would have continued for longer had it not been lunch time! This is a significant finding given that researchers involved in the Oxford pre-school project (Bruner 1980) showed surprise when 3-year-olds concentrated on an activity for five minutes.

These observations led me to believe that these activities had succeeded in beginning to answer my first question: the waterplay session and gluing sessions had indeed provided further opportunity for exploratory play. My next step was to have a brainstorming session with nursery staff to produce examples of other exploratory play ideas, as my observations made me think there is certainly a need to provide this age group with plentiful opportunities for this type of play. As Abbott (1994: 80) points out, 'Hutt showed clearly that exploration is a powerful forerunner to full-blown play. Many teachers and other educators are guilty of hurrying children on to "production" when the joy, excitement, and learning to be gained from exploring the materials comes first.'

To help answer my second question – does the type of play change if the toys are different? – I set up two activities, deliberately choosing equipment aimed at play which Hutt *et al.* (1989: 224–5) found to produce ludic behaviour. The first activity was an outdoor physical play session with bikes, cars and trucks, and the second session was one in which imaginative toys were provided, such as small cars and a road mat, dinosaurs, farm animals, zoo animals, and play people.

What I observed from the outdoor play was that during the first five to ten minutes, play was relaxed and the children were at ease as they pedalled the bikes and cars around. After that the children became less boisterous, and I observed children examining pedals, looking closely at wheels, poking twigs between spokes and generally becoming more intent. What had begun with a group of nine children aged 13 to 24 months, all displaying ludic behaviour, changed after five to ten minutes to individuals behaving in an epistemic manner.

This pattern repeated itself during the imaginative play session. Again, to begin with, there were lots of examples of imaginative play – with the cars being rolled along the floor with 'brum brum' noises and animals being walked along with 'clip clop' noises – but again after five to ten minutes children began to examine the toys, turning them over, feeling them, placing them, examining them, etc.

So, therefore, from my observations the answer to my second question is that different toys and equipment can affect whether 1-year-old children play in an epistemic or ludic manner, but not as much as might be expected. But a third question might be – what exactly should be the adult role in these different kinds of play behaviours?

Staff involvement

I feel that children of this age in our nursery already have well-developed epistemic behaviour, and that while staff have an important role in providing the materials, equipment, a suitable setting and a calm atmosphere for exploratory play, there is little need for intervention during such play – this could well disturb a child's concentration or opportunity to learn through doing something for him or herself. I feel an important role for staff during such play is that of observer, thus enabling the future needs of the individual children to be assessed. However, this is something I will continue to monitor since Hutt clearly points to the important role of adult availability to support children's epistemic play.

However, in contrast to Hutt I felt that the children's play which displayed ludic behaviour – the physical and imaginative play – could benefit much more from adult intervention, as the children demonstrated their ability to initiate ludic behaviour play but were unable to sustain it for very long, unlike older children, who I have observed playing imaginative games over several days without adult intervention. It must be remembered that Hutt's research was with 3- to 5-year-olds, and clearly there are differences between this age group and the underthrees in their ability to sustain ludic play.

In order to support children I believe staff need to become fully immersed in the play, so that they are a part of it. It may be that staff initiate games such as chase in the garden, or perhaps they look to extend existing play, for example, by becoming the car park attendant when the children are playing on the bikes and cars. There may be instances where the staff play together themselves in order to provide model examples, such as holding telephone conversations using toy telephones.

However, in whatever way staff become involved in children's play, it is useful to bear in mind the conditions needed to ensure good quality play as identified in the Rumbold Report (1990) and described by Abbott (1994: 85):

1. sensitive, knowledgeable and informed adult involvement and intervention;
2. careful planning and organisation of the play setting in order to provide for and extend learning;
3. enough time for children to develop their play;

4. careful observation of children's activities to facilitate assessment and planning for progression and continuity.

[. . .]

Conclusion

Imaginative, exploratory and key workers' activities are now an established part of our nursery life for children under 3.

Of these activities it is the exploratory play sessions, I feel, that represent the biggest change. This would probably be the same for most pre-school establishments, as Hutt *et al.* (1989: 226) point out: 'Pre-school environments are structured in such a way as to encourage primarily ludic rather than epistemic activity . . . Free play, or ludic activity, clearly has an important effect on psychological development, but it requires appropriate counter-balancing by epistemic behaviour.'

I feel the quiet atmosphere and attentive behaviour of the children in exploratory play sessions can be likened to the behaviour of children when being taught in a whole-class situation – an idea to which I previously would have been averse.

However, my observations have led me to believe that the quiet atmosphere of these sessions and the attentive behaviour of the children provides them with excellent opportunities for learning.

References

Abbott, L. (1994) 'Play is ace!': developing play in schools and classrooms, in J. Moyles (ed.) *The Excellence of Play*. Buckingham. Open University Press.

Bruner, J. (1980) *Under Five in Britain*. Oxford: Grant MacIntyre.

Goldschmied, E. (1987) *Infants at Work* (training video). London: National Children's Bureau.

Hutt, J., Tyler, S., Hutt, C. and Cristopherson, H. (1989) *Play, Exploration and Learning*. London: Routledge.

Rouse, D. and Griffin, S. (1992) Quality for the under threes, in G. Pugh (ed.) *Contemporary Issues in the Early Years*. London: Paul Chapman Publishing/National Children's Bureau.

Smilansky, S. (1968) *The Effects of Sociodramatic Play on Disadvantaged Preschool Children*. New York: Wiley.

Chapter 11

Exploring the great outdoors
Ian Shirley

> The theme of this chapter concerns the opportunities and potential learning value of outdoor spaces. Ian Shirley discusses practical ways that practitioners might offer children access to outside locations where, through all their senses, they can experience the wonders waiting to be discovered. He argues that encouraging direct personal exploration, including consideration of emotional responses to familiar and unfamiliar places, can foster children's creativity and stimulate learning.

The great outdoors

It has always amazed me how differently children behave outside the classroom. Whatever the purpose of going outdoors the children and I always seemed to return in higher spirits. Science investigations, arts activities, sports and data-gathering tasks all became much more relevant the moment we left the sterile world of the classroom. But each of these tasks is usually part of a practitioner-initiated activity. How much more relevant and exciting could the learning be for our children if we allowed them to take some of the decisions about spaces to be explored and activities to be undertaken?

Recently, in the centre of a local town I took some time to watch the world go by. Soon I became aware that a large, slightly raised, aluminium circle in the centre of the square was causing a great deal of interest. Children couldn't resist it. They walked along its edge, trying not to fall off; they walked to the centre and jumped hard, testing its springiness and sound qualities; they scraped their shoes along its rough surface. One boy just stood in the centre and admired his new, slightly elevated perspective. Soon I noticed adults, too, were tempted by this object. Some, the responsible ones, walked around it. Some skirted the edge, feeling it beneath their feet, using their senses to get a good feel for the object. Some were openly inquisitive: they strode straight to the middle of the circle with a sure step, thoroughly enjoying the texture of the metal and the spongy bounce of this makeshift playground installation. To me it was a form of community performance art. I enjoyed the way a simple object affected the spirit of these shoppers for a minute – a brief diversion from the humdrum and predictable activity we call retail therapy.

We should be aware of this phenomenon. Napier and Shankey (in Wyse, 2004) remind us of the importance of the play model of learning developed by Hutt *et al* (1989):

> Without opportunities to explore, the child has a limited knowledge of the materials, their properties and the possibilities of use. Exploration allows children to develop their knowledge, skills and understanding. When these are in place children can progress to more creative or conventional responses.
>
> (Wyse, 2004, p. 150)

It seemed obvious to me that all the shoppers I observed were enjoying the intrinsic pleasure of this exploration process. Human beings are naturally inquisitive and it is up to practitioners to exploit this natural trait. Indeed some pedagogies, such as Reggio Emilia, denounce a given curriculum in favour of a curriculum determined by the child, as Thornton and Brunton (2005, p. 8) explain:

> In Reggio, there is no predetermined curriculum; children's learning is developed through their involvement in long and short-term projects . . . At the centre of the Reggio pedagogy is the child who . . . embodies a curiosity and open-mindedness to all that is possible.

That a simple object, such as the one in the town centre, caused so many people to observe, hypothesise, test and analyse suggests we should be making more use of naturally inquiring minds. It also suggests that novel and unfamiliar situations cause us to question. For this reason, and as already discussed above, practitioners should try to find novel and unfamiliar places for children's investigations. Certainly we need to go outdoors but where might remain unexplored? Every school will differ but locations chosen should be rich in features, safe and appropriate for intended purpose; familiar in outline but unfamiliar in detail. Here are some suggestions of locations that might be worth considering:

- underneath a hedge
- the car park
- under a window ledge
- a porch
- a bench
- a garden
- under a mobile classroom
- a wall of a building
- a tree
- under a stone or other object
- the path to the school
- the pond area
- the bin/skip storage area
- the playground

- the playing fields
- under a bridge
- in a nearby church yard
- the other side of the fence.

Getting started

In a recent arts project, students at Canterbury Christ Church University worked together with children in local primary schools. Part of their brief was to investigate the potential of the school grounds for motivating learning across the curriculum. One group had decided to focus on a seemingly dull grassy enclosure. It was a long narrow strip, the size of a regular back garden, protected by a fence on three sides and a low wall which met up with the playground on the other. Beyond one side of the fence lay an attractive and well-maintained garden; the remainder provided a boundary with the outside world. A significant feature of the enclosure was a large tree whose canopy dominated the air-space. Clearly this place was familiar but largely unexplored, rich in feature and, as it was enclosed, safe. No doubt the children noticed this space every day, as it lay very close to their classroom and outdoor play area. The students wanted the children to think about it in a new and highly focused way; they wanted to give the space an identity beyond anything that it had achieved so far. The idea was to develop the garden as a space for wishes – a 'wishing garden' in fact. The medium was to be the arts and the children were encouraged to think about the space through a range of sensitising experiences.

Sensitising experiences

We only make sense of places through action and interaction. Without this kind of experience we cannot know the 'essence' of a place. Such action and interaction involves a process of sensitisation by which places become familiar and understood. We use touch, smell, sight and hearing to reference the space and, consequently, we are able to select spaces for appropriate activities such as taking photographs, playing games, having a picnic, setting a story or holding an outdoor summer concert. In order for the children to design and build the 'wish garden' it was vital that they got to know the space really well first. They needed to know about its shape and form. They needed to experience its atmosphere and to become familiar with the artefacts that made the space special. For this a series of suitable 'sensitising experiences' were undertaken which had the additional benefit of encouraging the children to work collaboratively and, perhaps more importantly, in original and novel ways. Ways that were more related to children's imaginary play than to regular 'content-driven' learning.

Such experiences rely on the children being immersed in an environment through all senses. It is not enough to go on a sound walk and simply talk about what is heard. The children need to be encouraged to select, reject, sort, engage, create, develop and synthesise these sounds. They need to be encouraged to focus on detail. As Shirley Brice-Heath (2004, p. 44) notes:

[Children's] . . . attention to detail runs contrary to established and expected notions of the attention span of very young children. Their shifts in before and after drawings . . . attest to children's willingness to look and look again if given the encouragement and . . . the chance.

Perhaps we ought to give ourselves the chance to look again too. The tasks that follow are meant to stimulate interest in and awareness of the environment. While they will certainly work with children, you may equally enjoy doing them yourselves, with colleagues or with your family. One of the greatest joys of teaching is being a lifelong learner and being open to unexpected and unplanned moments of discovery. Rediscover your childlike inquisitiveness and never lose hold of it!

Sounds

Let the children experience the sounds of a place. Unusual spaces can be interesting sites for listening. Encourage them to explore the sound qualities of materials available: beating bins, running a stick along a fence, beating a metal pole with different types of beaters, real and found. Try tapping, flicking and patting with fingers. Explore shouting through pipes and tapping on different lengths of drainpipe. Most importantly, question the children about the noises they make. Get them to use appropriate language to define what they have heard. Talk about timbre – the way different objects sound. Explore what effects the sounds would be good for. Talk about pitch – how some sounds are higher than others. Get them to notice the connection between size and pitch. Create rhythm phrases. Play echo games and question and answer responses. Get the children to explore loud and quiet. Think about sounds that travel and sounds that are difficult to hear. Create maps of a sound walk through the space or plot sounds on a spatialisation plan like the one given below.

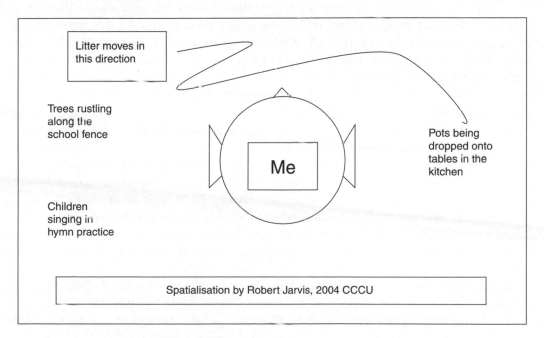

Many artists use such sounds to create soundscapes that suggest the nature of a place or an idea. The sounds can be collected on a simple tape recorder or, more interestingly, on a digital recording device. They can be analysed and described in terms of their main features and children may enjoy guessing what these sounds are. The children could be invited to produce a graphic score, showing the sounds as they appear, like a piece of music. Older children may go on to manipulating these sounds with simple computer programmes such as Windows 'sound recorder'. They can loop the sounds, play them in different directions and add echo effects before they are added to acoustic instruments as part of a musical composition.

The ultimate aim of this is to make children sound-aware so they enhance their familiarity with spaces they encounter every day. They can then make decisions about suitable spaces based on the sound environment they will be working in.

Sights

Encourage the children to notice what they see in these spaces. Allow them to work in twos, taking each other to interesting places, each child positioning the other carefully to notice something interesting exactly as they want it to be seen. One child could lead the other, eyes closed, and then squeeze their hand for as long as their eyes are to be open. They should be encouraged to describe accurately what they have seen. They should use words about colour, size, shape and texture to achieve real and cognisant sensitisation to the place.

Cameras are a useful and familiar device for getting to know a place. Set a limit to the number or types of photographs that can be taken. For example, ask children to take ten photographs that feature a shape or a colour. Or take ten photographs that reflect the atmosphere of a place. The children should work in groups and there should be much discussion about what photographs are to be taken. Digital imaging allows the children to accept and reject images more freely. You might want to restrict this by stating that they can only reject two pictures. All others must be carefully discussed and prepared before the shots are taken. The children could provide a presentation of their photographs. They can describe the features of a place they like or dislike. They can describe their reactions to a place and discuss how feelings within the group differed. Once again it is important to focus on the detail and help the children find words that express their thoughts and intentions. Imagine the discussion that could erupt over an upturned bin, or a building half demolished or half built.

Get the children to identify places where two interesting materials meet, such as where a piece of bark has been stripped away on a tree. Contrasting materials, juxtaposed, provide an interesting resource for close observational drawing. Focus on colour, texture and contrast and encourage the children to enjoy the interesting effects created by both natural and man-made objects. In focusing on such detail you will help the children to become observant and fastidious in their approach to all aspects of their work.

Ask them to collect items from around the space which are of special significance and provide something of the essence of the space. These could be used in a collage or as visual aids in a display of poetry. Use the objects as a basis for literacy. Ask the children to describe them in detail, on paper or to a friend. Play a game of 'guess who I am' or write riddles, where the person describing has to try to keep the identity of the object hidden, but nevertheless has to tell the truth. This will help them focus on the smallest details of the object.

The ultimate aim of all this is to make children visually aware. They will become used to looking for the detail and observant enough to suggest suitable spaces for a variety of activities in the future.

Concepts

> We learn by touching, smelling, hearing, seeing and responding emotionally and spiritually to stimuli. We can reinforce the experience by talking, reading, and writing, but the starting points have to be direct, personal experiences.
>
> (from *The Coombes School Handbook* in Jeffrey and Woods, 2003, p. 28)

Coombes School in Berkshire places equal value on learning outdoors and in, as this extract from its *Handbook* illustrates. Emphasis is on helping children understand what has been learnt. Equally, we should be looking for opportunities for children to notice their responses to spaces and activities throughout their tasks. So we need to encourage children to think about how they are affected by the activities and the spaces they are working in; that is, to consider the emotional charge of a space. Such thoughts encourage aesthetic awareness, and this not only helps children become cultured and thoughtful but can have a significant role in their spiritual development (see Radford, 2004, p. 87 for further discussion).

Ask the children to consider the place in a novel way. Perhaps they could collect photographs featuring a chosen number, such as study of 'Three' or maybe they could investigate shades of colour, such as a study in 'Yellow'. These could then be used as an introduction to the work of artists such as Paul Klee, who became obsessed with colour.

Ask the children to consider their emotional response to different places. Ask them to find comfortable places, sad places, scary places, peaceful places. Allow them to draw these places, perhaps getting them to think about how colour can help to create an atmosphere. Then get them to photograph the places using a variety of techniques, such as colour photography, black and white photography and close-up shots. Use the pictures for a class discussion about their feelings and to compare their findings.

Move a stone in a damp area and ask the children to watch the activity of minibeasts closely. They should sit and listen quietly, noting the different forms of movement of the creatures, their appearance and activities. Ask them to make suggestions about life under the stone. What are the characteristics of the creatures? Who's the boss? Who are the naughty ones? Get them to sketch one creature. Get them to take close-up photographs with zoom-lens cameras. The very act of getting down and dirty in the mud and clay provides sensory experiences children need. The conversations and shared experiences help to develop a community of researchers who are keen to find out about the world and who build on each others' knowledge and opinions.

Rich tasks

Once internalised, these observations can become synthesised in a rich task. An associate and creative pedagogue, Peter Dixon, suggested many delightful activities to help children learn through play and exploration. One memorable activity was to provide each child with a small chunk of clay so that they could go into the school grounds to find (create) a beautiful bird or fearsome monster. The children would collect materials and stick them into the clay. They had to provide accurate details for their creation, such as its common and scientific names, feeding habits, life cycle and other notable features.

I once did this activity with student teachers. They produced some beautiful and exotic birds which were celebrated in a variety of performances such as a Buddhist-style homage on the university lawn, and a Bill Oddie style nature programme in the science department gardens. Similar opportunities could be provided for young children by inviting them to create a dance for the creatures with musical accompaniment. They should be reminded of how the minibeasts moved so they can decide the kinds of movements to use in their dance. If this is to be a dance about birds they need to spend time watching birds, in the air and on the ground. It should be possible to create a bird hide in the school grounds, perhaps behind a set of steps or near a tree.

Older children could create nature programmes, lasting no longer than two minutes, using video cameras and the movie facility on digital cameras and mobile phones. Again, they should be encouraged to focus on the detail and to plan the action carefully in advance, but only after they have had chance to explore and play first. They could use a story board to present their developing ideas and groups of children could be encouraged to compose incidental music.

Collect the children's emotional responses to places by producing a huge, wall-sized display in the form of a map, where individual groups' feelings are plotted. These can be illustrated by their drawings and photographs and by the objects collected from the spaces. The very process of making such a display is a rich learning opportunity. Capture the conversations, the small acts of collaboration and the creative moments and reinforce these by rewarding the children as they are observed.

Such rich tasks allow children to make decisions about their own learning. You should allow them to get on with the tasks uninterrupted, only stepping in to keep the activity going and to show you value what they are doing. Sometimes you may need to contribute more to help a group move on. The temptation is to take over by giving specific directions. Usually it is more useful to ask questions that provoke the children to think, or even encouraging them to backtrack so that threads can be picked up and redirected. Either way, the benefits of such work is that the children have a strong sense of ownership.

Student teachers are often anxious about embarking on activities of this kind and express fear of coping with children's behaviour outside the classroom. However, many are surprised by how engaged the children are outdoors. Experience suggests that if the activities are fun, engaging and worthwhile, behaviour will not be an issue. Children are naturally inquisitive. They learn through observing, testing and accommodating behaviour. Margaret Donaldson (1978, p. 113) sums up these fundamental urges as 'to be effective, competent and independent, to understand the world and to act with skill'. If we are to truly allow our children to learn and to become independent beings we must provide opportunities for them to exercise control and to make decisions in groups and on their own. As Donaldson observes:

> It is arguable that in some ways we do not encourage competence – that we keep our children too dependent for too long, denying them the opportunity to exercise their very considerable capacity for initiative and responsible action. (*ibid*)

Allow the children to talk in groups and pairs. Show them you value their thoughts and discussions. Working in unusual spaces, away from classrooms, allows children to converse and explore without fear of disturbing other classes. The children will need to negotiate tasks and processes in order to move ahead. They will have to plan together and discuss their findings. They will have to use appropriate language to communicate nuance and to find ways of sharing their findings with the rest of the group. They may need to find ways of expressing the characteristics of a place to the whole class.

Find a reason to congratulate each child and make a point of stressing why their actions and achievements are good. Use domain-specific language to articulate the actual nature of their success and be prepared to step in and show good practice at any point during the activity. Commending children in this way not only provides them with a clear understanding of what good work looks like but also gives them a reason to go on. Simply believing you are good at something has a significant effect on actually becoming good at something.

Conclusion

The outside world offers a context for many of the activities children do and we shouldn't overlook the unfamiliar aspects of familiar places. Of course, we can view such places scientifically: we can draw them, measure them, record them, describe them, discuss them and analyse them. But we can also use the magic that is inherent in such places. We can play in them, perform in them, change them, transform them, redesign them, recreate them, speculate about them and represent them. We can try to remember how we used all kinds of places as settings for our own play as children. Our skill as practitioners allows us to step in to make appropriate interjections that will help move children on in their learning. We must try to provide a scaffold to support their learning through listening and observing but we must not hijack their ideas.

We practitioners should seek the potential of our school grounds and local environment to facilitate learning. We should provide opportunities for the children to take decisions about their learning and to take ownership of their curriculum. The school and all it represents is an important part of childhood. Even the more unusual locations need to be explored, demystified and valued if we are to encourage children to become creative and responsive to the ever changing world. We need opportunities to throw off the shackles of our over-prescriptive curriculum in order to do this. The answer may be to extend an approach to education more in keeping with the Foundation Stage as is becoming policy in Wales. For it is at this stage that we see teaching and learning as more in tune with one another. If only governments would defer to practitioners.

Sadly, as Wragg remarked (2004, p. 98), this couldn't happen in England because 'trust in professionals is simply missing'. So how can we maintain children's 'enthusiasm . . . imagination, playfulness, resourcefulness and genuine creativity' (Wyse, 2004, p. 128) throughout all stages of the primary phase? True engagement for adults and children alike is derived from an inner drive. I do not propose that simply moving children's learning outdoors will magically enhance learning. My contention is that exploring, playing in and re-inventing familiar and unfamiliar places that are easily accessible, near and free will foster genuine creativity, inquisitiveness and the construction of learning.

References

Brice-Heath, S. and Wolf, S. (2004) *Art is all about Looking: Drawing and Detail* London: Creative Partnerships.

Donaldson, M. (1978) *Children's Minds* London: Croom Helm.

Hutt, S. J., Tyler, C., Hutt, C. and Christopherson, H. (1989) *Play Exploration and Learning* London: Routledge.

Jeffrey, B. and Woods, P. (2003) *The Creative School: A Framework for Success, Quality and Effectiveness* London: Routledge.

Radford, M. (2004) The Subject of Spirituality, in Hayes, D. (ed) *The RoutledgeFalmer Guide to Key Debates in Education* London: RoutledgeFalmer.

Thornton, L. and Brunton, P. (2005) *Understanding the Reggio Approach* London: David Fulton.

Wragg, E.C. (2004) *Education, Education, Education: The Best Bits of Ted Wragg* London: RoutledgeFalmer.

Wyse, D. (ed) (2004) *Childhood Studies: An Introduction* Oxford: Blackwell Publishing.

Chapter 12

'Hi Granny! I'm writing a novel'
Literacy in early childhood: joys, issues and challenges

Marian Whitehead

In this chapter Marian Whitehead provides a brief overview of the complex issues and challenges surrounding the development of language and literacy in the early years of childhood. The main focus of the chapter is on the teaching of initial reading and the controversies and dilemmas arising from compulsory synthetic phonics instruction in early years settings. Guidance on good practice permeates the chapter.

Introduction

This title incorporates the first words of a brief transatlantic telephone call from my grandson, Dylan, who was just one month short of his 8th birthday. His claim may still rest on the fragile evidence of scattered pieces of paper on his bedroom floor and the energetic filling of a notebook with page after page of boldly scrawled conversations and descriptions. But many adult novelists do the same and Dylan is bouncing with literary pride. He has come a long way in the years since his birth when he first shared picture books with his immediate family and learnt about the roles of readers and the significance of pictures and print (Whitehead 2002). Dylan's own literacy history can best be summed up as one of meeting joyful challenges on a passionate pilgrimage from reading people and pictures to reading words and the world (Freire and Macedo 1987). There is nothing unusual about this story and Dylan is an ordinary little boy bursting with physical energy and enthusiasm for cycling and football, skateboarding and basketball, computer games and chess. However, he does have a family who believe in him as a reader and writer, share their own literacy activities with him and have always held firmly to the view that all young children require time, confidence, interested adults and enjoyment if they are to become readers and writers – or even novelists.

These views can no longer be taken for granted, not even in schools and early years settings, and joy in early literacy has increasingly given way to stress, boredom and failure. But this is nothing new, although we might have hoped to have moved on from narrow and punitive approaches to teaching literacy to young children. In fact, literacy has always been a site of controversy and prejudice because it is bound up with social and political power and citizens have always been judged and ranked by their levels of literacy (Whitehead 2004). However, when these crass judgements filter down into early years settings and classrooms and adult prejudices and misunderstandings are treated as respectable theories of literacy, young children are caught up in some very unpleasant 'reading wars' and good sense is the first casualty. The following challenges and issues will be focused on in this chapter:

- Literacy is not rooted in letters and words, but in non-verbal communication and close relationships.
- A narrow reliance on one kind of phonic approach in the initial teaching of literacy in English will always fail many children.
- At the heart of reading is a search for meaning and understanding – stories, books and visual, technical and cultural literacies are central to this.
- There is a dauntingly high price to pay for promoting bog standard literacy in the twenty-first century.

Communication, language and living

I am enjoying my coffee and watching a baby of about 6 months with a young father just a couple of tables away. The whole period of informal observation (or eavesdropping) takes 40 minutes and the play between child and father entertains many of the coffee bar customers, as well as me!

Initially baby is sitting on dad's lap and they play a game of peep-boo with a muslin square that dad regularly drops over baby's head and then whisks away for the exciting moment of discovery and shout of 'boo!'

A second activity starts up: dad makes exaggerated facial grimaces, baby chuckles and both take turns to poke their tongues out. This exchange continues intermittently throughout the next 30 minutes and for most of this time baby is also eating a biscuit.

Dad moves baby into a high chair and produces a rattle that he shakes rhythmically and then passes to the baby. Baby gives it a few hefty shakes before passing it back to dad and these musical exchanges continue, to the delight of both players.

From the vantage point of the high chair the baby begins to take an interest in the people sitting near by and goes in for some serious people-watching and attempts to make eye contact. Most people do respond with a smile and this elicits a triumphant answering smile from the baby. However, an elderly man at the table next to the baby is totally unresponsive and baby seems puzzled and confused, staring long and hard at this stranger who will not communicate.

This episode covered a substantial period of time and had its own rhythms of excitement, repetition, concentration and investigation. It could be described as 'getting your carer to entertain you' and, although there was a rich variety of play, communication, movement, sound, taste, texture and engaging with people, it was all done in a context of ordinary pleasures, familiar routines and a safe relationship. It should come as no surprise, then, that I wish to claim that some highly significant literacy developments start long before the early years of schooling. Literacy has its roots in the earliest inter-actions between babies and carers and in the play and investigations of toddlers on the move. These earliest stages of communication and language are shared with important adults, and sometimes with siblings, and coloured by powerful feelings and emotions about human relationships, identity, attachment, love and loss.

The work of Trevarthen has focused on babies 'learning in companionship' (2002: 20) and identified the prime need infants have to get to grips with the world and to do so in the course of sharing meanings with an older and wiser companion. This approach builds on the work of Vygotsky (1986) who described the optimal levels of learning and understanding reached by children when they are doing things in partnership with an older and more experienced member of the culture. This social construction of thinking highlights the importance of the rich thick textures of life and everyday experiences that make it possible for infants to get a grip on communication, relationships, objects and culture (Gopnik et al. 1999). These are complex ideas but we can bring them down to earth by reminding ourselves of the baby in the coffee bar. We can also make more sense of these ideas if we trace their links with early literacy learning:

- Literacy is communication, but communication starts with the non-verbal and verbal interactions between babies and carers and the baby partners are pro-active and skilled communicators.
- Literacy is an extension of oral culture and of our lifelong fascination with eaves-dropping, gossiping, singing, dramatizing, rhyming and punning, dancing and ritual. Here are the roots of linguistic patterns, phonological sensitivity, drawing, writing and reading.
- Literacy uses signs and symbols to carry meanings and infants also sign their needs and intentions with gestures and facial expressions and make significant marks in food, mud, moisture and dust, as well as 'pretending' that they are eating, sleeping, and so forth.

Perhaps the following observation is illuminating:

> I am observing the play of children in the large garden of a Children's Centre in an urban setting in the east of England. I decide to take a brief break to read through my notes and think about what I have seen, so I sit down in an empty willow arbour. In less than two minutes I am joined by three girls (4-year-olds) who sit close to me, take a great interest in my notebook, ask me what I am doing and ask me what I have written. They listen carefully to my answers (mainly focused on 'finding out what interesting things they can do in their garden') and then they suggest, very firmly, that they want to write about themselves in my notebook. I can hardly refuse and the results are below (Figure 12.1).

The important thing about this encounter is the children's clear grasp of what writing does, what it is for and their own roles as writers and recorders of events in their daily lives.

Trevarthen (2002) captures the richness of early communication, language and living, in a broad sweep of activities from birth to the early years of school:

Infants play with emotional narratives long before they talk, and toddlers create dramas together before they have any demonstrable 'theory of mind'. This gives both the reason and the means for language learning. From 2 to 6 children make things, tell and listen to stories, create drama, acting fantastic parts, dance and exhibit all sorts of musical skills. Their appetite for cultural forms of life is enormous and their perception of human roles is rich and penetrating. We may well ask what goes wrong!

(2002: 16–25)

We may well answer that children's own enthusiasm for communicating, learning and investigating gets smothered beneath a deluge of unimaginative information and unrelated facts. Children's achievements are also masked by a bureaucratic passion for recording what they cannot do. This arises from a worrying obsession with what comes

Figure 12.1 The little girls' drawing

after the early years and a failure to focus on the quality of children's lives here and now (Petrie and Apter 2004). The teaching of reading to very young children is often the chief villain in this story of lost opportunities, inappropriate educational provision and insensitive practitioners.

Phonic fibs – neither first nor fast

There is a wonderful story about teaching letter sounds in isolation that goes the rounds and, apocryphal though it may be, it has much to say to teachers, parents and communities. It was retold in a national newspaper (Mangan 2005) to great effect. The setting is a class of 4-year-olds in rural north Wales and their new, young teacher is attempting to teach the letter 'S' using a large colour photo of a sheep and demanding, with absolutely no success, that the children tell her what it is!

Eventually, one brave soul put up a tiny reluctant hand. 'Yes!' she cried, waving the photo aloft. 'Tell me what you think this is!' 'Please, Miss,' said the boy warily. 'Is it a three-year-old Border Leicester?'

The moral of the story is, never underestimate the young, thoughtful meaning-makers (Wells 1986) who are on the receiving end of such inept and grossly over-simplified approaches to the teaching of phonics. The recent 'fuss about phonics' is a case in point, and the fact that government ministers have thrown their lot in with the latest panacea for teaching reading quickly and cheaply is the worst possible reason to go along with it! Professional educators and carers have a responsibility to be thoughtful and to educate themselves about phonics and share their knowledge in accessible ways with worried parents and community groups. A confident understanding of the terms that are frequently bandied about makes a good start:

- *phonics* is a method for teaching reading that focuses on the relationship between sounds (phonemes) and letters (graphemes). A phoneme is the smallest unit of sound in a language but not necessarily a single letter, e.g. 'ee' in 'bee' is a phoneme. Linguists identify approximately 44 phonemes in English.
- *synthetic phonics* is the focus of attention in England, but it is also the oldest and most traditional of phonic methods. It assumes that simple decoding is all that is required in reading and teaches the sounds of individual letters and the 44 phonemes of English. Children are taught to sound out the letters in words and 'blend' them together. So we somehow make 'mer'- 'a'-'ter' into 'mat' and fail dismally when we get to the more complex word patterns in a simple text, e.g. 'said', 'the', 'any'.
- *analytic phonics* is based on modern linguistic research and children are gradually taught to look at segments of words and at the frequent patterns in sounds and words. This approach begins by focusing on the beginning, or initial, sounds of words, called 'onset', and the end phonemes called 'rimes'. This involves lots of enjoyable play with the alphabet and the sounds of letters (alphabetic awareness) and children can be helped to enjoy the *alliteration* of same initial sounds in tongue twisters and the same, or similar, end rimes found in words that *rhyme* in songs, poetry and verse.

Even these simplified definitions should make it clear that perhaps using phonics in the initial teaching of reading is not going to be a straightforward and unproblematic strategy for all children and all teachers. However, there are some phonic fibs currently being promoted at the highest governmental level in the UK, namely, the insistence that there is one, and one only, foolproof method for teaching all children to read! Fibs are those rather trivial little lies that we all resort to in order to manipulate a situation, or oversimplify a case, and phonic fibs are currently doing just that.

Even without historical evidence, recent professional experience and academic research, much of it from the USA, is highly ambiguous about the advantage of one kind of phonics over another (Meyer 2002; Altwerger 2005). It is more likely that different aspects of phonics are effective at different stages in young children's literacy development. Furthermore, we all get better at using a range of phonic strategies once we are able to read! There is no research support for the notion that every phoneme and every possible spelling 'rule' for English (166 and counting, plus a large number of exceptions) must be taught systematically to every child (Dombey 2006). Children really do teach themselves to read as they get involved with texts and many children who have been studied closely by academics learn to read at an early age without being taught by professional teachers (Clarke 1976). This is not to suggest that we abandon the teaching of reading, but we do have to include the achievements of such children in any respectable theory of learning to read and we have to analyse the grounds of their success. Some things are clear: the success of these children is rooted in warmly supportive homes, literacy-rich environments and experiences that help them make sense of meaningful print in the out-of-school world they share with their families and communities. They all seem to have encountered stories and printed texts, including books, as well as talk and play with language, songs, chants, hymns, rhymes and poems. Visits to libraries, places of worship, shops, clinics and offices also played a crucial role in the children's literacy, as did lots of markers and masses of scrap paper and steamed up widows! The children were supported by caring relationships with one or two special adults, as well as siblings, and their daily lives also offered opportunities to be quiet and undisturbed.

These general factors are a powerful challenge to the 'fib' that synthetic phonics must be 'first' in any approach to initial reading and, combined with the earlier discussion on communication and language development, they put paid to the notion that reading only starts when teachers 'do sounds'! The hidden, and often forgotten, mass of the literacy iceberg is beneath all the surface fuss over sounds, blending and word-building games. We must be aware of its significance and, putting 'first things first', help young children to bring their deep knowledge of language and communication to bear on the literacy of schooling.

The other 'fib' that is now permanently linked with 'first' is 'fast' and as a slogan for early education and literacy it is totally inappropriate. Those who work with young emerging readers and writers are privileged to be at the start of lifetimes of change, development, unpredictability, challenge and pleasure. Speedy solutions and quick-fix techniques are the worst possible approaches for young learners who need time for thinking, investigating, going 'off message' and playing. In the early years of care and education children must have quality experiences and their unique patterns of learning must be respected. Getting ready for the next and later phases of schooling is an unacceptable justification for nineteenth-century reading dogma and a compulsory early start to schooling! Young children are not chrysalides waiting for the ultimate stage in their educational metamorphosis: they are human beings living their lives here and now.

It is not surprising that a 'one size fits all' reading method appeals to bureaucrats and politicians. It makes the teaching of reading no more complex than buying socks in a department store and hides all the difficulties of individual differences in development and life experiences, complexities of language processing in the brain, or differences between the phonological system of English and other languages. Most important of all for the quick-fix advocates, the buying-new-socks theory of reading makes it possible to employ any well-intentioned adult to read the instruction books, pass on the information to the children and conduct the rote learning choruses! Thus freeing the early years of schooling from the expense of employing specialist graduate teachers!

Learning to read isn't that simple, unless adult practitioners know the one easy lesson about teaching reading: respond to what the child is trying to do (Smith 1994). This adult responsiveness involves understanding that the child must get the big picture about reading at the start: 'What's it for?', 'How does it work?', 'How do you do it?', 'What are the black marks for?', 'What are the pictures for?', 'What's it got to do with talk and telling stories?' And, What's it going to do for me? So many children are pushed through endless reading lessons without ever getting the chance to formulate, let alone ask, these initial questions about reading. Yet these are the basics for learning to behave like a reader: asking questions of the text and recreating the narrative. Young beginner readers have huge demands made on their language processing skills when they tackle text, but the more background knowledge they have of books and reading as a meaning–making activity, the better the trade-off between visual letter and phoneme decoding and constructing meanings (Crystal 2005).

Stories, books and new literacies

Stories are a timeless and universal way of making sense of experience. They are the means by which we impose order on random events and try to understand the significance of what happens to us and why people behave as they do. This is why we gossip and tell tales about our daily lives. This is why we listen to the stories of other people, or watch them narrated in plays, films and television: we hope to gain more stories, more meanings and more explanations to try out. This is why we read. It is also why very young children listen, chatter, tell tales, talk about their day, draw and make marks, dance and enact play scenarios, and mull over the puzzling world in which they find themselves. Stories are ways of thinking and are crucial to young thinkers as they set out on their daily meaning–making activities. Books give children and adults a hugely expanded resource of more stories for thinking with, and for understanding and exploring new worlds of experience. They are not optional extras in the early years, nor are they rewards for those who survive phonic training and are deemed eligible to move on to real reading. Stories and books are 'the basics' at the start of becoming literate and the only reason for doing so. The most dangerous aspect of the new synthetic phonics orthodoxy is the advice to use only approved phonically regular schemes, rather than real books written by knowable authors who share stories and facts about the human condition.

Stories and books also come with an added linguistic bonus! They use language in all its varied rhythms and patterns, including important phonic features such as alliteration, or same initial sounds, and the rhyming qualities of word endings that sound alike and sometimes look similar – but only sometimes! Stories and books offer very rich examples of new, unusual and exciting vocabulary for the emergent reader. I have seen a group of children in a nursery school so captivated by the 'sploshing' and 'squelching' of the traditional rhyme, *We're Going on a Bear Hunt*, that they rushed into the garden and created their own mud and river in a large sand tray so that they could squelch and splash through it while chanting the story word for word. Now that is the power of rhymes, stories and picture books!

Our children inhabit a complex world in which many forms of literacy exist and enter into their consciousness, as we realize when they 'read' the signs on the motorway, identify the appropriate public toilet door, play a computer game, operate a DVD player and a mobile phone. Modern research into early literacy now describes the multi-modal nature of literacies and many practitioners bring these insights to bear on classroom provision and the teaching of reading (Hall 2003; Larson and Marsh 2005; Pahl and Rowsell 2005). At a time when technology is transforming literacy, it is bizarre to tackle early literacy instruction with the tools of the nineteenth century! Our youngest children can read pictures, follow digital icons, operate sophisticated ICT systems, and many can move between two or more languages and cultures. How often do we use these powerful tools for thinking to help children access the written texts that we all want them to read? The 'new literacy studies' emphasize the old truths: the teaching of literacy must be situated and meaningful and draw on the everyday literacies of homes and communities.

Bog-standard literacy: paying the price

There is considerable concern among educators and authors that if we promote a narrow, utilitarian and outdated approach to literacy, we will pay a high price in alienation from schooling and all things educational, high rates of functional illiteracy and political disengagement and passivity. These are not exactly the lessons we would wish to teach in a democracy. This new/old approach has been wittily described as bog-standard literacy, but its modest achievements are bought at an extraordinary price (Powling 2005: 6). Perhaps we should remind ourselves of the price that will be paid in the early years.

Synthetic phonics does not improve young readers' understanding of texts and this seems to be reflected in a decline in reading for pleasure, helped along by a school system that now spends far, far more on testing than on books.

Young bilinguals are short-changed if they are only trained to bark at print and discouraged from using the complex bilingual literacies, stories and symbol systems of their homes and communities. In their early days in education settings and schools they need access to a richly symbolic and playful curriculum and the chance to communicate in many different ways.

Many young boys will pay a high price if the reading experiences they are offered are passive, rote-based and seat-bound! Boys are sometimes slower to get involved with formal reading instruction and need to be physically active learners for many years, but they also thrive on adventurous texts that are factually rich as well as imaginative.

Parents will pay a high price, namely the loss of the very special contribution they can make to their children's literacy development, if they are persuaded that there is only one way to teach reading. If reading at home with mum, dad or grandma, deteriorates into imitating the worst kinds of teacherly activities like sounding out individual letters and blending them, we will have lost one of the most empowering literacy strategies to have emerged in the twentieth century.

Conclusion

It is misguided to teach children the tricks of decoding simplified print and hope that they will apply these 'rules' to genuine texts at a later stage. The quality and content of children's first reading books matter if our children are to become passionate, critical readers. Complexity is central to children's earliest communications, language development, social experiences and thinking. Young children are sensitive to subtle differences and variations in printed material if the contexts involve meaningful and emotionally rewarding encounters with people, ideas and events.
[. . .]

References

Altwerger, B. (ed.) (2005) *Reading for Profit: How the Bottom Line Leaves Kids Behind*. Portsmouth, NH: Heinemann.

Clarke, M. M. (1976) *Young Fluent Readers*. London: Heinemann.

Crystal, D. (2005) *How Language Works*. London: Penguin Books.

Dombey, H. (2006) How should we teach children to read? *Books for Keeps*, 156: 6–7.

Freire, P. and Macedo, D. (1987) *Literacy: Reading the Word and the World*. London: Routledge and Kegan Paul.

Gopnik, A., Meltzoff, A. and Kuhl, P. (1999) *How Babies Think: The Science of Childhood*. London: Weidenfeld and Nicolson.

Hall, K. (2003) *Listening to Stephen Read: Multiple Perspectives on Literacy*. Buckingham: Open University Press.

Larson, J. and Marsh, J. (2005) *Making Literacy Real*. London: Sage.

Mangan, L. (2005) Do citizenship tests work? Ask a silly question. *The Guardian*, G2, November 2 p. 36.

Meyer, R.J. (2002) *Phonics Exposed*. Hillsdale, NJ: Lawrence Erlbaum.

Pahl, K. and Rowsell, J. (2005) *Literacy and Education: Understanding the New Literacy Studies in the Classroom*. London: Paul Chapman.

Petrie, P. and Apter, T. (2004) Will educating pre-school children in literacy and numeracy help to create a capable population? *RSA Journal*, pp. 6–9.

Powling, C. (ed.) (2005) *Waiting for a Jamie Oliver: Beyond Bog-Standard Literacy*. Reading: National Centre for Language and Literacy.

Smith, F. (1994) *Understanding Reading*, 5th edn. Hillsdale, NJ: Lawrence Erlbaum.

Trevarthen, C. (2002) Learning in companionship, *Education in the North: The Journal of Scottish Education*, 10: 16–25.

Vygotsky, L.S. (1986) *Thought and Language*. Cambridge, MA: MIT Press.

Wells, G. (1986) *The Meaning Makers*. London: Hodder and Stoughton.

Whitehead, M.R. (2002) Dylan's routes to literacy: the first three years with picture books, *Journal of Early Childhood Literacy*, 2(3): 269–89.

Whitehead, M.R. (2004) *Language and Literacy in the Early Years*, 3rd edn. London: Sage.

Chapter 13

Creativity across the curriculum
Bernadette Duffy

Young children's creative and imaginative experiences can too often be limited and superficial. In this chapter Bernadette Duffy argues that creativity is part of every area of the curriculum and all areas of learning have the potential to be creative experiences. In order to ensure that *all* children have access to a broad range of creative and imaginative experiences, practitioners must be aware of the importance of all children feeling valued and their voices heard. The author stresses the importance of working with parents and carers in encouraging creativity. The chapter concludes with examples of creativity in action across the curriculum.

[. . .]

The importance of access to a wide range of experiences

Each experience a child has offers possibilities for learning and if we are not aware of these we may miss opportunities and impede children's progress. We need to ensure that the creative and imaginative experiences we offer are:

- *broad* – they must include the full range of experiences
- *balanced* – they must not concentrate on one area of experience and restrict or neglect the rest
- *accessible* – children's access should be monitored and their learning and development systematically assessed.

While some of the experiences will be available all the time and provide our core provision, others may be introduced for a limited period in response to children's interest and needs. By giving children access to a variety of experiences we offer them the opportunity to learn and develop:

- attitudes, feelings and dispositions
- knowledge and understanding
- skills and abilities

and to use these in their own creative and imaginative ways. Each of these features of learning is important. For example, there is little point in teaching children the technical skills involved in reading if they do not also have the desire to use these skills. Conversely, it is frustrating to have a burning desire to create a sound but to lack the technical skills necessary to achieve it. While knowledge and skills can be taught, attitudes and feelings cannot be learned through direct instruction but only develop in an environment that is encouraging and values these attributes. Creative and imaginative experiences encourage a wide range of:

DISPOSITIONS AND ATTITUDES

fun   appreciation   confidence   self-motivation   values

enthusiasm   experimentation   persistence   sharing

curiosity   perseverance   enjoyment   cooperation

willingness   acceptance   excitement   reflection   self-esteem

concern   self-discipline   evaluation   concentration

helpfulness   pleasure   lack of inhibition   respect for others

---

As adults we divide experiences into different areas of learning or subjects. Children will not divide or perceive the experiences on offer in this way. For them, experiences are not compartmentalized and attitudes, knowledge and skills do not develop in isolation from each other. The example of Leeanne shows this.

Example

Leeanne, aged 5, was involved in acting out the story of Cinderella. This had gone on over a number of days and with each retelling the narrative became more complex and detailed. She reached the point in her drama when she needed the ball gown. With the help of a nursery nurse student, Leeanne created the gown from lengths of cloth fastened with safety pins and decorated with stapled-on braiding. Once the gown was completed she returned to her imaginative play and continued the story. At the end of the session she chose to record her experience by drawing a picture of the ball, which she shared with her mother at home time. Leeanne's learning covered a number of experiences: she engaged in imaginative play, used textiles and drew. She demonstrated a variety of attitudes, knowledge and skills. For example, cooperation, perseverance, knowledge of fabrics and their properties, knowledge of fairy tales, how to measure lengths of cloth, fine and gross motor skill. For Leeanne these were not experienced as separate, but as a whole.

Access for all

[. . .] Creative and imaginative experiences are not only for those identified as gifted. Everyone has an entitlement to the full range of experience and to reach their full potential. [. . .] But the society we live in assigns different value to different groups of people based on their:

- race, religion, culture, class and ethnicity
- gender
- additional needs such as special educational ones or disabilities.

People in particular groups are seen as inferior, for example, people whose skin is not white, people who have certain medical conditions (HIV, mental illness), or people who come from particular religions (Muslims, Jews). Children who belong to families in these groups can find that their access to the creative and imaginative experiences they need is limited because of beliefs based on the view that they are inferior.

Children from some groups appear to display marked ability in certain aspects of creativity and imagination. However, we need to be cautious about ascribing this to innate ability. It is just as likely to be the result of upbringing and expectations. For example:

- Some groups of Chinese children have highly developed drawing skills at an early age due to the value placed on and early instruction in these skills by the communities in which they live (Cox 1992).
- Boys often appear to be better than girls at creating three-dimensional representations with construction materials. While this may be partly the result of innate differences, most of the difference is due to the greater encouragement boys receive (Moyles 1989).

Children are aware of the values and judgements of the adults around them from a young age. The distorted opinions that develop from exposure to beliefs that are based on prejudice and discrimination will stay with them. Young children need to preserve, develop and value their own worth and the worth of those around them. This does not mean treating all children in the same way but ensuring that all children feel valued. If all children are to achieve this the adults who are part of their lives must be aware of:

- the prejudice that exists in society
- the ways in which beliefs based on prejudice affect children's opportunities to learn and develop their creativity and imagination
- the steps that can be taken to challenge and overcome prejudice and ensure equal opportunities for all children.

The range of abilities evident in any group of children make it extremely unwise to simply assume competence, or lack of it, on the basis of membership of a certain group.

The abilities they display may be the result of innate ability but can also be the outcome of encouragement from the adults around them. We need, therefore, to ensure that all children have access to a broad range of experiences.

Valuing children's race, religion, culture, class and ethnicity

The materials, equipment and experiences we offer should reflect a wide variety of cultural experiences. This is especially important for monocultural settings where children may not have the opportunity to encounter cultural diversity in their community, and when home cultures emphasize clearly defined roles for each gender. Creative experiences and imaginative play offer children the opportunity to explore lifestyles outside their immediate family and to gain an insight into the lives of others. It is important to avoid reinforcing stereotypes, for example, that all Indian women wear *saris*, or adopting a 'tourist' approach, such as only showing images of people from ethnic minorities in artificial and exotic settings. The aim is to increase children's understanding by showing them images that reflect the real-life experience of families from a variety of cultures.

Stereotypical ideas of class may limit children's access, for example, some forms of creative expression such as ballet and opera are seen as not being relevant to working-class children. Children from different religious groups can also find their access curtailed, for instance it is sometimes assumed that children from Muslim families are not allowed to depict the human form. In fact the depiction of the human form is only prohibited in mosques. There are many wonderful examples of Muslim artists representing the human form, for example in miniatures.

The experiences children have in their homes and communities will affect their uptake of the creative and imaginative experiences we offer. The experience of imaginative and creative play alongside an older sibling or friend can enhance younger children's play. In communities where they are part of an extended family or a network of close friends, young children will often have skills that children of a similar age, without access to these networks, lack.

Valuing children's gender

Young children are interested in gender differences and explore the roles adopted by each. While it is essential that children develop a positive self-image, part of which involves their identification with others of the same gender, we need to make sure that this does not limit their access to creative and imaginative experiences. The challenge is to confront stereotypes which limit access, and offer experiences which extend children's horizons. We need to think carefully about the labels we use, for instance, calling the imaginative play area of a classroom the 'Wendy house' or 'home corner' will not discourage boys to use it. Similarly we need to monitor children's use of the physical environment to ensure equal access. For example, girls may be reluctant to use construction materials if these have been monopolized by boys and are therefore seen as 'boys' toys'. Bloom and Sosniak (1981) examined longitudinal studies of creative people and found that early experiences which de-emphasized traditional roles were significant.

Valuing children with additional needs

Children with additional needs are sometimes offered a limited curriculum with the view that they need to give all their attention to the acquisition of so-called basic skills – though what could be more basic than the desire to create? However, in many ways the experiences that form the creative and imaginative range have particular relevance to children with additional needs. These experiences encourage an open-ended approach to learning and enable children to use all their senses, including those which may be impaired. When children have a condition such as autism, art and music may offer a means of self-expression and creativity when spoken language fails them. Creative and imaginative experiences can offer children with special educational needs the opportunity to order their understandings and inner worlds and share these with others. Music and dance can express meanings which surmount the need for words.

Children who have marked abilities may also experience difficulties. Marked ability in one part of the creative and imaginative range of experience, for example music, may lead to an over concentration on that area and a neglect of other aspects of creativity.

It is essential to ensure that children with additional needs are not intentionally or unintentionally excluded. The challenge is to adapt or expand the experience so that everyone can get involved. The example of Anderson shows how a group of practitioners tried to do this.

Example

Anderson, aged 4 years and 6 months, was visually impaired. His key worker observed his reluctance to engage in forms of representation which involved fine detail and confined locations, such as drawing while seated at a table. She responded by rearranging the outside space to include large sheets of paper attached to the wall for painting and drawing. Anderson responded with enthusiasm. He concentrated for long periods and returned to his drawings to refine and develop the images (see Figure 13.1). The opportunity to work on a large scale enabled him to make full use of his available sight and the more spacious surroundings allowed him to move without fear of bumping into a person or object. By assessing Anderson's particular needs and altering the way in which he had access to drawing experiences his key worker helped him to engage in an aspect of creative expression he had previously been denied.

Valuing children's voices

The content of children's imaginative play often gives us an insight into their pre-occupations, for example the superhero play that many young boys often engage in

Figure 13.1 Anderson engaged in representing a snail.

(Holland 2003). But we need to be aware that our attitudes may stop us listening to the voice of the child. Anning and Ring (2004) found that boys' use of drawing for meaning making was unacknowledged by practitioners until they were at the stage of visual realism. Holland (2003) also found practitioners reluctant or unable to accept the child's voice in superhero play.

Children with additional needs can also find their voices are unheard. In some cases access to the arts is limited because programmes for the children focus on what they can't do and practitioners concentrate on plugging the gaps. In other cases lack of imagination on the part of the adults leads to children not having access to opportunities because the additional support they may need is not forthcoming. In both cases children's voices are left unheard.

Working with parents and carers

The importance of working in partnership with parents is a key theme in the *Early Years Foundation stage* (DCSF, 2008) and this is especially true when it comes to encouraging creativity.

We need to think:

- How do parents feel about creativity?
- Do all parents feel the same?
- Are there differences based perhaps on age, culture, gender, class and faith?

There is no such thing as a typical parent! Values and traditions differ between parents, and it is important that practitioners respect this and give parents opportunities to discuss and share their views. Some early years practitioners express concern, and on occasion annoyance, at certain parents' unwillingness to allow their child to freely explore materials such as paint, clay or water. The example of Simon shows the importance of taking parents' concerns seriously and working with them.

Example

During a home visit to Simon's family it became apparent that his parents were concerned by the emphasis that the centre put on creativity and the arts or 'getting messy', as his mother and father put it. They explained to the staff that they did not see the point in encouraging the children to get messy and in the process ruining their clothes, and would like Simon kept away from such activities. Simon's parents were not alone in this view. While respecting the parents' viewpoint the staff also felt that it was important for parents to have an opportunity to understand why the centre valued creativity and the arts.

Staff organized a series of workshops on mark making which gave parents an opportunity to come and explore the creative process with their children. Some were organized during the day and others in the evenings. Children and parents had the opportunity to create large-scale paintings while listening to music, to paint on silk, and to use inks and other materials to explore colour mixing and printing. At the end of each workshop there was time for staff and parents to talk together about what had gone on and what they thought the children had got from the experience. Feedback was very positive. For a number of parents this was the first time since their own school days that they had the opportunity to paint and they rediscovered their own pleasure in mark making. Parents were impressed at the level of concentration the children showed when they were absorbed in representing their ideas. After a few weeks Simon's parent started to bring his younger sister to the workshops so that she could enjoy getting messy. As Simon's mother said, 'If they come home messy you know they've had a good day!'

Depth

Not only do we need to make sure that children have access to broad and balanced provision, we also need to be aware of the importance of ensuring that children are able to deepen their understanding. There is a danger that in trying to ensure that children have access to the breadth of provision our approach becomes superficial and they end up with a series of activities rather than the opportunity to delve into an experience. Children need time to explore and opportunities to repeat and return to experiences, so as to deepen their understanding.

Access to differing experiences allows children to increase their understanding by solving problems in different ways. Representing the same experience or idea through the different media enables children to explore it in depth. Using an unlikely medium to represent an image or idea, for instance, drawing a loud sound or making the sound of sunshine, challenges children's thinking and skills. The medium they finally choose reflects:

- their mastery of that medium
- the properties the medium brings to solving the problem they wish to solve.

For example, children can explore and deepen their understanding of pattern by encountering the same concept in a variety of media:

- *pattern you can hear* – music, for instance rhythm – ta, taa ta, taa, ta or repeated phrases in a song
- *pattern that moves* – dance, for instance – up and down, up and down or a sequence of steps
- *pattern you can feel* – texture and textile, for instance – under and over, under and over, in and out, in and out, or the feel of the weave
- *pattern you can see* – draw, model and paint, for instance, light and shade, decoration, repeated sequences of colour or shape.

Seeing patterns is a key element in the creative process and is crucial in many subjects, especially mathematics and science.

Children can also deepen their understanding through opportunities to represent their experiences and ideas using action, images and traditional symbols. Bruner (1982) describes these three ways of processing information as:

1 *The enactive mode* – based on action, learning through doing, for example, children representing fast and slow using their body movements.
2 *The iconic mode* – replacing the action with a drawing or using an image to stand for an object or concept, for example, children representing fast and slow using marks and signs they have devised themselves.
3 *The symbolic mode* – using traditional symbols (musical notation, writing, numbers), for example, children using music notation to represent fast and slow.

Through these modes children are able to produce their own representations, store and retrieve information (see Figure 13.2). At different ages different modes will predominate. For example, young children will readily use actions to represent their experiences, whereas they are less likely to use codes such as music notation. There is sometimes a tendency to neglect the enactive mode as children grow older but it is important to ensure that all the different modes continue to be available to children as each can offer new insights and deepen understanding.

If children are going to have the opportunity to delve into experiences and deepen their understanding they need:

- access to materials and equipment
- time to explore materials and equipment
- an understanding of the properties of materials and equipment
- the chance to develop their skills and understanding
- time and opportunities to use their skills and knowledge to create their own representations
- a variety of social contexts: working alone, alongside others, in pairs, in groups.

Figure 13.2 Alison, aged 4 years 6 months, who is starting to use traditional musical notation to represent tunes

Differentiation

While it is essential to ensure that all children have the opportunity to experience a wide range of experiences, it is also crucial to recognize that the needs of individual children will vary over time and that the needs of the children in any group will vary at any one time.

Children's learning needs will vary according to their:

- ability
- stage of development
- interest (see Figure 13.3).

In response we need to differentiate the experiences we present, to match the experience we are offering to the learning needs of the individual children we are offering it to. For example, through the questions we ask, and the responses we expect from different children, we can increase the complexity of the experience on offer. By breaking the experience and explanations we give into smaller, more manageable steps we can maximize understanding for less able children. Creative and imaginative experiences offer children the freedom to use the materials in an openended way. As there is no pre-prescribed end product individual children are able to use the materials in a way that matches their own learning needs.

The adults' expertise is in enabling children to develop mastery and the freedom to explore at their own level by finding ways to develop the skills and concepts children need at the time they need them. To do this we must be sensitive to:

- what to introduce, and when, by being aware of the typical stages children go through and what is developmentally appropriate
- the processes involved in creativity
- when to intervene and when to stand back.

Figure 13.3 We need to match what we offer to the interests of individual children. Georgia, aged 3 years 10 months. The caption under the representation reads 'Georgia was fascinated by the stuffed owl (she asked) "Was it real?". She represented it using pen, buttons and feathers. She remembered to draw its "beak, wings, and talons" '.

Some examples of creativity and imagination across the curriculum

Personal, social and emotional development

Goleman's (1995) work on emotional intelligence, our ability to tune into others and empathize with them, shows the link between imagination and emotional development. Without imagination we cannot gain an insight into the experience of others, guess what they are feeling or think or decide what may be socially acceptable. Working together encourages a sense of self-respect and valuing of others. This area of learning also includes the development of dispositions, attitudes and self-confidence. Creativity builds on children's curiosity and encourages a positive approach to new experiences.

Children display a high level of involvement and are able to select and use resources independently. Through the creative process children can develop concentration, problem solving, planning and seeing things through to completion.

Literacy

Approaches to literacy which emphasize the mechanics of reading to the exclusion of creativity limit children's development as readers and writers. Reading development builds on representation through making marks. Ascribing meanings to these marks helps children to understand the symbolic nature of written language. The narratives children develop through their imaginative play provide the basis for writing stories as can be seen from the example of Laura.

Example

Laura, aged 3 years, was fascinated by fairy tales. Her interest had been supported by her parents and key worker at the nursery she attended. Laura had spent much of her time during the previous week engaged in acting out her own versions of fairy tales and at the suggestion of her key worker recorded these in a book. She wrote various letters to which she ascribed meaning and read these to the adult in charge. She illustrated the story as she went. Her story told of a little girl who wanted to be a princess. To achieve this she needed a princess dress but her mother would only let her have a workday dress and told her she was a little girl not a princess and that it was time for bed. Laura drew together elements of her understanding of real life and used her knowledge of fairy tale to create her own story, with its own meaning.

Mathematics

Mathematics and creativity are sometimes seen as mutually exclusive and the way many of us were taught mathematics, with an emphasis on getting the right answer rather than creating our own understandings, has left some practitioners with a distinct lack of enthusiasm! Grey's (1997) work shows that children who are successful mathematicians are those who have learned how to develop new facts from old ones in a flexible way. Seeing patterns is at the heart of mimetic and the example of children exploring patterns shows 4-year-olds demonstrate this.

Example

A group of 4-year-olds had been exploring pattern with their teacher. They became aware that repletion is the key to patterns and began to identify patterns in the environment. For example they recognized the waltz rhythm – 1, 2, 3; 1, 2, 3; 1, 2, 3. They created their own patterns when they organized the fruit snack: apple, orange, banana, pear, apple, orange, banana and pear. While examining the number square two the children discovered another pattern: the number at the end of each row ended with a zero 10, 20, 30, 40, 50 and so on. No one had drawn the children's attention to this. They had used their knowledge of numbers and their growing awareness of patterns.

If we see mathematics as a set of skills to learn rather that problems to be solved we will discourage children's creativity. Real-life problems such as organizing a class celebration can give children opportunities to use their mathematical skills (Hanley 2004).

Science and technology

Science is all about being open to possibilities, living with uncertainty, thinking 'what if'. It is about finding patterns rather than knowing facts and it is a highly creative subject. Scientific understanding is developed through the investigations that occur when children are presented with unfamiliar materials and resources and exposed to a variety of materials and their properties. The glue example shows one such exploration.

Example

During her observations of a group of 2- and 3-year-olds Sam noticed that they were far more interested in exploring the properties of the glue she had provided for them rather than using it to stick the materials available in the workshop. Sam decided to encourage this exploration so she set aside a table covered in a plastic sheet for the glue exploration. The glue was available to the children throughout the day and was left overnight ready for them to continue their exploration the next day. Over the next few days the children poured and dripped glue onto the plastic sheet. They added other materials to the glue – food colouring, glitter, bits of paper – to see what happened. As the glue dried the children observed that it changed from opaque to clear and they could see the different materials embedded in the layers. This process went on for over a week.

The practitioners observed the children as they created the glue surface and recorded the children's development in the different areas of learning. For example, the children worked together as a group and developed dispositions such as persistence and concentration thus promoting personal, social and emotional development. They explored the properties of materials and developed their knowledge and understanding of the world. The children were given time and space to explore. Their ideas were valued and responded to.

Design and technology fosters curiosity. They involve solving problems to create something of use. In design technology there is a need to play with ideas and materials to discover how they work and how they can be used. The example of Victor shows how he uses his understanding of technology.

Example

Victor, aged 5, was part of a group of Year 1 children discussing a forthcoming visit to a farm during which they would find out how milk was made into cheese. The children were encouraged to explore a range of possibilities and various suggestions were made. Some thought that it was to do with magic while others remembered their experience of shaking cream in a jam jar to make butter. Victor listened carefully and commented that it would take a long time to shake the milk and the farmer must have a quicker way. After the discussion Victor went away to ponder the problem and created his own diagram of a cheese-making machine. Victor drew on his knowledge of butter making and his understanding of machines and combined these to reach his own conclusion.

Creativity and information and communication technology (ICT)

Like creativity ICT has a cross-curricular role. Through the appropriate use of ICT we can enhance our learning across the curriculum. For the youngest children objects such as mobile phones are often the props they use to engage in imaginative play. As children get older ICT enables them to try out their ideas on screen before they try them out in real life, for example seeing how a design looks from different angles. This enables them to explore a wider range of possibilities than would be possible in real life and take risks with their design that they may be reluctant to take with an actual model.

Creativity, geography and history

Geography, or a sense of place, involves introducing children to maps as a means of representation. In creating a map we do not record everything we see but make decisions about what the key things to record are and why. Topography is in some ways an act of fiction. Not only do we choose what to represent but also how to represent it. Geography is about our relationship with the world around us, both natural and man made, and involves the ability to imagine different environments and their possible impact.

History is about connecting events and hypothesizing about causes. It involves imagination and being able to put ourselves into someone else's shoes as the example of Nina illustrates.

Example

Nina, aged 4 years and 6 months, went to visit the Foundling Museum and during the visit was told about Captain Coram. A few days later she was playing in the garden and started acting out a story based on her knowledge of Captain Coram 'I'm Nelly and I am a little girl at the Foundling Hospital and nice Captain Coram is looking after me because my mummy can't'.

Conclusion

Children are not empty vessels. They have their own ideas and thoughts, their own desire to create. Our responsibility is to ensure that we build children's current skills and understanding and expand this by providing new opportunities that develop their attitudes, skills and knowledge across a broad range of experiences.

Creative development is an area of learning in its own right in the Foundation Stage and the guidance emphasizes the link between creativity and the arts. [. . .]

References

Anning, A. and Ring, K. (2004) *Making Sense of Children's Drawings*. Maidenhead: Open University Press.

Bloom, B.S. and Sosniak, L.A. (1981) Talent development vs schooling. *Educational Leadership*, 27: 86–94.

Bruner, J. (1982) 'What is representation?', in M. Roberts and J. Tamburrini (eds) *Child Development 0–5*. Edinburgh: Holmes McDougall.

Cox, M. (1992) *Children's Drawings*. London: Penguin.

Department for Children Schools and Families (DCSF) (2008) *The Early Years Foundation Stage*, http://www.standards.dfes.gov.uk/eyfs/. Accessed 08.12.08.

Goleman, D. (1995) *Emotional Intelligence*. London: Bloomsbury.

Grey, E. (1997) 'Compressing the counting process: developing a flexible interpretation of symbols', in I. Thompson (ed.) *Teaching and Learning Early Number*,

Hanley, U. (2004) 'Mathematics in creativity in the primary curriculum', in R. Jones and D. Wyse (eds) *Creativity in the Primary Curriculum*. London: David Fulton.

Holland, P. (2003) *We Don't Play with Guns Here: War, Weapons and Superhero Play in the Early Years*. Maidenhead: Open University Press.

Moyles, J. (1989) *Just Playing?* Buckingham: Open University Press.

Chapter 14

Children growing and changing
The interpersonal world of the growing child

Patti Owens

Patti Owens considers the interpersonal world of the child through three key themes which inform developmental theory. She then examines in some detail Stern's model of infant development, in particular attachment theory. She considers the implications of Stern's work for early years practitioners in the context of a climate where 'success' may be measured in terms of achievement rather than children's emotional well-being.

What is so important about interpersonal development?

As an early years practitioner for over twenty years, I have had the opportunity to observe a lot of young children and adults interacting as they spend time together. Nowadays I also work as a psychotherapist with adult clients. Time and again I hear stories of love and care offered to these people as children by nursery nurses, nannies, teachers and playgroup workers, as well as parents. And, of course, I hear the bleaker tales of rejection, humiliation and sometimes abuse at the same hands. Our responsibility as early years practitioners is a serious and important one in human terms; we play a key role in both the *intra*personal and *inter*personal development of human beings. Our work with the youngest children has a profound effect on the way they come to feel intrapersonally, or 'inside themselves', and on the manner of being they adopt as adults, in interpersonal relationships with others.

Interpersonal development is [. . .] an area of human development that we could be more aware of. [. . .]

[. . .] Poorly informed professionals can not adequately support a child's interpersonal development, and we pay the cost in society as children grow up into adults who do not relate effectively to others, or even feel good about themselves. [. . .] Despite the great contribution made by past theorists, it is easy to criticise some of their ideas from a modern perspective. Without an understanding of important research conducted more recently, early years practitioners can be left feeling that it is better to trust one's intuition in these matters, rather than a faulty or mistaken developmental theory.

A new approach to developmental theory

[. . .]
I have identified three themes which together inform [. . .] developmental theory and create a background for my discussion, later on in this chapter, of Daniel Stern's model of interpersonal development in very young children (Stern 1985).

1. There is now an emphasis on 'whole' child development. In effect this means that we are no longer easy with the notion of separating out areas of development. When I focus here on interpersonal development I keep in mind that this is only one, though a very important, aspect of every child's experience and perception. The notion of 'whole-ness' also transcends old-fashioned terms like 'phase' or 'stage' of development, favoured by earlier theorists. We concentrate on young children, but of course interpersonal development continues throughout human life, and it is often experience rather than ages, phases or stages, that triggers off new learning at a particular point.
2. The old debate about 'Nature versus Nurture' does not in fact get us very far, much as this has preoccupied past theorists (Bee 1992). We now give due recognition to the fact that human development takes place in a social context. The process whereby a child grows in human character and understanding is more like a 'transaction' than a battle where one side is dominant. We are learning much more about the complexity of neonate and infant experience (Kagan 1984, Berry Brazelton and Cramer 1991). [. . .] Researchers, furthermore, have identified the critical influence that even young children bring to bear on their carers and their environment, so changing the course of their own development (Woodhead et al. 1991).
3. Unlike major theorists such as Freud, who seems never to have actually observed an infant whilst constructing his theories about human developmental psychology, recent researchers base their theoretical models on close, detailed infant and child observation. Whilst accepting that observations provide the evidence for ideas about how children develop, most researchers also see the practical impossibility of a totally objective 'scientific' stance. The observer will be influenced by, amongst other things, their own early experiences, often seeing events through the filter of their own childhood memories (Houston 1995). [. . .] Daniel Stern (1985), for example, uses the notion of the 'participant observer' where he checks out his own observations and intuitions against those of any other adults, usually parents or carers, who are participating in the observation.

Without a theory, such observations and intuitions can be very interesting and rewarding to follow up, but they remain un-grounded. Current researchers, therefore, construct models of development that offer a kind of map, or template against which we can orient our observations. Unlike past developmental theorists whose work has often been presented as scientifically true, or even proven, modern researchers tend to take a more humble attitude, but one that enables them to continually check their theory against what they actually observe, revising the model in the light of further research. In this way, a theory can only ever be more or less 'useful', not more or less true.

These three characteristics of modern developmental theory are evident in the work of Daniel Stern, and it is to that research I now turn.

Daniel Stern's model of infant interpersonal development

Daniel Stern draws on two perspectives in constructing his model of infant development: psychoanalysis and developmental psychology, notably attachment theory (Bowlby 1965, Barnes 1995). As a developmental psychologist he is a committed infant observer; as a psychotherapist he makes some inferences about the infant's 'inner' psychological world, based on his experience of taking adults through the process of psychoanalysis. Stern gives a detailed account of the first two years of life, during which period he argues that the infant goes through the process of developing four distinct 'senses of self'. Each sense of self begins its development only when the infant has particular experiences and gains particular human capacities, during the process of wider growth and change. Stern refers to these sets of experiences as 'domains of experience' – not stages or phases of development.

In the first eight weeks or so of life the infant's sense of self is 'emergent' and the primary need seems to be for 'relatedness' with the primary care giver, usually the parent(s). Stern sees as crucial the infant's capacity at this point to perceive events and experiences with their 'whole' self. Think for a moment of a baby feeding: he or she touches, smells, sighs, desires to be fed, experiences satisfaction. These experiences do not distinguish between the physical and the emotional, for the infant's perception of the world takes place using their whole being. Correspondingly, Stern notices the importance of a key 'parental assumption', namely that this infant is a person with developing human characteristics. Consider how we might say to a very young infant things like, 'You want your nappy changed don't you?', or 'I bet you wish your sister was here.' Stern thinks, rightly in my view, that past developmental theorists have been wrong to see this neonate behaviour as purely based on physical survival needs. In doing so they have 'looked right past' what was happening in front of their eyes, as infant and parent/carer make those significant initial contacts; the beginnings of human relatedness. Hence Stern's labelling of this first domain of experience, the 'domain of emergent relatedness'.

Then between about two and six months of age, the infant develops what Stern calls a 'core sense of self', based on experiences and perceptions in the domain of 'core relatedness' to another human being, usually the parent or carer with whom the infant spends most interactive time. If we imagine for a moment that the infant could speak, he or she might say, 'I am a being with a physical presence. I can feel physical sensations, which for me are not separate from my emotional feelings. If I am happy I feel good in my body; if I am distressed I feel pain. I am aware that other beings (parents/carers) can influence how I feel.'

What is more, Stern's observations lead him to hypothesise that the infant begins at this time to remember the most often repeated events, and then make generalisations based on these rememberings. Stern calls this process the establishment of RIGs, or 'Repeated Interactions that are Generalised'. The experience of, say, having a bib put on comes to be associated in the infant with nourishment, which is a physical need. But the experience is also strongly associated with closeness to the parent/carer, and with that more of a sense of himself or herself as both distinct from, and related to, that other person. If the physical nourishment goes along with welcome, appropriate interaction from a parent/carer who tunes in to the infant on more than just a physical level, these experiences can be generalised to form special RIGs that will persist very strongly throughout their coming life. Good experiences of this kind, which include the special interaction with another person who gives emotional, as well as physical, nourishment, can help the infant to experience what Stern calls an 'evoked companion', or the experience of being 'not alone' psychologically, even when this is materially the case. Work with insecure children and adults suggests that where this process has not happened for some reason, the individual can not 'evoke a companion'; they can not believe that they will be protected and nurtured, however safe they are in fact (Gillie 1999).

The third sense of self, the 'subjective' sense, begins to be experienced, according to Stern's observations, around seven to nine months. This is the domain of 'inter-subjective relatedness' where, all being well, the infant comes to trust that his or her own feeling states are both unique to himself or herself, and capable of being understood by significant other people, mainly parents or carers. The infant realises for the first time, perhaps, that 'I have a mind, and so does this other person'. Intimacy can be more or less deep and fulfilling for the infant, depending on how he or she experiences the other person in relation to himself or herself. Crucial to this new development is the 'care-giver's empathy', or indeed lack of it. This is the first time, says Stern, that the care-giver's 'socialisation of the infant's subjective experience' becomes an issue. The parent or carer has responsibility for affirming or denying the infant's inner, subjective experience. A child can learn that some of their feelings – the need to weep, the urge to reach out and love another, for example – are, or are not, acceptable. These attitudes, as Stern notes, tend to move forward with us into adulthood, as strong and persistent RIGs.

All three domains of experience and perception continue through infancy and beyond, and we need to bear in mind that these are not stages or phases of development like those traditionally outlined, but ways of experiencing ourselves and other human beings that have their beginnings in our infant histories. These early experiences become part of our adult ways of being; part of how we experience ourselves in relation to others, helping to form our habitual attitudes and predispositions to the ever-changing circumstances of ordinary human life.

The fourth domain of 'verbal relatedness' depends on language acquisition and comes to the fore, according to Stern, at around fifteen to eighteen months. The infant becomes capable of making clear to others that they know things, using symbols and words. This gives them another way of thinking about themselves, others and the wider world; they begin to develop a 'verbal self'. Central to this process is the forging of 'we meanings'. Think of the kind of example where a toddler tries to make himself or herself understood; fails at first, then succeeds. Such verbal agreement, though necessarily symbolic (words are in themselves abstract entities) adds a kind of concrete-ness to the child's reality. Before words, a lot depends on the child's ability to respond to, then initiate, interactions with their parents and carers, in conjunction with the parent/carer's empathetic and welcoming response to the child's efforts. Now, says Stern, words can be used to solidify the sense that 'we' understand things together. The child can gain enormously in confidence and ability to relate and communicate with others, in generalising from these verbally supported RIGs. As with the other domains of infant experience, however, there is also the possibility to distort or fracture the child's experience. Words add another even more powerful dimension in such cases. An all too common example is the child who experiences violence or abuse from a 'carer' who at the same time speaks kind words like 'I love you, I don't want to hurt you, but . . .'. Or there is the example of the child whose attempts to reach out in affection to another person are met with words that should express reciprocation, but do not; the child instead hears harshness of tone, or experiences emotional coolness, not the warmth the words alone might suggest. As psychotherapists know, there are many ways in which the experience of 'words not matching my reality' can become part of the adult's way of being in the world, and their habitual expectations in relation to others.

Some implications of Stern's research for early years practitioners

So what are we to make of Stern's model of infant interpersonal development, as early years practitioners? Many of us will have dealings with infants and very young children so the relevance may be immediately apparent. Others will be working mainly with older children in the 0–6 years age range. It might be interesting then to notice how Stern's notions of 'domains' of experience, and development of different 'senses of self', for instance, can inform your observation and understanding of older children's interpersonal development.

With these issues in mind, I want to finish this chapter with an infant observation [. . .] I undertook and analysed in the light of Stern's model of infant interpersonal development.

Observation of Thomas

I observe Thomas [. . .] when he is ten months old (43 weeks). He is with his father, who shares childcare with Thomas' mother; both parents do paid part-time work. They are at a toy library group close to their home, which Thomas has visited twice before with his mother. Thomas and his father are playing on a large mat where four other children, all under a year, are using the selection of colourful and soft toys set out by the toy library leader and her assistants.

Observation method

As the observer, I have known Thomas' parents for several years. Thomas is their first child, and I have observed Thomas in the home setting on a number of occasions since his birth. I try to keep myself in the background, though if Thomas approaches me I will interact with him as normally as possible. Thomas' father has agreed to be a participant observer, and discuss the observation with me after it has been completed. The observation lasts about 5 minutes.

Record of observation

Thomas has been sitting near an eleven month-old girl, picking up and dropping squares of coloured felt fabric. He rolls from a sitting position into a crawl, moving across the mat for a couple of metres. He sits up, head turned to the right, and points, making excited 'Ee-ee-ee-ee!' sounds. Thomas' father, who has been watching him, looks in the direction of Thomas' pointing finger. Thomas first looks at his father's face, then back in the pointing direction. Thomas' father says, 'What do you want, Tom? Yes, cubes . . . they look exciting, don't they?', and pointing at them himself, says, 'Ye-e-e-e-eh – cubes!'. Thomas looks at his father's face again and chuckles, then points, looking at his own hand, then at his father's face again, then his father's hand. Thomas suddenly lurches into a crawl, going over to the soft, coloured cubes. He sits up again, and bangs his hand down a few times on one of the cubes, making the 'Ee-ee-ee!' sound again. Thomas' father comes over. 'Bang, bang, bang!' he says, tapping his fingers on the cube. Thomas watches him do this then looks away, this time pointing in front of himself towards another cube. He makes as if to crawl towards it then stops and looks up at his father's face. Seeing his father look away (he has noticed another child throwing toys in a rather dangerous looking manner) Thomas whimpers then starts to cry, banging his arms and kicking his legs. 'Oh, what's the matter?' whispers Thomas' father, 'Wasn't I looking at the cube with you?' He strokes Thomas' face and Thomas stops crying and points again to the cube in front of him. 'OK Thomas,' says his father, 'This cube is a yellow one – Ye-e-e-llow!' Thomas laughs and looks up, touching his father's smiling mouth.

My response to this observation, in the light of Stern's research

This observation reflects very clearly some of the key points in Stern's model of the development of a 'subjective sense of self'. Thomas is apparently seeking what Stern calls a 'shared subjective experience' with his father. He is not content merely to enjoy his own knowledge (That's a cube over there!) and mastery (I can sit, crawl, grasp, be excited, feel happy, be worried, point my finger and make daddy look . . .). He wants to do what Stern calls 'sharing the focus of attention' with his father. Being 'preverbal', Thomas needs experiences of the kind that do not require language, though his 'Ee-ee-ee-eeh!' sounds communicate excitement effectively enough. He uses pointing himself, to make his father look in a particular direction, as well as looking in the direction that his father points, rather than simply looking at his hand as a younger infant might have done. All this indicates a shared experience where Thomas is both aware of his own physical and feeling state, and trusting that his father will understand that too, because somehow the father seems to have similar feelings.

These early interpersonal experiences rely on a special kind of empathy that Stern labels 'affect attunement'. I noticed that Thomas' father responded to his son's excited

'Ee-ee-ee-eeh!' sounds with words spoken at a similar vocal pitch: 'Ye-e-e-eh, cubes!', accompanied by a sort of wriggle in his upper body. When I asked Thomas' father why he might have done this, he said that although he had not thought about it at the time, on reflection this 'wriggle' was another way of letting Thomas know that his excitement was 'contagious' – a shareable human experience. Stern thinks that these experiences of affect attunement 'recast the event, and shift the focus of attention to what is behind the behaviour, to the quality of feeling that is being shared'. So here Thomas learns that he can have feelings of excitement, enthusiasm, concern, fear, all of which are capable of being understood by this important other person, his father. And further, Thomas can know more about his own inner feelings now, as well as responding to more overt parental behaviour.

Of course, Stern's model leaves some things unanswered and may generate some objections. Stern himself wonders if 'different societies could minimise or maximise this need for intersubjectivity'. He is aware that in a society like many in the West, where individualisation of human experience is highly valued, we run the risk of losing out in interpersonal terms. Certainly the many signs of personal and social breakdown seem to point to this trend, so it is not surprising that Stern, like myself and others in the field of psychotherapy and counselling, should see a need to attend to the interpersonal, as well as the individual development of the infant (PCSR 1997, AHPP 1999). Stern's model, however, may not be generalisable across the spectrum of different human societies.

Conclusion

Writing as an early childhood educator, I can see that Stern's ideas lend more weight to some of the principles we already hold dear, such as the guidelines on appropriate adult to infant childcare ratios [. . .] or the principle that 'children need relationships with significant responsive adults' [. . .] (Rouse and Griffin 1992). If we are to have infants and very young children in institutionalised childcare situations at all, these must be centres not just of excellent educational practice, with trained professionals to care for the children in a well resourced environment, but also places where these 'unseen' inter-personal processes can be nourished in the growing child. Whether an infant or young child is cared for in their own home, by a trained childminder, or in some other early years setting, 'what is at stake here is nothing less that the shape and extent of the sharable inner universe of the child' (Stern 1985).

Writing as a psychotherapist, I see daily the effects of neglecting the interpersonal world of the growing child, in favour of other kinds of 'success'. The majority of people who attend my practice are outwardly successful and have achieved a great deal 'out there' in the world. Their lameness is internal; their pain is often silent and hidden from others. Long ago, they lost the trust that others will be capable of understanding how they feel; as adults their apparent self confidence is not supported by the internal strength that can only grow, it seems, in the company of another person who affirms and encourages interpersonal efforts.

I make use of Stern's idea that the 'domains of experience' go on developing through-out a human life. It is never too late, I suspect, to experience another's empathy and attunement to one's inner world; this experience can bring healing, even to adults quite advanced in years. How much better then, to show our children that feelings matter as much as mental arithmetic; that caring for each other is no less important than learning to read. [. . .] Our support for the interpersonal development of young children is no 'optional extra'; it provides the solid ground on which to build a healthy and happy human life.

References

AHPP Publications (1999) *Association of Humanistic Psychotherapy Practitioners*. London.

Barnes, P. (1995) *Personal, Social and Emotional Development of Children*. Milton Keynes and Oxford: Open University and Blackwell.

Bee, H. (1992) *The Developing Child*. New York: HarperCollins.

Berry Brazelton, T. and Cramer, B. G. (1991) *The Earliest Relationship*. London: Karnak House.

Bowlby, J. (1965) *Child Care and the Growth of Love*. Harmondsworth: Penguin.

Gillie, M. (1999) 'Daniel Stern: A Developmental Theory for Gestalt?', *British Gestalt Journal*, December 1999.

Houston, G. (1995) *The Now Red Book of Gestalt*. London: Gaie Houston.

Kagan, J. (1984) *The Nature of the Child*. New York: Basic Books.

PCSR Publications (1997) *Psychotherapists and Counsellors for Social Responsibility*. London.

Rouse, D. and Griffin, S. (1992) 'Quality for the under threes', in Pugh, G. (ed.) *Contemporary Issues in the Early Years*. London: NCB/Paul Chapman.

Stern, D. N. (1985) *The Interpersonal World of the Infant: A view from psychoanalysis and developmental psychology*. New York: Basic Books.

Woodhead, M. *et al*. (1991) *Becoming a Person*. London and New York: Routledge.

Chapter 15

Promoting healthy eating in early years settings

Deborah Albon and Penny Mukherji

Children's well-being is a central tenet of the *Every Child Matters* agenda (DfES 2003), and the *Early Years Foundation Stage* in England (DCFS 2008) is concerned with health promotion. Deborah Albon and Penny Mukherji focus on healthy eating as an important aspect of health promotion and offer strategies for developing, monitoring and evaluating a health promotion programme in early years settings.

All those of us involved in the care and education of young children have a responsibility to promote their health and well-being, a responsibility that is enshrined as one of the *Every Child Matters* (DfES 2003) outcomes: being healthy. Early years settings are increasingly being recognised as key agents for health promotion, for both children and their parents. The *Early Years Foundation Stage* (EYFS) (DCSF 2008) implies a holistic approach to health promotion, empowering children with the knowledge, skills and attitudes that will help them to make healthy choices about eating, sleeping and keeping themselves clean. Within the EYFS principles there is also an emphasis on the promotion of emotional well being. In this chapter we focus attention on just one aspect of health promotion – healthy eating – and explore the following five areas:

- Why we should promote healthy eating in the early years
- What we mean by health promotion
- Promoting healthy eating and the early years curriculum
- Inclusion, diversity and listening to children
- Developing a health promotion programme.

Why we should promote healthy eating in the early years

There are two main reasons why we should promote healthy eating in the early years. One is that an unhealthy diet in early childhood can cause a lifetime of ill health for the individual. The second is that recent evidence has identified early years settings as having a key role to play in laying the foundations for healthy eating in young children (Mooney et al. 2008).

The long term effects of an unhealthy diet in early childhood

It is estimated that 'food related ill health is responsible for about 10% of mortality and morbidity in the UK and costs the NHS about £6 billion annually' (Rayner and Scarborough 2005: 1054). The roots of food related illness often lie in early childhood (Jackson and Robinson 2001). The most obvious effects of poor nutrition can be seen if children either do not receive enough food, or receive too much. Whilst, in the United Kingdom (UK), we are struggling with an obesity epidemic, we should not forget that worldwide, 25% of children are underweight (UNICEF 2007). In contrast, in the UK, by 3 years of age, 18% of children are overweight and 5% of children are obese (Hansen and Joshi 2007).

Children need energy to grow and to keep active. This energy is supplied by the fats, proteins and carbohydrates in their diets. If they consume foods containing more energy than they need, then the excess energy is converted to fat, which is stored in the body ready to be used at times when food is scarce. Looked at in these simplistic terms, the cause of the epidemic of obesity and overweight is self-evident, children are eating more than they need. However, the reasons why children consume more than they need are extremely complex. Dehghan et al. (2005) suggest that any explanation has to take account of a wide variety of influences, 'including genetic factors, environmental factors, lifestyle preferences and the cultural environment of children' (Albon and Mukherji 2008: 32).

The two main influences on childhood obesity are diet and exercise. Since the middle of the 20th century there has been a considerable change in the way we eat. There has been a shift away from eating meals cooked at home from basic ingredients, to eating more pre-prepared foods and snacks that are high in fat and sugar, with the result that 94% of children in the UK now eat more than the recommended level of saturated fat (BMA Board of Science 2005). We have also seen an increase in the consumption of sugar rich fizzy drinks and fruit juices. This type of diet is known to be obesogenic, which means that it encourages obesity. However, there is little evidence that children are consuming more calories per day than they used to in previous generations. In fact Dehghan et al. (2005) report that some studies show that children's diets today contain fewer calories than in previous years.

As with diet, the activity levels of children have dramatically changed compared to past generations. The increase in television viewing and use of computer games, together with fears about children's safety, has led to a reduction in children's activity levels. Children are also less likely to walk to school than previously, which many more journeys being made by car. Research has confirmed that children with low levels of activity are more likely to be overweight or obese (Swinburn and Egger 2002). However there is evidence that the amount of exercise children undertake in school, and mode of travel to school, seem not to be related to levels of obesity (BMA 2005). Indeed, in one study undertaken in nursery schools in Scotland, an intervention that provided children with three, thirty minute periods of focused exercise a week, had no effect on levels of overweight (Reilly et al. 2006).

Obesity in children is a serious condition as it can lead to a variety of health related conditions as they grow older. These include:

- Type 2 diabetes
- Coronary heart disease
- Psychological difficulties (BMA 2005).

In addition to diseases of over or under nutrition, there are other health consequences of poor nutrition in the early years. These include:

- Oral disease (too much sugar can lead to dental cavities) (FSA 2008). 41% of children have evidence of tooth decay by the age of five in the UK (Harker and Morris 2005).
- Iron deficiency anaemia: 3% of boys and 8% of girls aged 4–6 are anaemic (Ruston et al. 2004).
- Vitamin D deficiency, which can lead to rickets (FSA 2008).

The importance of early years settings in promoting healthy eating

For some children in full time day care, the nutrition they receive in their setting makes up the majority of their nutritional intake. The *Early Years Foundation Stage* (DCSF 2008) makes the provision of healthy, balanced and nutritious food a specific legal requirement. However, those responsible for the care and education of very young children are becoming increasingly aware of the responsibility placed upon them, not only to provide a healthy diet, but also to help children develop healthy eating habits. This responsibility is emphasised by the National Institute of Clinical Excellence (2006).

What we mean by health promotion

There have been many attempts to define 'health promotion', but all definitions carry within them the idea that health promotion is about empowering individuals and communities to take control of their own health, as far as they are able. The following definition is a typical example: 'Health promotion is the science and art of helping people change their lifestyle to move toward a state of optimal health' (O'Donnell 1989: 5). However we would argue that health promotion strategies must take account of the many social and political influences that lead to health inequalities. These may adversely impact on an individual's ability to address their own health issues. Naidoo and Wills (2000) have identified five main approaches to health promotion:

1. *Medical or preventative*: interventions focus on measures designed to prevent ill health, such as immunisations.
2. *Behaviour change*: interventions designed to encourage individuals to adopt health behaviours such as healthy eating.

3. *Educational*: interventions designed to supply the underpinning knowledge about health, so that individuals can make healthy lifestyle choices.
4. *Empowerment*: interventions designed to give people the confidence to be able to take control of their own health, both at an individual and a community level.
5. *Social change*: interventions designed to change the underlying social structures that impact on a population's health, for example anti smoking legislation and initiatives designed to reduce poverty and health inequalities (Albon and Mukherji 2008: 119).

Health promotion campaigns that include all, or most of these approaches, are likely to be more successful than a campaign that uses just one approach. Below we look at promoting healthy eating in the early years curriculum as well as suggesting ways practitioners might develop a health promotion programme in their setting. These ideas are linked to Naidoo and Wills' (2000) approaches to health promotion listed above, falling within 'behaviour change', 'educational' and 'empowerment' categories.

Promoting healthy eating and the early years curriculum

Promoting healthy eating should be viewed as an integral part of the early years curriculum. However, it is important to consider what is meant by the term 'curriculum'. It is easy to think of the early years curriculum as the activities carried out during the non-routine times of the day but it should be regarded as far more than this. Manning-Morton and Thorp (2003), for instance, encourage practitioners to view the curriculum broadly, in terms of all of the children's experiences during the *whole* day. This view of the curriculum encourages practitioners to consider routines as an important part of the early years' curriculum.

Of key importance are mealtimes and snack times. If you consider the amount of time spent during the day engaged in eating and drinking, it is evident that there are plenty of opportunities to promote healthy eating as part of the day to day activities in the setting. Routines such as mealtimes provide a 'rhythm' to the day (Viruru 2001; Albon 2007) and should be thought through carefully (Albon and Mukherji 2008). Yet research has shown that many early years' practitioners do not view mealtimes and snack times as activities imbued with potential for learning (Sepp et al. 2006).

In Sweden there is a concept of the 'pedagogic meal', which emphasises the importance of mealtimes as occasions when practitioners act as positive role models for healthy eating (Sepp et al. 2006). Alongside this, children are able to visit the kitchens in order to see how food is prepared, stored and cooked. This can be contrasted with an approach that overly accentuates safety and hygiene, with kitchens viewed as needing to be separate spaces away from the children's daily experience. The Practice Guidance for the *Early Years Foundation Stage* (EYFS) (DCSF 2008) makes reference to healthy eating in its 'self care' section under Personal, Social and Emotional Development and in the section 'health and bodily awareness' under Physical Development. The EYFS, however, does not go as far as the Swedish curriculum in promoting the value of a 'pedagogic meal'. Indeed in many reception classes, teachers, nursery nurses and teaching assistants rarely eat with the children.

The organisation of snacks needs careful consideration as it is an area that is often overlooked (Cheater 2001). Whilst water should be freely available at all times, early years practitioners need to reflect upon whether to have a set snack time or whether to organise snacks and drinks in such a way that children can help themselves to a drink or a snack when they are hungry or thirsty. The former approach enables practitioners to monitor the children's food and drink intake more closely and is often underpinned by a concern that children might snack in such a way that spoils their appetites at mealtimes. The latter approach is underpinned by a perspective that recognises that children know their own bodies and can communicate when they are hungry or thirsty (Albon and Mukherji 2008). Of course a mid-way position is also possible, where a practitioner sits at the snack table whilst children come and go to eat and drink when they choose to. In this way the practitioner is able to monitor children's dietary intake as well as be available for conversation about what is being imbibed.

Mealtimes are also highly significant events during the day. Giovanni (2006) argues that the rituals associated with lunchtimes are important as they are key opportunities for young children to participate in the group-life of the setting. She points to how mealtime rituals are linked to a particular group's sense of identity and help to create an emotionally warm, calm environment in which communication can flourish between children and their peers and children and adults. By creating a calm and convivial atmosphere for mealtimes, eating healthily may be viewed as a positive experience – one that contributes to a sense of well-being. However, we are not suggesting that children sit as one big group for meals. It is important that the child's key person is the practitioner that eats with them (Elfer et al. 2003). Ideally children should be in small key person groups as this provides a warm and supportive context for children to try out skills such as pouring their own drink and feeding themselves (Petrie and Owen 2005). It is now a requirement of the EYFS that early years settings operate a key person approach (DCSF 2008).

As well as mealtimes and snack times, play activities and adult-directed activities during non-routine times can help to develop a positive attitude to healthy eating. Cooking experiences are important here because they are an opportunity for children to learn a variety of cooking techniques, develop a positive attitude towards nutritious foods, and extend their knowledge about nutrition. Often, cookery experiences are viewed as an opportunity for learning about mathematics, for instance, because they offer a meaningful context for measurement. Whilst this is very important, developing a curriculum *about* food, rather than purely *through* food, is also vital (Albon 2007). Children can also help with preparing food for snack times and mealtimes. Even very young children can help wash and tear lettuce leaves for their group's snack table and by doing this, learn about the importance of hygiene in food preparation as well as taking care over the preparation of food (Manning-Morton and Thorp 2003). Through engaging in such experiences, where they prepare food for each other, children are also learning about the way food plays a key role in cementing social relationships (Albon and Mukherji 2008).

Rivkin (2007) describes other activities that can promote healthy eating in early years settings. These might include growing fruit and vegetables in the garden and using these in cooking activities, snack times and mealtimes, as well as going on outings in the local area to markets or a local allotment to explore seasonal fruit and vegetables. Rivkin also recommends role play that incorporates real foods as a context for learning about healthy eating.

This can be viewed as a contentious position. There may be an ethical dilemma if using food as a plaything when there are people in the world with little food to eat. This view can be contrasted with a perspective that sees playing with food as vital in order that children come to associate food as an enjoyable activity rather than one associated with anxiety. We believe that early years practitioners need to reflect on the ways that play can contribute to promoting a positive attitude towards healthy eating (Albon and Mukherji 2008).

In addition to the above points about the early years curriculum, early years practitioners need to plan carefully for inclusion and equality (Albon and Mukherji 2008). This is discussed in the next section, in which the importance of listening to children's views about food and eating is also emphasised.

Inclusion, diversity and listening to children

As with any aspect of the curriculum, issues of inclusion and diversity should permeate throughout the curriculum rather than being a tokenistic one-off activity. An example of this might be inviting a parent of Indian origin on a one-off occasion to make barfi with the children. McAuliffe and Lane (2005) point out that stereotypical assumptions are sometimes made about groups of people based on food – especially if the food is unfamiliar to the people who are eating it. They argue that it is important to remember that eating familiar foods offers security for young children. Therefore, whilst encouraging children to eat unfamiliar foods that encourage them to widen their cultural experience is a useful way to learn about diversity, it may reinforce negative attitudes. The interweaving of food, culture and identity is complex and early years practitioners need to avoid sending messages, albeit unwittingly, of cultural superiority or ethno-centrism about food. McAuliffe and Lane (2005) cite the use of 'ethnic foods' and 'normal foods' as language to avoid as we all have ethnicity and what is 'normal' for one person or group, may not be 'normal' for another.

The requirements of children with special educational or additional needs should also be considered carefully. Practitioners should tune into the individual needs and interests of children rather than purely seeing their disability or condition. Some children may like to feed themselves at the start of a meal but may prefer someone to feed them after a while, if they are getting tired and/or the food is getting cold (Council for Disabled Children 2004). Further to this, Albon and Mukherji (2008) argue that children who need to have their food liquidised before eating may rarely have had the opportunity to taste the individual foods that comprise their meal. Again, good practice should aim to allow children to try individual foods, enabling practitioners to develop an understanding of the children's perspectives on the food they are eating.

Tuning into children's perspectives about the food they are eating is very important. When thinking about promoting healthy eating, practitioners should listen to children in order to build on their current understanding, interests and attitudes towards the foods they eat. With very young children and babies, a key tool that aids practitioners in this is observation (Manning-Morton and Thorp 2003).

Young children and babies will often 'speak' to us using their bodies as well as through making vocalisations. Practitioners need to tune into their facial expressions, and the movements of their head and tongue especially, in order to gain an understanding of their likes and dislikes when feeding (Albon and Mukherji 2008). Young children and babies may be telling us something about the pace of the mealtime experience, the food on offer, the size of teat hole in a feeding bottle, or possibly that they want a break from feeding in order to bring up wind. As with adults, young children are likely to have idiosyncratic ways of getting their feelings across to the people that care for them. A key person approach is important here in developing the kind of close relationship with the child that fosters an ability in the practitioner to 'read' these cues as well as a confidence in the young child that the practitioner who is with them during mealtimes is one s/he is familiar and comfortable with and one who knows how to respond to him or her sensitively.

Children's perspectives can also be incorporated into menu planning. McAuliffe and Lane (2005) discuss a range of strategies for this, including working with the cook in early years settings to devise menus that are both nutritionally balanced and responsive to the children's preferences as well as running tasting sessions with the children. Parents could also play a significant role in such sessions and could be encouraged to share recipes that their children enjoy at home.

In summary, tuning in to children's perspectives about the food they eat can be embedded as part of good practice. Planning for diversity and inclusion should also permeate curriculum planning. We conclude this chapter by considering how early years practitioners might plan for a health promotion programme.

Developing a health promotion programme

It may be appropriate for settings to develop a specific programme about healthy eating. This could be because practitioners have identified a specific need in the children and families with whom they work, or as a result of a local or national initiative. Occasionally the initiative comes from the families that use the setting.

Mooney et al. (2008) undertook a study which looked at health promotion work undertaken in early years settings in the UK. They identified four factors that influence the success of heath promotion activities:

1. Health promotion interventions should be based on existing early years curriculum frameworks.
2. There needs to be effective partnerships between early years professionals and health professionals.
3. Both parents and practitioners need to be involved.
4. Health promotion activities need to be resourced adequately at both national and local levels (Mooney et al. 2008: 163).

Parental involvement is key to any health promotion activity, and the promotion of healthy eating is no exception. Lumeng (2005: 18) makes the following recommendations for practitioners when involving parents:

- The limits of parental influence should be acknowledged (we would also add the practitioners' influence).
- Parents should be empowered so that they are confident to suggest changes to food and drink provision in the setting.
- Parents should not be encouraged to change feeding practices unless there is strong research evidence to support the suggestion. In the UK we would suggest that any such advice is based on the Food Standards Agency 'eat well' guidelines (FSA 2008).
- Early years practitioners can act as advocates for parents when campaigning for policy change at local and national level. For example, working with parents to increase the availability of affordable healthy foods for parents on a low income.

These factors need to be taken into consideration when planning any health promotion programme. In addition, Albon and Mukherji (2008: 132) recommend that it is helpful if the following steps are taken during the development of the programme:

- Identify needs and priorities
- Set aims and objectives
- Decide on the best way to achieve your aims
- Identify resource needs and available resources
- Formulate an action plan
- Implement the plan
- Evaluate the programme.

Identify needs and priorities

What are the underlying reasons for implementing a healthy eating programme? You may have identified that some of the children in your care are overweight, or you may have been invited to join in a locally organised initiative. The staff team and the parents should be involved and invited to contribute to the planning and implementation of the programme. At this stage you need to identify outside agencies and health professionals who may be able to help you. Proper research at this stage may save you time. For instance, you may find that your local health authority already has a healthy eating programme set up which you just need to adapt for your setting.

Set aims and objectives

Without having clear aims and objectives you may find that your focus of attention becomes too broad, and the impact may be lost. Objectives should be precise, e.g. you want a 20% increase in the number of children eating fruit at snack time by the end of the health promotion programme. If objectives are based on accurate data you will have information upon which to base an evaluation of the success of the programme. You should also consider how your aims and objectives link into the requirements of the *Early Years Foundation Stage* (DCFS 2008).

Decide on the best way to achieve your aims

Once you have clear aims you will be able to identify the people who could help you. This will almost certainly include the staff team, children, parents and other professionals, but could also include the local community. Discussions with all involved will help you identify the methods you will be using.

Identify resource needs and available resources

Having decided on your aims and objectives you will have some idea about resource needs. Discussions earlier on in the planning process may already have identified possible sources of funding or materials that you could use.

Formulate an action plan

It helps to produce a clear action plan that identifies what needs to be done, by whom and by when. A member of the team should have oversight of this to monitor progress and to be the main point of contact.

Implement the plan

This phase marks the end of the planning stage. Regular review meetings will help identify if any aspect of the plan needs modification.

Evaluate the programme

Evaluation measures should be based upon the objectives of the programme. If one of the objectives was to increase the number of children eating fruit at snack time you would have needed to have collected data on this before the start of the programme and repeated this after the implementation phase. In addition to data collection the staff team need to meet for a de-briefing session where all involved report back on things that went well, and things that could be improved upon. It will be an opportunity for staff to report on the children's involvement and level of understanding, so that opportunities for future activities can be identified. All records and resources should be archived so that they can be referred to in the future. Finally all those involved need to be informed of outcomes and formally thanked.

Conclusion

We have argued that promoting healthy eating is an important part of early years practice. As the National Institute for Clinical Excellence (2006: 149) pronounced:

Although parents are primarily responsible for their child's nutrition and activities, childcare providers can also play an important role by providing opportunities for children to be active and develop healthy eating habits and by acting as important role models. Crucially, a child's positive experience in childcare outside the home may influence their behaviours in the home and thus help promote healthy lifestyles to the family as a whole.

References

Albon, D. (2007) 'Food for thought: the importance of food and eating in early childhood practice', in J. Moyles (ed) *Early Years Foundations: Meeting the Challenge*. Maidenhead: Open University Press.

Albon, D. and Mukherji, P. (2008) *Food and Health in Early Childhood*. London: Sage.

British Medical Association (BMA) Board of Science. (2005) *Preventing Childhood Obesity*. London: BMA Publications.

Cheater, S. (2001) Pupil snacks: the extent to which food and drinks policies in Wirral schools promote health, *Health Education Journal*, 60(4): 303–312.

Council for Disabled Children (2004) *The Dignity of Risk*. London: NCB.

Dehghan, M., Akhtar-Danesh, N. and Merchant, A. (2005) Childhood Obesity, Prevalence and Prevention, *Nutrition Journal*. 4(24): 1–8.

Department for Children, Schools and Families (2008) *The Early Years Foundation Stage. Setting the Standards for Learning, Development and Care for Children from Birth to Five*. http://www.standards.dfes.gov.uk/eyfs/site/index.htm accessed 28-07-08.

Department for Education and Science (2003) *Every Child Matters Green Paper*. London: The Stationery Office.

Elfer, P., Goldschmeid, E. and Selleck, D. (2003) *Key Person Relationships in Nursery*. London: Sage.

Food Standards Agency (2008) *Eat well, be well*. http://www.eatwell.gov.uk/ Accessed 28-07-N08.

Giovanni, D. (2006) The Pleasure of Eating, *Children in Europe*, 10: 10–11.

Hansen, K. and Joshi, H. (eds) (2007) *The Millennium Cohort Study. Second Survey. A User's Guide to Initial Findings*. London: The Centre for Longitudinal Studies.

Harker, R. and Morris, J. (2005) *Children's Dental Health in England 2003*. London Office for National Statistics.

Jackson, A. and Robinson, S. (2001) 'Dietary Guidelines for Pregnancy: a review of the current evidence', *Public Health and Nutrition*, 4(2): 625–630.

Lumeng, J. (2005) 'What can we do to prevent childhood obesity?', *Zero to Three*, 25 (3b): 13–19.

Manning-Morton, J. and Thorp, M. (2003) *Key Times for Play: The First Three Years*, Maidenhead: Open University Press.

McAuliffe, A.M. and Lane, J. (2005) *Listening and Responding to Children's Views on Food*, London: NCB.

Mooney, A., Boddy, J., Statham, J. and Warwick, I. (2008) Approaches to Developing Health in Early Years Settings, *Health Education*, 108(2): 163–177.

Naidoo, J. and Wills, J. (2000) *Health Promotion: Foundations for Practice*, 2nd edition. Edinburgh: Bailliere Tindall.

National Institute of Clinical Excellence (2006), Guidance on Obesity: The Prevention, Identification, Assessment and Management of Overweight and Obesity in Adults and Children, available at: http://www.nice.org.uk/guidance/index.jsp?action=byID&o= 11000 accessed 27-07-08.

O'Donnell, M. (1989) Definition of Health Promotion: Part III: Expanding the Definition, *American Journal of Health Promotion*, 3(3): 5.

Petrie, S. and Owen, S. (2005) *Authentic Relationships in Group Care for Infants and Toddlers – Resources for Infant Educarers (RIE): Principles into Practice*, London: Jessica Kingsley.

Rayner, M. and Scarborough, P. (2005) The Burden of Food-related Ill Health in the UK', *Journal of Epidemiology and Community Health*, 59: 1054–1057.

Reilly, J. R., Kelly, L., Montgomery, C., Williamson, A., Fisher, A., McColl, J. H., Lo Conte, R., Paton, J. Y. and Grant, S. (2006) Physical Activity to Prevent Obesity in Young Children: Cluster Randomised Controlled Trial, *British Medical Journal*, 333: 1041–1043.

Rivkin, M.S. (2007) Keeping Fit in Body and Mind, *Early Childhood Today*, 21(5): 28–36.

Ruston, D., Hoare, J., Henderson, L., Gregory, J., Bates, C.J., Prentice, A., Birch, M., Swan, G. and Farron, M. (2004) *The National Diet and Nutrition Survey: Adults Aged 19–64 Years. Volume 4: Nutritional Status (Anthropometry and Blood Analyses) Blood Pressure and Physical Activity*. London: The Stationery Office.

Sepp, H., Abrahamsson, L. and Fjellstrom, C. (2006) Pre-school Staff's Attitudes Toward Foods in Relation to the Pedagogic Meal, *International Journal of Consumer Studies*, 30(2): 224–232.

Swinburn, B. and Egger, G. (2002) Preventative Strategies Against Weight Gain and Obesity *Obesity Reviews*, 3(4): 289–301.

United Nations Children Fund (UNICEF) (2007) *The State of the World's Children 2008*. New York: UNICEF.

Viruru, R. (2001) *Early Childhood Education: Postcolonial Perspectives from India*. London: Sage.

Chapter 16

Playing with song
Susan Young

Although usually enjoyable experiences for young children, Susan Young asserts that they often have limited, or no, opportunities for contributing to the song singing sessions in their early years settings. In this chapter, discussing the observations she made of two and three, and three and four year olds in different settings, the author draws practitioners' attention to the ways young children spontaneously play with 'song' in their everyday activities. She describes the inventive way one observed practitioner fostered 'song play' with the children in her nursery. She concludes by encouraging all early years practitioners to re-think and reflect on the potentially rich learning experiences they can provide children by engaging in and fostering 'playing with song'.

In this chapter I make a distinction between 'performing songs' and 'playing with song'. Separating out these two activities in this clear-cut way is a little artificial and in reality there are many shades of singing activity which blend performing and playing. But making this distinction will be useful because it will draw attention to certain aspects of song singing which can otherwise be a taken-for-granted activity in early childhood settings.

Performing songs

Usually in educational settings, songs are performed. The adults perform songs for children and children perform songs with the adults. Typically, the adult gathers children in a group, then initiates and leads a short session in which a number of songs are sung, once through, in succession. The songs are usually well-known 'favourites' which children learn from repetition. This session carries certain expectations of the children – that they will join in with singing the song with everyone else [. . .] and participate in the activity in ways which are determined by the adult. Children often have little or no opportunity to make their own contributions, save, perhaps suggesting some simple variations of movement, or words. I have noticed that the song-singing session in early years settings often serves an extra-musical purpose. Group singing is a time when children are encouraged to conform to behaviours associated with formal schooling (James, Jenks and Prout, 1998); to sit still, cross-legged on the floor in one position for a relatively long period of time, to participate in uniform, communal activity, not to talk, to follow instructions and to watch the lead adult carefully to imitate non-verbal models. The session is usually enjoyed by adults and children alike and contributes to a cheerful atmosphere, with song words and actions suggesting fun, humour and happiness. And this sense of fun helps to disguise the highly regimented nature of the activity. You might think I am unjustifiably casting a negative shadow over an activity which is a valuable and cherished mainstay of early childhood education. But often the most taken-for-granted activities are those which benefit from some rigorous rethinking.

Playing with song

The Roehampton and Richmond First Steps (RRiF) Project

In order to present my contrasting version of 'playing with song' I provide observations of young children's spontaneous singing taken from some recent research projects. The main project from which I draw, the RRiF project ran for over a year in a range of settings in South West London (Young, 2003). The project was guided by the following questions:

- What spontaneous musical abilities do children reveal in early childhood contexts?
- How do they engage with musical activities that are presented to them by adults?
- How might adults best foster children's musicality?

The project was driven by the conviction that to observe, listen to and recognise young children's own ways of being musical is essential so that these can become the starting points for adults to connect with, follow, respond and build on. There is a surprising shortage of research studies which have explored children's spontaneous musicality (Barrett, 1998). The majority of research, framed within music psychology, has sought to identify children's developmental pathways in skills associated with the formal, conventional practices of music and for this purpose, most research has focused on how children perform in set tasks (Young, 2002). So, for example, researchers interested in singing have explored children's ability to remember given melodies, to sing them in tune or to learn to pitch their voices with accuracy (e.g. Davidson, 1983; Dowling, 1982). There has been little interest in how children sing when left to their own devices.

The RRiF Project aimed to combine research with the development of practice. So findings from the research aspects of the project directly informed experimental approaches to practice explored collaboratively with staff working in the various settings. In the final part of this chapter I [. . .] describe some of these approaches.

Observing children

In keeping with the overall RRiF project aim to discover more about the spontaneous musical activities of young children, an important strand of the research project was to focus on the spontaneous singing play of young children. I observed a group of 6-8 children (the numbers varied due to irregular attendance) aged between two and three years over 6 weekly visits during a one hour free-play period in the main play-room at their daycare [. . .] (Young, 2002). During the first week I simply jotted down all the spontaneous singing I heard, jumping from child to child as I heard something interesting. I used every means I knew to jot down their vocalisations: words, phonics, various made-up symbols, rhythm notation and sol-fa. I also collected information not just about the children's vocalisation but how it was embedded in their general play with things and the other children and adults in their environment. The first problem I encountered was that their singing play was much more prolific than I had anticipated. So in subsequent visits I no longer randomly observed all the children, but systematic-ally tracked individual children over 10-minute periods. I used the same set of mixed symbols for my jottings, but with practice evolved them into more of a system. [. . .]

In the last week I recorded the sounds in the play-room using a portable cassette recorder with built-in microphone. Although this was a fairly crude method of collecting the children's singing, it enabled me to review these with a colleague and check them against my field jottings. How my colleague described what she heard did not always tally exactly with my own versions, but we decided the discrepancies were slight enough for her to confirm that my field notes were sufficiently accurate for the purposes of this project. [. . .] Importantly I was trying to get a sense of how the children's spon-taneous singing was woven into the fabric of their play – not something abstracted and isolated from it. The simplicity of my methods seemed appropriate and adequate enough for this research purpose.

Playing with song: two and three year olds

These young children used their voices, some almost continually, in a wide range of expressive forms of singing which were integrated with their play [. . .] (Young, 2004; Campbell, 1998; Sundin, 1998; Kartomi, 1991). As I collected field notes, I could begin to identify some recurring types of singing play and to group these into different categories.

Playing with known songs

Songs which the children knew, either from their experiences at home from TV pro-grammes or CDs, or from the daycare, would re-appear, perhaps in short, remembered snatches, perhaps longer sections, often with altered melodies and words. The repetitive singing of short sections, or altered melodies, may arise because they do not yet remember the song exactly, or their vocal range and voice technique are not yet developed enough to manage the full pitch range. All these are interpretations which researchers with 'developmental agendas' have tended to suggest and they are probably contributory (Welch, 1986). But I also think children have no purpose or need to sing the complete song from beginning to end or in its conventional musical form or with its full, usual lyrics. Certainly with some three- and four-year-olds, I was struck by how they were often able to sing a song they knew well from beginning through to end if I asked them to, but in their play they rarely did so. It is, after all, much more fun, more interesting, to play with the song, to fit it around what you are doing at the moment, make it match a movement, make the words fit the toy you have, to add some melody of your own making. If you, yourself, have a song 'on the brain' as we say, I am sure it surfaces in association with what you are doing, in variations of your own making and in short phrases.

Free melody

When you listen to children singing of their own volition, they are not only using song melodies of known songs but also improvising their own melodies. There were two types of self-made melody. One type consisted of long, freely meandering threads of melody on open vowel sounds ([. . .] Bjørkvold, 1989; Moorhead & Pond, 1941). It typically occurred during focused solo play and often with small objects and toys requiring concentration. This is a typical example. Callum was threading beads on a lace, and as he did so, he sang quietly to himself with a fluid, free-floating melody on an open syllable sound 'aah!' When two beads were threaded he altered his melody to short dipping phrases to match the beads swinging to and fro on the lace. Just as mothers sing to babies to help calm and soothe, so I have the idea that young children can sing themselves down into a state of physical calmness required for mental focus (Trehub, 2003). [. . .] As adults we often use music to help regulate our physical and emotional state in much the same kind of way (DeNora, 2000).

Chant

Another type of melody was typically a short melodic idea or phrase, with a rhythmic pattern which children would repeat over again. Often these types of melodic chant were sung to significant words or short phrases, again, fitting closely with their play ([. . .] Campbell, 1998). Kasha was playing at the water tray and had tipped a plastic figure out of a small boat into the water. As it bobbed about, she dipped her hand in to paddle the figure along and sang, 'swim, swim, swim', in a regular grouping of three. Each group sat on three regular beats with a pause between and the pitches were clear, the middle 'swim' being sung a note higher than its two neighbours. Interestingly, her singing was almost imperceptible but that day we were filming in the nursery for a video on children's musical activity and the sound recordist's sensitive equipment had picked up her song. I had thought that I was good at hearing young children's singing, but I missed this completely. It goes to show how easy it is to become complacent that we are hearing and seeing young children and how we must continually struggle to remain alert.

Movement singing

Children's vocalisations were also fused with movement – either their own physical movement or the movement of the things they were playing with (Young, 1995). We saw how Callum's bead-threading song changed as the beads swung to and fro, his vocalisations changing to match the swing. Similarly my field notebooks became full of examples of children singing their movements, it is as if they are wired up on all systems and physical energy and exuberance are also expressed with their voices. [. . .] One interesting example illustrates the close integration of the movement of toys and self-movement. Ben was lobbing a little cloth doll about two metres into the air so that it arced just ahead of him and fell to the floor. As he lobbed he chanted 'up the choo' (this is how I heard it) and the 'choo' matched the doll's flight elongated and curved in his voice. The 'up the' he sang as he held the doll in both hands readying to throw. Having lobbed the doll three times, he then took a couple of steps, saying 'up the' as he did so and jumped himself into the air with the 'choo'. The transfer of doll movement to his own movement seemed to pivot on his rhythmic, contoured, verbal chant. To transform an activity into vocalisation converts it into a very flexible form. It gives the child a kind of 'grip' on an experience, it emphasises certain aspects of how the movement is structured – its timing is a translation of flight in space, its contour a translation of the curve of the throw – but a very flexible grip which helped to support a quick conversion of the time-space idea into self-movement (Young, 2006).

Singing for toys

The way in which children sing for vehicles, animals and people, often giving them prosodic markers – gruff animal sounds, the ubiquitous siren, engine sounds and so on – helps them in the process of animating the toys (Sawyer, 1997). For example, Leah makes the usual descending-pitch string of 'chuc, chuc, chuc' sounds for rotating blades as she flies the helicopter in to land. But a moment later, when she grips the paramedic, she makes the same singing sound to indicate that he needs to fly off again. Her helicopter 'song' [. . .] is now detached from the flying movement and is representative of that toy, indicating the next move in her game.

Playing with song: practitioners

Having discovered the quantity and variety of spontaneous singing among the two- to three-year-olds in daycare I transferred my attention to the three- and four-year-olds in a nearby nursery run by the local education authority (Young, 2003). Among these children I could hear continuations of the types of singing play that had been so prolific among the younger children. As we explored children's spontaneous singing and how it was integrated into their play in the RRiF project, we discussed how this might influence practice. Practitioners in the nursery had become interested in finding ways of integrating songs into their everyday activity with children. As is usual practice, the nursery set out a number of areas within its room which were intended to provide a stimulus for certain kinds of play. So they set out song play areas.

Adults fostering song play

One practitioner, Ann, became particularly inventive in designing and playing with children in these set-ups. In one activity, she chose the song about jelly-fish jumping off a rock. An area of the floor was spread with a blue cloth and on it she laid out plastic sea creatures of all kinds, including jellyfish, some wooden blocks to be 'rocks' and fishing nets. She sat on the floor in this area and when children arrived who were interested to play, she would sing the song with and for them while they acted out its sequence of jumping jellyfish. In one play episode, Tyler sings only one part of the song, but sings this repeatedly with a deep, wobbly voice on the word 'jellyfish' which he obviously enjoys. At the same time he clutches a plastic jellyfish which he wobbles as he sings and then flings into the blue cloth 'sea'. Two girls join in the play. They sit on Ann's knee being the jellyfish themselves. Ann 'wobbles' them on her knee, they laugh, enjoying the emotionally warm, one-to-one contact with an adult they know well. Acting out the jellyfish, they jump off Ann's knee and into the sea, singing as they do so. They then play with the fishing nets and Ann watches and listens as they continue to sing not only bits of this song, but also make up a new melody to the same words. Finally, they 'catch' Ann in a fishing net by popping it on her head – a joke which everyone enjoys.

Learning to be a singer

Within all this activity the song was sung, in snatches, with added vocalisations, with interesting voices, in its entirety and with other transformations and variations to fit with their activity. [. . .] The children improvised their play with and around the song. I suggest that these kinds of song-play activities allow the children to be more autonomous and creative in their song singing than is the case during adult-guided song singing sessions (Young & Glover, 1998). What's more, the songs were repeated several times over, either by the adult to accompany the children's play or to support their own singing, or by the children in solo singing. The songs were sung slowly and deliberately in ways which fitted with how the children were singing and gave them ample opportunity to 'get on board' with the song. Songs 'performed' by adults in group sessions are usually sung too quickly for young children, particularly if taken from commercial recordings (Young & Glover, 1998). Ann sometimes prompted a child's singing by starting and then withdrawing her own voice, or sometimes lightly joined in when the child's singing faltered. Importantly, her contributions were not leading but were contingent and responsive to how the children were singing (Young, 2005a; also, Maxwell, 1996). She watched and listened carefully and tailored her input accordingly (Tarnowski & Lerclerc, 1994).

Significantly, the several repetitions of the same song at slow speeds and opportunity for individual practice, which are ingredients for successful learning of songs and the development of song-singing skills, were automatically built into the song-play activities (Young, 2003). These are approaches advocated by music education pedagogy and which are also rarely included in the usual, song 'performing' sessions. I am not suggesting that this kind of song play activity replaces communal song-singing sessions, but that careful thought is given to the purpose of singing activities and to what children are learning and gaining. In this nursery, staff became inventive at incorporating songs into all kinds of ongoing activities. For example I heard a little ditty made up between adult and child about going to hang up her coat; I heard an improvised song included for outdoor play on bikes which reminded children to stay within some lines and I heard a made up song for children playing with plastic animals in a farm.

Playing with song: in the home and daycare

This kind of informal, embedded, playing around with songs, using songs in many different kinds of context for many different purposes has much more in common with the way parents and carers sing with babies and very young children at home (Trevarthen, 2002; Trevarthen & Malloch, 2002). Music making among women with children in the domestic spaces of home and child-care settings has always, traditionally taken place – hence the repertoire of rhymes and songs for children – and is something that, from research, we have found women do comfortably and easily (Street, Hargreaves & Young, 2004). They use whatever songs they know or have picked up from various sources – current pop songs as nappy changing songs, an old, half-remembered nursery rhyme for a Bumpsie Daisie up the stairs song. And the songs, little more than short ditties many of them, are part of the everyday, routine activity inventively adapted. There is no expectation to 'perform' the song, to necessarily sing it completely, to present it with good vocal tone, with rhythmic and pitch accuracy as in the conventions of Western art music and its derivative practices of music education. We have allowed the music education practices which have become associated with older children to scale downwards into practice with young children instead of encouraging the skills of embedding song into everyday childcare activity to become a 'bottom-up' model for early childhood music education practice (Young, 2005b).

For it is often said that practitioners lack confidence for music and that this is given as a reason for needing extra support or even to hand over music to specialists. It is the belief that music in education requires the formal skills, for example to model complete songs in performance mode, that is the source of anxiety. I have described how young children play with songs and have suggested that a continuation of that play in practitioner-designed song play activities is both more appropriate and motivating for children, and at the same time provides a rich learning experience in which they have the opportunity to become creative and autonomous song singers. This version, this 'playing with song' version of using songs hopefully prompts some rethinking of what is important and valuable about singing.

References

Barrett, M. (1998) 'Children Composing: A View of Aesthetic Decision-Making', in B. Sundin, G.E. McPherson, G. Folkestad, (eds) *Children Composing: Research in Music Education* 1998: 1. Malmo Academy of Music, Lund University.

Bjørkvold, J. (1989) *The Muse Within: Creativity and Communication, Song and Play from Childhood through Maturity*, (W.H. Halverson, Trans.). New York: Harper Collins.

Campbell, P. Shehan, (1998) *Songs in Their Heads: Music and its Meaning in Children's Lives*. Oxford: Oxford University Press.

Davidson, L. (1983) Tonal structures of children's early songs. Paper presented at the International Conference on Psychology and the Arts, Cardiff. *Bulletin of the British Psychological Society*, 36, pp. 119–120.

De Nora, T. (2000) *Music in Everyday Life*. Cambridge: Cambridge University Press.

Dowling, W. J. (1982) Melodic information processing and its development, in D. Deutsch (ed.) *The Psychology of Music*. New York: Academic Press.

James, A., Jenks, C. & Prout, A. (1998) *Theorizing Childhood*. Cambridge: Polity Press.

Kartomi, M.J. (1991) Musical Improvisations by Children at Play, *The World of Music* 33 (3), pp. 53–65

Maxwell, S. (1996) 'Meaningful Interaction', in S. Robson & S. Smedley (eds) *Education in Early Childhood: First Things First*. London: David Fulton Publishers.

Moorhead, G. & Pond, D. (1941) Music of Young Children Book 1. Chant in G. Moorhead & D. Pond, (reprinted in 1978) *Pillsbury Foundation Studies: Music of Young Children*, Santa Barbara: Pillsbury Foundation [now available from the MENC Historical Center, University of Maryland, USA].

Sawyer, R.K. (1997) *Pretend Play as Improvisation: Conversation in the Preschool Classroom*. Maywah, New Jersey: Lawrence Erlbaum Associates.

Street, A., Hargreaves, D.J. & Young, S. (2004) Singing to Infants: How maternal attitudes to singing influence infants' musical worlds. Paper presented at the ISME Early Childhood Commission Conference, *The Musical Worlds of Children* Escola Superior de Musica de Catalunya, Barcelona, Spain, 5–9 July.

Sundin, B. (1998) Musical Creativity in the First Six Years, in B. Sundin, G.E. McPherson & G. Folkestad (eds) *Children Composing: Research in Music Education* 1998: 1. Lund, Sweden: Malmo Academy of Music, Lund University.

Tarnowski, S. and Lerclerc, J. (1994) 'Musical Play of Preschoolers and Teacher-Child Interaction', *Update: Applications of Research in Music Education, Fall/Winter* 1994, 9–16.

Trehub, S. (2003) Musical Predispositions in Infancy: An Update, in I. Peretz & R. Zatorre (eds) *The Cognitive Neuroscience of Music*. Oxford: Oxford University Press.

Trevarthen, C. (2002) Origins of Musical Identity: Evidence from Infancy for Social Awareness, in R. MacDonald, D.J. Hargreaves & D. Miell (eds) *Musical Identities*. Oxford: Oxford University Press.

Trevarthen, C. & Malloch, S. (2002) Musicality and Music Before Three: Human Vitality and Invention Shared with Pride, *Zero to Three: Journal of the National Centre for Infants, Toddlers and Families*. 25 (1), pp. 10–18.

Welch, G.F. (1986) 'A Developmental View of Children's Singing', *British Journal of Music Education*, 3 (3), 295–303.

Young, S. (1995) Listening to the Music of Early Childhood, *British Journal of Music Education*, 12, pp. 51–58.

Young, S. (2002) Young Children's Spontaneous Vocalisations in Free-play: Observations of two- to three-year-olds in a day-care setting, *Bulletin of the Council for Research in Music Education*. 152, pp. 43–53.

Young, S. (2003) *Music with the Under Fours*, London: RoutledgeFalmer Press.

Young, S. (2004) Young Children's Spontaneous Vocalising: Insights into Play and Pathways to Singing, *International Journal of Early Childhood*, 36 (2) pp. 59–74.

Young, S. (2005a) *Musical Communication* between Adults and Young Children, in D. Miell, R.McDonald & D.J. Hargreaves (eds) Musical Communication. Oxford: Oxford University Press.

Young, S. (2005b) Changing Tune: Reconceptualising Music with Under Threes, *International Journal of Early Years Education*.

Young, S. (2006) Seen but not heard: Young children, Improvised Singing and Educational Practice, *Contemporary Issues in Early Childhood* Vol. 7, No. 3.

Young, S. & Glover, J. (1998) *Music in the Early Years*. London: Falmer Press.

Chapter 17

Young children, learning and ICT
A case study in the UK maintained sector

Mark O'Hara

ICT has become an integral part of learning and teaching in many schools. Provision in the early years is much more variable. In this chapter Mark O'Hara draws on research in four early years classrooms to explore how, when and for what purposes ICT are used. He suggests that ICT has the potential to support young children's learning but that changes in the way it is used and the opportunities for it to be used to support children's learning are necessary if all children are to engage with and learn through new technologies.

Introduction

For the Organisation for Economic Co-operation and Development there exist three overlapping and converging reasons for the inclusion of ICT in education (OECD, 2001a). Economically, learning about and through ICT improves pupil employability and national prosperity. Socially, ICT capability is a prerequisite for participation in both society and the workplace, and its inclusion in the curriculum offers a means to ameliorate any possible digital divides between the haves and the have-lesses that exist within populations (Selwyn & Bullon, 2000; OECD, 2001b). Pedagogically, ICT offers practitioners and pupils opportunities to increase the breadth and richness of learning, including the development of higher-order thinking skills such as analysis and synthesis. ICT can facilitate learning in different locations (both real and virtual) and offers the possibility of empowering the learner by accommodating different learning styles and preferences (OECD, 2001c).

[. . .]

Pedagogy in UK maintained settings is heavily influenced by constructivist and social-constructivist theories of learning, but practice in the sector can vary widely when it comes to ICT (O'Hara, 2004). Some practitioners, academics, policy-makers and commentators have embraced the use of ICT (Ager & Kendall, 2003; Freedman, 2001;

Siraj-Blatchford & Siraj-Blatchford, 2002). For these individuals and organisations, ICT is categorised as a new tool that could and should be incorporated into existing early years practice in developmentally appropriate ways, supplementing, not replacing, other important first-hand experiences and interactions and accompanied by quality adult input to help children learn about and through the technology (Sarama, 2003; Turbill, 2001). In addition, play is thought to be expanded and enhanced by the introduction of ICT as children use equipment such as floor robots, walkie-talkies or computers. ICT therefore is seen as offering a range of potentially valuable pedagogic tools when properly utilised (Cooper & Brna, 2002; Savage, 2004).

However, ICT has had a less than well-developed identity in other settings, often being conceptualised as little more than computers and with little in the way of guided interaction on offer for children as practitioners rely on less pedagogically effective reactive supervision (Plowman & Stephen, 2003). What Meade referred to as the need for participatory interaction and assisted performance may not always be translated into practice where the use of ICT is concerned (2000). ICT has also been regarded with suspicion by some and been described as inherently unsuitable for application in early years settings by some commentators, who feel that it flies in the face of good early years practice and the widely accepted needs of young children, including first-hand experience, play and talk (Kelly, 2000; Oppenheimer, 1997). [. . .] Computers in particular have been viewed as inappropriate tools that risk stunting children's intelligence and social skills and of damaging their health (McVeigh & Paton Walsh, 2000). The fiercest critics of the introduction of ICT into early years settings have cited potentially harmful effects of prolonged computer use on young children in terms of their physical and social well-being. Over-preoccupation with the development of computer skills may impede the establishment of good social skills and concern for others (Meltz, 1998; 'Modern life leads to more depression among children', 2006). Critics also fear hidden health costs such as vision strain, repetitive strain injuries, or sedentary lifestyles leading to obesity (Alliance for Childhood, 2000, 2004; BBC, 2004).

The research

The aim of the research which informs this chapter was to illuminate aspects of the technological dimension to childhood and in particular young children's interactions with ICT in education. It set out to explore the ICT experiences and capabilities of children in four foundation-stage classes in the UK maintained sector. Its purpose was to investigate and weigh up some of the pedagogical claims and counterclaims made in relation to ICT in the early years.
[. . .]

In recognition of their existing competences and to play to their strengths as research participants, nursery and reception children were observed and interviewed whilst involved in activities featuring ICT (Clark, 2004). The observations and discussions were conducted in the normal surroundings of children's nurseries and classrooms by familiar adults and included opportunities for appropriate debriefing, praise and thanks (Gollop, 2000, in Clark, McQuail, & Moss, 2003).
[. . .]

The settings

The research aimed to tell a story that would resonate with readers with an interest in the UK maintained sector. As a result it was necessary to ensure that the cases eventually chosen would not prove to be hopelessly atypical. A baseline survey involving 100 maintained early years settings across different local authorities made it possible to sketch a picture, albeit fuzzy, of a typical setting at that point in time, in that region (Bassey, 1998). The typical setting had a wide range of ICT available when one included items such as digital cameras and other shared resources. The typical setting had an ICT suite as well as individual PCs (normally one or two) located in each classroom and nursery, and reception pupils were timetabled to use the ICT suite each week. In the typical setting, ICT was largely equated with PC use by practitioners, with relatively little attention paid to the potential for integrating ICT more fully into role play, creative areas or the outside environment. In the typical setting, opportunities and time for staff training and development were limited; and this contributed in part to a mismatch between the availability and the usage of the ICT resources within settings.

The research eventually focused on foundation-stage children in two schools in the state-maintained sector, in the same local authority and each having both nursery (3–4 years) and reception (4–5 years) classes. Both schools approximated well to the typical setting in terms of the incidence and use of ICT. Tower School was a nursery/infant school. Children made good progress during the foundation stage, with teaching and learning characterised at inspection by Ofsted as either good, very good or excellent. Both classes had a single PC in them and this resource was supplemented with timetabled visits to the school's ICT suite, which contained approximately 20 laptops, an electronic whiteboard for staff use and two Pixie floor robots. Park School, meanwhile, was a nursery, infant and junior school. This school provided a satisfactory standard of education overall; however, within this, the foundation stage was singled out as a strength, as children progressed and achieved well in all areas of learning. Both classes contained two PCs. In addition, they both contained interactive whiteboards set at a child-friendly height to enable children to work directly with the boards. The foundation stage shared floor robots such as the Pixies with the rest of the school. The school also possessed a well-equipped ICT suite that the reception children used on a timetabled basis.

Discussion

[. . .]
The following a discussion is organised into the following five themes:

- Learning about ICT;
- Schema;
- Problem-solving, perseverance and motivation;
- Social skills and peer tutoring;
- Creativity.

Learning about ICT

In addition to planned learning and teaching involving ICT, some staff also identified new opportunities for young children to learn about ICT. In one nursery, children were encouraged to answer the telephone, albeit under supervision. In another, a teaching assistant took small groups of children to the staff room to photocopy work. Practitioners also commented that technologies such as the listening station were on open access and that children were using them 'all the time'. A reception practitioner remarked to her colleague when discussing children's use of the PC in the classroom: 'they're perfectly able to use them [CD-ROMS] aren't they, get them out and put them in and load them up and all sorts'. In her reception class, children were also making regular autonomous use of the CD player/radio.

Learning about ICT was greatly enhanced by practitioners who were sensitive and responsive to the children's capabilities and competences, not least their language skills. An attempt to explain to three reception children what was happening as images from a digital video camera were being transferred to a PC prompted the sceptically amused response from one of the children: 'Cameras can't talk!'. [. . .] Concentration levels and the quality of outcomes were improved as a result of timely and appropriate adult intervention. In one instance, a 4-year-old had been asked to draw a picture using a drawing package on a laptop. To begin with, the child worked alone and produced a purple mark in the middle of the page. Finding it hard to make further progress, she became dispirited and was on the verge of abandoning the task. At this point an experienced nursery nurse intervened. She was able to revive the child's interest; offered technical advice and guidance; and encouraged a sense of pride and achievement, judging by the child's eagerness to print her final picture.

One potential impediment to learning about ICT arose as a result of the high levels of initial excitement that the introduction of new technologies sometimes produced. The introduction of a public address system into a nursery 'Post Office' was a good example, resulting in little or no imaginative play on the theme of the Post Office at first. Instead the children sang songs, hailed friends or practiced funny voices. It was only a few days later that children were observed integrating the equipment into their stories in a much more matter-of-fact manner. The children had to be allowed sufficient time to develop skills and acquire familiarity with the technology.

Schema

Data supporting the notion that the children were acquiring knowledge of other subjects or areas of learning as a result of interacting with ICT were largely absent. On one occasion, for example, three nursery children were using a software package designed to help pupils with number recognition. Whenever the right number was matched to the right image, the children were rewarded with a flashing screen and a simple jingle. In fact the children were not using their knowledge of number at all, and may not even have been aware of the purpose of the task. Instead, they were systematically matching every number to every image, using a process of trial and error, until they had cleared the screen of all the numbers and images. Good negotiation and management, perhaps;

but it is debatable to what extent the children were reinforcing their number recognition (Plowman & Stephen, 2003).

Yet it might be a mistake to assume that claims made for ICT as a means of enhancing and extending learning across the wider curriculum are unfounded. Some of the children observed demonstrated great enthusiasm for practising their recently acquired ICT skills and capabilities repeatedly. In one instance, the 4-year-old being observed was enjoying making bold left-to-right, right-to-left horizontal sweeps with the cursor, covering the screen in black bands, saying: 'Dark! I'm going to do a dark palace. I'm doing a black palace'. The sweeps continued until almost every part of the screen was coloured black. [. . .]

These behaviours and parallel behaviours observed as children worked with floor robots were reminiscent of the intense, absorbed and repetitive behaviour that have been associated with young children and schema (Athey, 1990). Children sometimes behave in ways that appear obsessive, for example repeatedly carrying things around in bags, posting objects or lining things up. In so doing they may be providing evidence of schema. There is no set order to the development of schema; parallel development is possible, and some children do not appear to engage in this kind of behaviour at all, perhaps having alternative approaches to learning about the world. Broad categories of schema include enveloping/enclosure, rotation, trajectory, transporting and connection. There was no corroborating evidence from other areas of the learning environments, but it was possible that the use of floor robots and generic drawing software as part of exploratory play may have supported the construction of schema relating to trajectory, rotation and transporting by some children.

Problem-solving, perseverance and motivation

Using ICT put some children into situations that made it necessary for them to make use of their problem-solving skills. During one observation, three children were using a digital camera to take pictures of spring flowers. The digital nature of the technology afforded the children the opportunity to review, retain or delete their pictures. This immediate feedback enabled the children to realise that they were obscuring the images with their fingers. The simple operating characteristics of the technology were being offset by the fact that it was quite difficult for little fingers to cope with the chunky design of the camera. However, once the children realised what was happening they became more systematic in their work, adopting a collaborative thinking-aloud strategy, advising one another and introducing what in effect amounted to a verbal checklist in which they reminded themselves of where to position various digits and how to take aim.

Problem-solving skills and the motivational potential of ICT were further displayed in the children's efforts to develop strategies to compensate for their less than fully developed fine motor skills. For one nursery child, moving the mouse and pressing the button simultaneously proved difficult. The child responded by adopting a sequential approach in which movement and clicking became discrete operations, resulting in a distinctive polka-dot pattern. [. . .] Another used his right hand to move the mouse, while using his left hand to trace a path on-screen showing where he wanted the cursor to go.

In another case, a child systematically tried as many different icons as possible in order to discover what effect they would have, exclaiming excitedly when something unusual or unexpected happened: 'Hey, look at that!'. The task set by the teacher came second to the child's agenda of discovering the capabilities of the software through exploratory play, trial and error. The child was highly motivated, and sought energetically to share his learning and excitement with his peers: [. . .] It was suggested by practitioner interviewees that some children who displayed short attention spans when faced with the majority of classroom activities, were attracted to ICT and would: 'concentrate on it for much longer than other things'. One practitioner reflected on her experiences with a specific child, saying:

> He just comes alive when he's on the computer. He knows he can do it; probably he plays games at home, I don't know. But if we didn't have that [PC] he would be struggling to succeed at much . . . that is something that he can do.

This said, another practitioner commented that the reverse was also possible and that she had a small number of children in her class who were confident, motivated and interested in most things but for whom ICT, and the PC in particular, seemed to hold little attraction. [. . .]

Social skills and peer tutoring

A key criticism of the increasing use of ICT in early years settings has been that it promotes isolated and individualised approaches to learning. The data gathered here suggested that this is not an inevitable consequence of its use. In one setting, practitioners worked with small groups using speaking books downloaded from the Internet on the interactive whiteboard. Children were encouraged to discuss the stories, share their ideas and move characters around using the touch-sensitive screen accompanied by much advice from their peers, solicited and unsolicited. Even ostensibly isolated activities, such as individual children using a PC, often belied the incidence of short (and not so short) exchanges with passing peers centring on the technology. In another class, practitioners organised a music area that included electronic keyboards and tape recorders to encourage children to sing and play together in small groups. Where settings incorporated ICT into imaginative and roleplay areas, the incidence of prosocial behaviour and communication was particularly high. In one reception class, the 'Travel Agents' roleplay area contained a telephone, a PC, an electronic cash register, walkie-talkies and calculators.

Other examples of social and collaborative endeavour were also observed during activities with the Pixie floor robots. These programmable vehicles presented children with a considerable intellectual and cognitive challenge, which resulted in a high level of autonomous peer support and tutoring as some children attempted to scaffold the learning of others. [. . .] In one example, two nursery children experimented with the Pixie using a process of trial and error in a self-initiated enquiry into distance as an older, more experienced, child reminded them: 'Remember what we showed you. You press that one, then that one, then that one'. In these instances, children were encouraged to discuss the activity and share their ideas. Social conventions and interpersonal skills such as turn-taking were as much a part of the learning objectives as the acquisition of technical competences. The active encouragement of collaboration when using ICT was seen by practitioners as having benefits for the helper as well as the helped:

> You do get more able children helping others . . . and sometimes . . . it's not necessarily the child that is more able generally . . . . That's good for their self-esteem.

However, while there was a social dimension to many of the ICT activities observed, it was not always positive or unproblematic; and operational exchanges centred on negotiation of access or management of the equipment of the kind reported by Plowman and Stephen (2005) were also observed. Paired or small-group work with ICT could suffer from a tendency for the more able, confident or experienced children to monopolise the activity. This manifested itself on occasion in low-level, short-lived squabbles over ICT resources. [. . .] One such victim remarked indignantly: 'We're supposed to share, aren't we?'

A further issue concerned gender, as there were occasional examples of some boys seeking to restrict or even block access to new technologies for girls. In a preliminary observation, for example, two boys had attempted to wrest control of a computer away from two girls in the role play area, where it had been integrated into the rest of the props and resources to promote imaginative play. In an inspired response, one of the girls suggested to the boys that: 'You be dogs!'. Having acceded, and once in role, the boys' attempts at a takeover were neutralised; dogs, as the girls were quick to point out, have little need for computers.

Creativity

Creativity involves a melding of imagination with purpose; has originality in the sense that something is original to the child; and has value, as calculated by whether the outcome works, is useful, offers a valid solution to a problem, or is aesthetically pleasing (DfES, 1999). On occasions, the affordances offered by ICT facilitated young children's creative impulses: 'That's the wind', as one 4-year-old proudly said when explaining and evaluating the aesthetic qualities of her drawing on the PC. One area in which the potential to encourage creative activity involving ICT was particularly pronounced was in imaginary play. Practitioners supported the idea that new technologies could provide new opportunities for children to meld imagination with purpose. Even with relatively limited use of ICT in this area, children were demonstrating their creative potential:

> We always try and model . . . when we've got telephones in the role play area . . . the sorts of conversations that you might have. The children will quite often . . . copy them and develop them into their own ideas. That's them being creative, isn't it? Especially using their own ideas and opinions, isn't it?

In one reception class, meanwhile, the teacher had initiated a small project on story-telling that made use of a digital video camera. She also used the interactive whiteboard with small groups to build storyboards and insert credits pages and special effects. In her view, the inclusion of the camera had been a catalyst for the children to begin making up their own stories. In an earlier example, four other reception children stage-managed and then enacted a news broadcast using a video camera and television monitor. The group demonstrated a surprising level of knowledge about the use of these technologies in the world around them, and were able to make use of this awareness in a highly original manner.

Conclusions

In some instances, children's interactions with ICT echoed the findings of Plowman and Stephen (2005), focused as they were on negotiation and management. However, in spite of the limitations associated with the reactive supervision sometimes adopted by practitioners, even apparently isolated tasks, such as children working independently on the class computer, offered positive social and collaborative experiences including periods of interaction, support and scaffolding between peers or between pupils and practitioners. This potential for supporting less isolated learning experiences for young children did need monitoring, however, as inequalities in skills and knowledge, accompanied on occasion by stereotypical views of boys' and girls' activities, could have adverse effects if not checked. The children's youth meant that their social skills were sometimes well behind their technical capabilities.

At times the day-to-day realities of trying to juggle a multitude of competing, and sometimes conflicting, priorities acted as an impediment to continuing curriculum development relating to ICT and resulted in the reactive supervision articulated by Plowman and Stephen (2005). Certainly competing pressures could act as a brake on the wider use of ICT as practitioners, not unreasonably, responded to the perceived expectations of colleagues, parents and policy-makers. In some cases, structural impediments, for example the non-existence of equipment or infrastructure, exacerbated the challenges still further. The nature of the foundation-stage teachers' role restricted the time and space to reflect on their understanding of ICT or to plan for its further incorporation into existing learning and teaching. However, there was also some recognition amongst practitioners that ICT might offer additional pedagogic benefits, as the technology offered new and different forums within which the children in these settings had opportunities to demonstrate generic learning competences and dispositions. These included problem-solving skills, high levels of motivation, con-centration, resilience, perseverance and exploring new outlets for inventiveness and creativity. For example, given time, some children showed that once any novelty had worn off they were able to incorporate ICT into their sociodramatic play in ways that were sometimes startling.

The observations also included many examples of ICT other than the PC (e.g., floor robots and audiovisual technologies), and for a number of the pupils it appeared that ICT offered an additional means for exploring how the world works; for example, it could be argued that exploratory play with floor robots offered new opportunities to investigate the schema of transporting. Equally, however, the high levels of excitement that could result from the introduction of new technologies into the classroom risked producing an initial drop in the quality of children's play and work until such time as the novelty had worn off. However, it must be acknowledged that there was also some evidence to suggest that the motivating power of ICT proved less influential with minority of the children. It may be that there are children with whom practitioners will struggle to locate any excitement or interest in ICT, and for whom they will need to adapt their teaching approaches. Much depended here on the decisions taken by practitioners as to how they would make use of the technology; ICT is not a panacea, but neither should it be treated as a pariah.

Recommendations

For most foundation-stage children in the UK today, ICT forms a part of their everyday experiences. This does not mean that practitioners should throw caution and professional judgement to the wind, rather that they should acknowledge that ICT offers tools that have the potential to extend and enhance existing provision. The degree to which ICT is appropriate or not in the foundation stage depends on how it is used; as Loveless (2003) points out, the issues involved are as much about teaching and learning as they are about the technology. While the design of an interactive whiteboard and its software may encourage certain teaching and learning styles, it does not preclude the adoption of alternative and possibly more appropriate pedagogies. At the same time, over-preoccupation with computers could result in a failure to recognise that a myriad other forms of ICT exist, some of which are already widely used in early years settings and others still with the potential to fit well with foundation-stage pedagogies. Practitioners must exercise their judgement about what to use and when and how to use it, in order to realise that potential. Planning and stage-managing the introduction of new technologies into all aspects of the early-learning environment would be a start; and this process would be made all the more easy for those practitioners who were clear that ICT involves much more than just the indoor area, the PC and drill-and-skill software. Participatory interaction and assisted performance help children to make the most of the learning opportunities they encounter (Meade, 2000). Practitioners already routinely get involved and scaffold children's learning in the role play area, during outdoor play, or at the writing and mark-making table; and the same guided interaction needs to be adopted in activities involving ICT (Plowman & Stephen, 2005).

Finally, addressing practice in the maintained sector is only half of the challenge facing policy-makers and practitioners. The parallel private and voluntary sector is a huge provider of early years care and education featuring every type and size of setting, from relatively large private fee-paying nursery schools to small local playgroups catering for a handful of children. This sector met the needs of 40% of the 10,000 birth to 5-year-olds in the local authority in which this research took place. To date, national research on the incidence or use of ICT in the private and voluntary sector is limited, but the suspicion must be that in the majority of cases the early years ICT expertise and resources of a small voluntary playgroup are unlikely to match those of a maintained school (Marsh et al., 2005). At the very least, the situation in the private and voluntary sector should be ascertained so that additional training and resources can be made available.

References

Ager, R., & Kendall, M. (2003). Getting it right from the start: A case study of the development of a foundation stage learning and ICT strategy in Northamptonshire, UK. Retrieved January 20, 2007, from http://crpit.com/confpapers/CRPITV34Ager.pdf.

Alliance for Childhood. (2000). Fool's gold: A critical look at computers and childhood. Retrieved August 31, 2001, from www.allianceforchildhood.org.

Alliance for Childhood. (2004). Tech tonic: Towards a new literacy of technology. Retrieved December 2, 2005, from www.allianceforchildhood.net/projects/computers/pdf_files/tech_tonic.pdf.

Athey, C. (1990). Extending thought in young children: A parent–teacher partnership. London: Chapman.

Bassey M. (1998, August). *Fuzzy generalisation: An approach to building educational theory*. Paper presented at the British Educational Research Association Annual Conference, Belfast, Northern Ireland. Retrieved April 26, 2005, from www.leeds.ac.uk/educol/documents.

BBC (2004, January 16). *'Couch potato' toddlers warning. Toddlers have as inactive a lifestyle as office workers, researchers have warned*. Retrieved March 14, 2007, from http://news.bbc.co.uk/l/hi/health/3399811.stm.

Bertram, T., & Pascal, C. (2002). Effective early learning programme: Child involvement scale. Retrieved December 2, 2005, from http://www.eddept.wa.edu.au/lc/pdfs/involvementworkshop.pdf.

Clark, A. (2004). The mosaic approach and research with young children: Commentary. In V. Lewis, M. Kellett, C. Robinson, S. Fraser, & S. Ding (eds), *The Reality of Research with Children and Young People* (pp. 142–156). Thousand Oaks and London: Sage.

Clark, A., McQuail, S., & Moss, P. (2003). *Exploring the field of listening to and consulting with young children*. DfES Research Report RR445. London: HMSO.

Cooper, B., & Brna, P. (2002). *Hidden curriculum, hidden feelings: Emotions, relationships and learning with ICT and the whole child*. Paper presented at the BERA Conference, Exeter, September, 2002.

Department for Education and Skills. (1999). Report of the National Advisory Committee on Creative and Cultural Education DCMS/DfEE.

Department for Education and Skills. (2007). The early years foundation stage: Setting the standards for learning, development and care for children from birth to five. Nottingham: DfES Publications.

Freedman, T. (2001, June 12). Primary effects. *The Guardian*. http://education.guardian.co.uk/elearning/story/0,,789479,00.ht ml. Retrieved April 26, 2004.

Kelly, K. (2000, February 9). False promise. *US News Online*. Retrieved April 26, 2005, from http://www.usnews.com/.

Loveless, A. (2003). *The Role of ICT*. London: Continuum.

Marsh, J., Brooks, G., Hughes, J., Ritchie, L., Roberts, S., & Wright, K. (2005). Digital beginnings: Young children's use of popular culture, media and new technologies. Report of the 'Young Children's Use of Popular Culture, Media and New Technologies' study. The University of Sheffield & Esmée Fairbairn Foundation.

McVeigh, T., & Paton Walsh, N. (2000, September 24). Computers kill pupils' creativity. *The Observer* http://education.guardian.co.uk/news/story/0,,372428,00.html. Retrieved April 26, 2004.

Meade, A. (2000). If you say it three times, is it true? Critical use of research in early childhood education. *International Journal of Early Years Education, 8*(1), 15–26.

Meltz, B.F. (1998, January 10). Computers: Software can harm emotional, social development. Boston Globe. Retrieved August 31, 2001, from www.boston.com/globe/columns/meltz.

Modern life leads to more depression among children. (2006, September 13). *The Telegraph*. Retrieved March 14, 2007, from http://www.telegraph.co.uk/news/main.jhtml?xml=/news/2006/09/12/nosplit/njunk112.xml.

O'Hara, M. (2004). *ICT in the Early Years*. London: Continuum.

Oppenheimer, T. (1997). *The computer delusion*. Retrieved from www.theatlantic.com/.

Organisation for Economic Co-operation and Development. (2001a). *Learning to change: ICT in schools*. Retrieved from http://www.oecd.org/.

Organisation for Economic Co-operation and Development. (2001b). *Understanding the digital divide*. Retrieved from http://www.oecd.org/.

Organisation for Economic Co-operation and Development. (2001c). *E-learning: The partnership challenge*. Retrieved from http://www.oecd.org/.

Papert, S. (1993). Mindstorms: *Children, computers and powerful ideas* (2nd edn). Cambridge, MA: Perseus Books.

Plowman, L., & Stephen, C. (2003, September). *Developing a policy on ICT in pre-school settings: The role of research*. Paper presented at the British Educational Research Association annual conference, Edinburgh.

Plowman, L., & Stephen, C. (2005). Children, play and computers in pre-school education. *British Journal of Educational Technology, 36*(2), 145–157.

Sarama, J. (2003). Technology in early childhood mathematics: *Building Blocks* as an innovative technology-based curriculum. Buffalo and Wayne State: State University of New York.

Savage, D. (2004). *Is Everyone Keeping Up?* London: ATL.

Selwyn, N., & Bullon, K. (2000). Primary school children's use of ICT. *British Journal of Educational Technology, 31*(4), 321–332.

Siraj-Blatchford, J., & Siraj-Blatchford, I. (2002). *Guidance for practitioners on appropriate technology education in early childhood*. Retrieved April 26, 2005, from http://www.ioe.ac.uk/cdl/datec.

Turbill, J. (2001). A researcher goes to school: Using technology in the kindergarten literacy curriculum. *Journal of Early Childhood Literacy, 1*(3), 255–278.

Part 3
Listening to children and adults

Linda Miller

Introduction

The chapters in the third part of this book encourage you to reflect on how you listen to the children and families in your setting through both verbal and non verbal communication, and most importantly how you take account of views that may be different from those you currently hold. Your relationships with children and other adults are critical in ensuring that children are able to thrive and learn. Themes that are considered in these chapters include: respect for children; listening to and working with parents, carers and children; 'listening' to children's voices and behaviours as part of observation and assessment; the challenges of ensuring successful transitions for children's well being and learning; and the role of grandparents in children's lives.

Transitions are an important part of all our lives and enabling successful transitions for children are crucial if they are to learn and thrive. Children usually look forward to starting at their early years settings or school and expect to do well, but hopeful beginnings need nurturing if they are to come to fruition. What has been described as the 'schoolification' of early childhood (OECD 2006) means that some settings do a better job of facilitating transitions than others. In the first chapter in this section, Chapter 18, Hilary Fabian identifies many of the hopes noted above, particularly those to do with learning, and outlines ways that practitioners can begin to increase the likelihood of a successful transition for all those involved. The chapter draws on examples from a small-scale comparative study between Lapland in northern Finland and north Wales to illustrate different approaches to the curriculum and the challenges for parents, children and practitioners as children make the move to school.

There have been significant developments in recognising children's rights and listening to their 'multiple voices' over the last ten years. Elizabeth Wood sees the development of the professional skills of observing and active listening as essential for reflective practitioners working in integrated service provision for children and families. In Chapter 19 she examines and discusses policy and theories underpinning these developments. Drawing on vignettes from research to exemplify how children are co-constructors of knowledge and meaning, she argues that developing a pedagogy of listening and observing, that is respectful of children's communications and understandings, informs practitioners' own understanding and challenges them to reflect on their own perspectives, values and beliefs.

The role of grandparents in children's learning is a neglected area of research. However, grandparents (and aunts, uncles and other family members) have always played a significant, although often unacknowledged, role in children's lives. In Chapter 20, Charmian Kenner, Tabera Arju, Eve Gregory, John Jessel and Mahera Ruby, members of a research team at Goldsmith's College, University of London, suggest their contribution is worth further consideration. Grandparents often have a close and special relationship with their grandchildren and the research team found many examples of them involved in a range of learning events in the home where the grandparents sensitively joined with children in a process of discovery or shared their knowledge and experience.

In Chapter 21 Naima Browne considers how children's understanding of gender influences who they choose to play with and what they choose to play. The theme of listening to what children say is again evident in this chapter as the author draws on children's conversations with her, carried out as part of her research, to explore children's perceptions of masculinity and femininity and what children consider boys' games and girls' games and why. The chapter focuses particularly on Superhero and weapons play and the debates that have taken place over the purposes of such play and whether or not to allow such play in early years settings.

Assessment is a key feature of the work of practitioners in early years settings. However, all too often external demands and considerations can mean that the focus is on outcomes and measurable achievement – assessment *of* learning rather than assessment *for* learning. In Chapter 22 Cathy Nutbrown argues that we need to reconsider why we assess young children's learning and to develop assessment practices that begin with respect for children and that will provide us with information to engage with and support children's learning and understanding. The theme of listening to children is again evident here as the author suggests that listening to children and observation are essential tools in achieving this.

Providing children with experiences outside the setting and contact with a range of different adults are important in helping children to develop the breadth and depth of their understanding. Art galleries are often not seen as places to take young children but there are indications that they wish to change this perception. Roger Hancock has been involved with Alison Cox and Synthia Griffin, Curators of Family and Community Programmes at Tate Modern, in a project to involve parents and children in joint learning experiences around works of art in the gallery. In Chapter 23, they describe what this involved using both words and a series of images to tell the story.

As Vicky Hurst and Jenefer Joseph note in Chapter 24, 'Life is one long transition for the under-6s'. In this chapter they explore the fundamental importance of the relationship between a child and her/his parents or carers in terms of children's emotional well being and early learning. They see this early experience as being crucial to successful transitions in 'the world beyond the familiar one'. They make the case for an inclusive approach to working with children and families which recognises and responds sensitively to diversity through a partnership approach.

It is widely agreed that partnership with parents and carers should be central to early years provision. Successful partnerships will depend to a large extent on practitioners' willingness to recognise the role of parents and carers in their children's learning and to listen to their views and perspectives. In Chapter 25, the last chapter in this section, Lucy Draper and Bernadette Duffy draw upon their work at Thomas Coram Children's Centre in London to explore the challenges and benefits of working in partnership with parents and consider why such a partnership is important in achieving positive outcomes for children and their families.

Reference

OECD (2006) *Starting Strong 11. Early Children Education and Care.* Paris: Organisation for Economic Co-operation and Development.

Chapter 18

The challenges of starting school
Hilary Fabian

Children usually look forward to starting at settings and schools and expect to do well, but hopeful beginnings need nurturing if they are to come to fruition. In this chapter Hilary Fabian identifies many of those hopes, particularly those to do with learning, and outlines ways that practitioners can begin to increase the likelihood of a successful transition for all those involved. The chapter draws on examples from a small-scale comparative study between Lapland in northern Finland and north Wales to illustrate different approaches to the curriculum and the challenges for parents, children and practitioners as children make the move to school.

Introduction

The start of schooling has been perceived as one of the major challenges of early childhood (Ghaye and Pascal 1988; Margetts 2003). However, it is not just children who are involved in the transition: children, parents and educators are all involved with this change (Dockett and Perry 2004). If it is to be successful, then it needs to be a process of co-construction through participation between the institution and the family communicating and working together (Griebel and Niesel 2002). In order to understand the complexity of transition, an ecological concept can be used (Bronfenbrenner 1979) comprising a series of nested structures (microsystems) linked together in a network (the mesosystem) and influenced by the wider society (the macrosystem): in other words, an interlocking set of systems comprising home, early childhood services and school, which provide a bridge between experiences and form a basis for on-going social interactions. The ability to manage a successful transition therefore involves not only the individual child but also the social systems of each setting.

The transition to a setting or school marks a significant change in the way that a child participates in the family and the community because commuting between the family and school setting demands adjustment and brings about changes in identity, relationships and roles. More than this, however, are the expectations of children, their parents and educators who all have high hopes at the start of the child's schooling (Fabian and Dunlop 2007). So how can children be helped to make a successful transition? It might be helpful to start with a definition of school success.

Ladd's definition of success in school is very straightforward, and encompasses several aspects of children's adjustment to school:

> A child can be seen as successful in school when she or he (a) develops positive attitudes and feelings about school and learning, (b) establishes supportive social ties with teachers and classmates, (c) feels comfortable and relatively happy in the classroom rather than anxious, lonely or upset, (d) is interested and motivated to learn and take part in classroom activities (participation, engagement), and (e) achieves and progresses academically each school year.
>
> (2003: 3)

These are aspects which are reflected in the UK's *Every Child Matters* outcomes (DfES 2003a) which put the emphasis on the child to adapt to the organization rather than bringing his/her own culture to the setting (Brooker 2002).

As well as taking account of *Every Child Matters*, this chapter draws on the findings of a small-scale study that explored children's, families' and educators' perspectives about the transition to school in Lapland and Wales (Fabian and Turunen 2006). Twenty-four children were asked about their expectations of school; 15 parents and 11 educators of prior-to-school children were interviewed to ascertain their views about transition, particularly in relation to curriculum continuity. In asking questions about the curriculum, a range of issues arose, because all those involved tended to view the transition as a whole rather than as a curriculum issue in isolation. The following sections identify some of the challenges for each group and raise questions that can be asked in any country about young children starting school.

Challenges for children

Most children look forward to going to school and settle quickly, but for a few it is a frustrating time that causes confusion such as not knowing where to go; anxiety about the rules of the classroom, as well as surprises such as everyone wearing the same school uniform (Fabian 2002).

Children enter the institutional world with already developing concepts of themselves (Donaldson 1978; Chapter 13) and by the time they start formal school children are thinkers and have a clear idea about what they like and dislike about learning. They see the school curriculum as a promise of something more than their prior-to-school experiences. They expect a richness to the learning that is greater than that previously experienced; that it will take them in new directions – unknown at this stage – but that there will also be some familiarity about the activities and the daily routines. For example, in Wales, children expected that play would continue as before 'with Lego and play dough' but that there would be additional activities such as 'Spiderman, spellings, letters and shapes'. In Lapland, children also expected 'to play outdoors and indoors, draw and paint, play games, listen to music, skate and ski' just as they did in pre-school but that these activities would be extended into 'learning about days of the week, manners and doing exercises'. These children expected to continue to learn in a similar way once they started school; to 'learn by doing, learning by themselves, remembering'. They also expected the learning environment to offer new and exciting challenges but one where it was safe to express ideas, ask questions and experiment with different approaches.

However, starting school can present curriculum challenges to children in the UK and Lapland as they generally move from a play-based curriculum which helps to develop independence and which flows with the child's agenda, to one in which the teacher directs the learning. They had an inkling that this would happen and asked if there would still be opportunities to go outside and appreciate their natural surroundings – for example 'to see butterflies'; and they wanted to know if there would be dressing up clothes at school. This gives a clear indication that they expected learning to involve play and be thematic. One of the challenges in becoming a school pupil is to transfer what has been learned in the familiar environment of the early childhood setting to the unfamiliar setting of school – to transpose 'symbolic capital' to school (Webb et al. 2002).

While these children were confident in their understanding about what takes place at school, some children in the study will continue to experience a diversity of contextual and cultural influences from their 'old' life as they return to their prior-to-school setting for after-school clubs or are collected by a familiar childminder. As they enter school, children often leave behind places or people who are familiar and face the challenge of making new friends and understanding new cultural contexts (Brooker 2002). They have developed their identity in a social and cultural environment with an emphasis on relationships, the contexts of those relationships and the cultural meaning of those relationships. However, on starting school, children might not be with their friends and will have to mediate new relationships often in unfamiliar surroundings.

Children will have gained expectations about school from relationships with friends, older siblings and other family members, but they might not realize that they are expected to adapt to a more formal way of working.

Challenges for parents

At the start of school parents tend to view their child's education in a more serious way (Griebel and Niesel 1999). They have high expectations and also anxieties about their child's behaviour and success; they want their children to acquire skills, knowledge and values that they believe to be important (Tizard and Hughes 1984); are concerned about the ratio of adults to children, playtime and lunchtime (Dowling 1988; Cleave and Brown 1991); and want their child to be happy and confident (Dowling 2000). In Wales, they were also concerned about how their children would cope with a longer day and whether or not their children would be respected and recognized as an individual. All this amounts to a growing pressure on schools to bring about an inclusive curriculum and meet a range of individual needs.

Parents undergo a transition – being a parent of a child at school – and are also concerned about their own role in supporting their child's education. For example, in

Wales, they asked whether or not they should be helping with reading before their child starts school. Parents wanted to know how to collaborate to help their child develop and what partnership meant in practice, particularly as they see the availability of teachers decreasing as their child grows older. Parents in Lapland held similar views. They felt comfortable in the prior-to-school setting as they were familiar with the building. They had great confidence in the staff because they always had time for parents, could meet the family's wishes and take their needs into account.

Socially isolated and/or single parents sometimes dread the prospect of their children starting school because the familiar would disappear: they would not know the staff in the new setting, would be unsure of their own future role and would have a gap in their own lives (Fabian 2003). Indeed, Dunlop and Fabian (2005, 2007) found that some parents planned to have another baby once their child started school in order to fill the gap.

Parents felt that the knowledge staff gained of their child was more important than the curriculum. In Lapland, educators devise an individual curriculum for children when they enter the early childhood setting. However, 36% of parents did not recognize that there was an individual plan for their child, based on the initial discussion with the staff. For others, the discussion was highly positive and parents felt they had a great deal of influence over the individual curriculum for their child. The most useful areas that parents identified in this personalized curriculum were social skills, developing friendships, play, daily routines, and specific subject skills, such as language, that would extend an already developed area. However, there was little conception of how the individual curriculum is used in the transition from early education to school. While the individual curriculum was considered a good starting point because it gives the basis for individual support of the child, parents hoped the staff at school would have time to read their child's transfer record and hoped it would not only reflect their child's ability but also the essence of their child. Some parents wanted to have a discussion with the pre-school teacher before the start of school as well as meeting the next teacher, thus co-constructing the transition.

Challenges for educators

Sometimes schools are 'fed' by a number of settings often with a range of organizational systems. For these schools, the challenge is recognizing the variety of settings from which children come and the concomitant variety of past learning experiences that have to be anticipated in order to accommodate and establish familiar routines for children. In other cases, the early years service is on the same site with the constituent parts of the system being interlinked and interdependent because the reception and early years educators visit each other's settings on a regular basis or have a system of looping (Gaustad 1998) where the children stay with one teacher for two years. In Lapland, the early years setting in the study was linked by a door to the school through which children visited the school for music and other lessons so staff and children got to know one another. The physical transition was not seen as an ordeal for children or families, even if the pedagogies were different.

Pedagogical differences between early childhood services and schools raise a challenge for teachers who usually expect children to be ready for school (Broström 2002). But what is 'ready'? Is it to do with competencies, skills and abilities? Learning is sometimes characterized by goals which reflect cultural perspectives such as those proposed in the *Early Learning Goals* (DfES 2007) or *Every Child Matters* (DfES 2003a) in the UK. Claxton and Carr (2004: 89) suggest that charting possible directions of growth and providing guidance to progress learning attributes are more important if children are 'to respond in a learning-positive way'. For this to occur, not only do children need to know about what takes place at school, how they are going to learn and how they are going to be assessed, but educators also need to be aware of the role they play in influencing learning. So instead of the child being ready for school, the school needs to take responsibility for being ready and creating a match between children and school (Lam and Pollard 2006). This raises issues concerning finding out about children's prior learning, knowing where to start in order to build on prior-to-school experiences to inform planning and design the child's learning. It might also avoid the problem that Stephens and Cope (2003) identified which was that the school expected the child to fit in with them and if children had difficulty with the transition, then teachers ascribed problems to the child, not to the school.

Multiple communications

Another challenge for educators is ensuring that everyone is involved and communicating with each other in a way that is understood. Parents and children want sufficient and accessible information and opportunities to understand the school environment, its curriculum and where they fit into the organization. Teachers want to know about the children's learning and previous experiences from parents and early years educators. If information is too substantial, given very rapidly or the terminology used is unfamiliar, then it can be confusing, cause misunderstanding and anxiety and hinder the transition process. One of the issues for educators is how and when to present information to parents – by brochure, website or meetings – to meet everyone's needs. Educational inclusion is as much about perceptions as it is access, so if parents think that they or their children do not match the norm, they might think that they will be seen as problematic.

This next section addresses ways of supporting transitions by going beyond those in the *Common Core of Skills and Knowledge for the Children's Workforce* (see Section 4: 16–17, DfES 2005) to look at social and cultural and familiarization and curriculum issues.

Social and cultural issues

In choosing a school, parents are also choosing values and beliefs, and have decided that they want their child to be part of the philosophical culture of that school. However, children also bring their own social capital with them which suggests that we may carry forward factors influencing our lives. If little capital accures to a child at the first transition, subsequently there may be less on which to draw (Dunlop 2007), so schools need to capitalize on the strengths that families have transferred to their child, while also helping them understand the language of school.

Well-being and pupil performance go hand-in-hand (Laevers et al. 1997). Children learn effectively if they feel safe and if they feel comfortable emotionally in the classroom (DfES 2003b, http://www.everychildmatters.gov.uk/ ete/personalisedlearning/). It is therefore important to help children feel that they belong to the school community by providing opportunities for social interaction, helping children to make friends and learn the rules of the classroom (Bulkeley and Fabian 2006). This in turn facilitates acceptance and helps children to develop a positive attitude regarding their identity as a schoolchild belonging to a particular school.

Friendships and relationships are central in helping children to learn well and profit from school (Fabian and Dunlop 2005) but at the start of school children have to cope with loss of friends from their prior-to-school environment and develop social relationships in the new class. To confirm their sense of self-esteem, a significant feature that helps children with starting school, and identified in several studies (Fabian 2002; Margetts 2003; Dockett and Perry 2004), is the ability to mix with other children and to start school with a friend.

Working with parents and colleagues in prior-to-school settings is a further significant aspect in bringing about a successful transition to school. Colleagues can learn from and with one another about their philosophy of educating and about individual children's needs. By building and cultivating networks both with parents and staff, expectations of school can be clarified, communication improved and parents helped to gain confidence to participate in their child's learning.

Familiarization issues

The new context usually means children have to adjust to changes such as the size of building, number of pupils in the class, different teacher–pupil ratios, different classroom layouts, a wider range of ages and often a different route to school. Teachers' beliefs about what is important at the start of school are reflected in the ways in which they introduce children to the school environment and learning at school. Broström (2002) found that the most frequently used method was the school inviting the child to visit the class before school starts and the teachers visiting the children in their early childhood settings. However, it is what takes place during those visits that makes a difference.

Parents in the Welsh study recognized the contribution that they made in supporting their children, and identified ways to help their children overcome insecurities and fears of their new surroundings such as helping them to develop independence and routines, for example, by 'being able to do up his shoe laces' and 'go to the toilet on his own', and talking to their children about what they might do and see at school. However, there is a danger that the picture that parents give their children of school does not live up to expectations, and children are left to handle the difference between the rhetoric and the reality (Dunlop 2001). Parents thought that the experience of eating a school meal with their child during a visit would give their child confidence. Staff felt children should have a more prolonged transition process and wanted support in developing their own skills in discussing parents' and children's wishes, in helping children respond to change and supporting them in their new, and sometimes challenging, environment.

Understanding the ways in which learning takes place is a major issue. At school there is greater importance given to outcomes and targets; sometimes homework in the form of reading and number activities; being taught subjects rather than areas of learning; and often a change in the teaching method. Parents are more likely to be able to support their child's learning if they are aware of the ways in which children learn at school and the support that they can give at home.

Curriculum issues

In Lapland, a personalized curriculum which involves an individual meeting between educators, children and their parents at the start of a child's formal education aims to take account of the child's individuality and parents' views on aspects such as the child's experiences, current needs and future perspectives, interests and strengths, and individual need for support and guidance. In Lapland, this included the concept of 'self' and emotional life; social, motor and cognitive skills; linguistic development; perception of the environment; working habits; self-expression; and music. In the UK, the *Every Child Matters* initiative (DfES 2003b) outlines a personalized approach to supporting children which means:

* tailoring learning to the needs, interests and aspirations of each individual;
* tackling barriers to learning and allowing each child to achieve their potential (http://www.everychildmatters.gov.uk/ete/personalised learning/).

It is focused on giving all children the support they require, whatever their needs, abilities, background or circumstances. By engaging parents in supporting their children's learning and progression, an understanding develops of formal and informal learning; academic and social learning; and the expectations and achievements of their child.

The difference in pedagogical styles and the curriculum content between early childhood services and school can cause problems with continuity. In Wales, the individual records were sent to school but only if the parents wanted this to happen. In Lapland, the staff ensured the child's individual plans were transferred to the school. Staff in Wales thought it would be helpful if teachers visited the nursery to meet the children and talk with them individually and discuss previous learning. In Lapland, transition activities for children with special educational needs depend on the child's individual circumstances. Whatever the need, there is intensive co-operation between parents, the future teachers and therapists to create the individual curriculum. In the UK, the *Common Assessment Framework* provides a simple process for a holistic assessment of a child's needs and strengths, taking account of the role of parents, carers and environmental factors on their development. Practitioners then are well placed to agree with the child and family about what support is appropriate (DfES 2003c, http://www.everychildmatters. gov.uk/deliveringservices/caf/).

Discussion

Every Child Matters has 'Ready for School' as a sub-heading under 'Enjoy and Achieve'. Readiness suggests a set of physical and cognitive skills that a child should possess to be ready to start school rather than a developing child who has abilities in a range of areas. There is consensus, however, based upon a wealth of research, that a child's readiness for school depends on his/her levels across five distinct but connected domains:

- physical well-being and motor development;
- social and emotional development;
- approaches to learning;
- language development;
- cognition and general knowledge (Rhode Island Kids Count 2005).

Most teachers want children to be healthy, confident, active and attentive, able to communicate their needs, feelings and thoughts, enthusiastic and curious when approaching new activities (Arnold et al. 2006). They also place importance on skills such as the ability to follow directions, not being disruptive in class, and being sensitive to others (Rhode Island Kids Count 2005). As Young (in Arnold et al. 2006: 7) says: 'The child who is ready for school has a combination of positive characteristics.' Starting school marks a boundary which demands that development has reached a particular point. Issues which affect children's intellectual capabilities, academic achievement and behaviour, include the home environment, poverty, care and nurture, food, safety, motivation, language and the child's view of themselves as a learner. Not being ready at a particular time can have a detrimental effect on future learning and self-esteem. So, rather than ensuring readiness for school, Broström (2002) suggests that schools become 'child-ready' to meet the wide range of individuals that enter at the set time. This is a school where 'staff members are welcoming and appreciative of children's efforts, ensure their safety and sense of security, and provide effective learning opportunities which enable children to interact effectively with their world' (Arnold et al. 2006: 19).

Educators and parents often have different ideas of school readiness. Teachers put more emphasis on the social domain, whereas many parents emphasize academic readiness. For example, in my study, parents had confidence that the prior-to-school setting gave their child a good start to their education socially but wanted their child to be prepared for more formal learning as the start of school approaches. Practices that establish and foster relationships among important individuals in the child's life are likely to reap the most benefit for the child (Early 2004). Starting school, therefore, is best supported by practices that engage the parents (and often grandparents) and early childhood setting prior to the first day of school in developing an understanding of how learning takes place at school, sharing information and identifying gaps, overlap and progression.

Conclusion

The start of primary school is a transition for children, parents and educators in children's life-long learning journeys. Children are agents in the transition process as they bring what they learned from home and early childhood settings to school, and have to be active in adapting and responding to the transition. They anticipate the school curriculum as being exciting, rewarding and different but also somewhat familiar. They expect school to be fun, but they are nervous about the unknown and the possibility of having to do things they do not want to do. Parents consider they have greater influence in the prior-to-school setting, have high expectations for their child's success at school and see partnership with school as the way of fulfilling this. Parents consider that the confidence their children gain at nursery has a significant impact on their child's ability to make friends and understand school. Although parents are unsure about curriculum content, they are more concerned that their child is able to maintain their own identity and individuality. Educators are faced with challenges to smooth the transition in terms of organizational systems, curriculum and pedagogy. A major challenge for all is communicating information to understand each other's perspectives.

Social and cultural aspects are central in supporting children in the transition to school and can be improved by developing communication networks and supporting children in developing friendships to gain a sense of belonging to the school community. Teachers usually help children become familiar with their physical surroundings; parents support the preparations for school by attempting to give their child greater independence. Personalized learning is becoming more common but discussions and profiles between early childhood settings and schools permit further enlightenment of educational goals at transfer. In the UK, the *Common Assessment Framework* will also help to improve integrated working by promoting co-ordinatèd service provision, thereby significantly advantaging the minority where further support is necessary.

A successful transition to school is achieved when all those involved understand their role in discussing the child's experience, strengths and needs and in planning the transition process. The well-being of the child then becomes a prerequisite for successful interaction and learning. The policy of *Every Child Matters* to co-ordinate services to maximize success among children as they enter school promotes integration of prior-to-school and school-age services. However, co-ordination is required to ensure that the transition process begins well before the first day of school to give sufficient time for key relationships to form and for continuity of learning to take place.

Acknowledgements

Many thanks to Tuija Turunen from the University of Lapland who worked with me on the research in Lapland and Wales. For additional support, see *International Journal of Transitions in Childhood*: http://extranet.edfac.unimelb. edu.au/LED/tec/

References

Arnold, C., Bartlett, K., Gowani, S. and Merali, R. (2006) Is everybody ready? Readiness, transitions and continuity: lessons, reflections and moving forward, background paper prepared for *Education for All Global Monitoring Report 2007 Strong Foundations: Early Childhood Care and Education*. Paris: UNESCO.

Bronfenbrenner, U. (1979) *The Ecology of Human Development: Experiments by Nature and Design*. Cambridge, MA: Harvard University Press.

Brooker, L. (2002) *Starting School: Young Children Learning Cultures*. Buckingham: Open University Press.

Broström, S. (2002) Communication and continuity in the transition from kindergarten to school, in H. Fabian and A.W. Dunlop (eds) *Transitions in the Early Years: Debating Continuity and Progression for Children in Early Education*. London: RoutledgeFalmer.

Bulkeley, J. and Fabian, H. (2006) Well-being and belonging during early educational transitions. Available at: http://extranet.edfac.unimelb.edu.au/LED/tec/journal_vol2.shtml

Claxton, G. and Carr, M. (2004) A framework for teaching learning: the dynamics of disposition, *Early Years*, 24(1): 87–97.

Cleave, S. and Brown, S. (1991) *Early to School: Four Year Olds in Infant Classes*. London: NFER/Routledge.

DfES (Department for Education and Skills) (2003a) *Every Child Matters* (Green Paper). London: HMSO.

DfES (2003b) *Every Child Matters: Change for Children*. Available at: http://www.everychildmatters.gov.uk/ete/personalisedlearning/ (accessed 7 November 2006).

DfES (2003c) *Every Child Matters: Change for Children*. Available at: http://www.everychildmatters.gov.uk/deliveringservices/caf/ (accessed 11 December 2006).

DfES (2005) *Common Core of Skills and Knowledge for the Children's Workforce*. London: DfES Publications.

DfES (2007) *Statutory Framework for the Early Years Foundation Stage*. Nottingham: DfES Publications.

Dockett, S. and Perry, B. (2004) Starting school: perspectives of Australian children, parents and educators, *Journal of Early Childhood Research*, 2(2): 171–89.

Donaldson, M. (1978) *Children's Minds*. Glasgow: Penguin.

Dowling, M. (1988) *Education 3-to-5: A Teachers' Handbook*. London: Paul Chapman.

Dowling, M. (2000) *Young Children's Personal, Social and Emotional Development*. London: Paul Chapman.

Dunlop, A.W. (2001) Children's thinking about transitions to school, paper presented at the 11th Annual Conference of the European Educational Research Association, Alkmaar.

Dunlop, A.W. (2007) Bridging research, policy and practice, in A.W. Dunlop and H. Fabian (eds) *Informing Transitions in the Early Years: Research, Policy and Practice*. Maidenhead: Open University Press/McGraw-Hill Education.

Dunlop, A.W. and Fabian, H. (2005) Transition day: who are the stakeholders? Inset day organised by Dumfries and Galloway, 1 December 2005.

Dunlop, A.W. and Fabian, H. (2007) *Informing Transitions in the Early Years: Research, Policy and Practice*. Maidenhead: Open University Press/McGraw-Hill Education.

Early, D. (2004) Services and programs that influence young children's school transitions. http://www.excellence-earlychildhood.ca/documents/EarlyANGxp.pdf (accessed 30 October 2006).

Fabian, H. (2002) *Children Starting School*. London: David Fulton.

Fabian, H. (2003) Managing the start of school for children from dysfunctional families, *Management in Education*, 17(5): 30–2.

Fabian, H. and Dunlop, A.W. (2005) The importance of play in the transition to school, in J. Moyles (ed.) *The Excellence of Play*, 2nd edn. Maidenhead: Open University Press.

Fabian, H. and Dunlop, A.W. (2007) The first days at school, in J. Moyles (ed.) *Beginning Teaching, Beginning Learning*, 3rd edn. Maidenhead: Open University Press.

Fabian, H. and Turunen, T. (2006) How might the transition of five-year-old children be supported by the curriculum? A comparative study between Wales and Finland. *OMEP UK Updates*, 120: 2–6.

Gausted, J. (1998) Implementing looping, *ERIC Digest* 123. Available at: http://eric. uoregon.edu/publications/digests/digest123.html

Ghaye, A. and Pascal, C. (1988) Four-year-old children in reception classrooms: participant perceptions and practice, *Educational Studies*, 14(2): 187–208.

Griebel, W. and Niesel, R. (1999) From kindergarten to school: a transition for the family, paper presented at 9th European Early Childhood Education Research Association European Conference on Quality in Early Childhood Education, 1–4 September, Helsinki, Finland.

Griebel, W. and Niesel, R. (2002) Co-constructing transition into kindergarten and school by children, parents, and teachers, in H. Fabian and A.W. Dunlop (eds) *Transitions in the Early Years: Debating Continuity and Progression for Children in Early Education*. London: RoutledgeFalmer.

Ladd, G.W. (2003) *School Transitions/School Readiness: An Outcome of Early Childhood Development*. Available at: http://www.excellence-earlychildhood.ca/documents/ LaddANGxp.pdf (accessed 30 October 2006).

Laevers, F., Vandenbussche, K.M. and Depondt, L. (1997) *A Process-oriented Child Monitoring System for Young Children*. Leuven: Centre for Experiential Education, Katholieke Universiteit Leuven.

Lam, M.S. and Pollard, A. (2006) A conceptual framework for understanding children as agents in the transition from home to kindergarten, *Early Years*, 26(2): 123–41.

Margetts, M. (2003) Children bring more to school than their backpack: starting school down under, *European Early Childhood Education Research Journal: Transitions' Themed Monograph Series*, 1: 5–14.

Rhode Island Kids Count (2005) *Getting Ready: Findings from the National School Readiness Indicators Initiative: A 17 State Partnership*. Available at: http://www. gettingready.org/matriarch/MultiPiecePage.asp_Q_PageID_E_318_A_PageName_E_ NationalSchoolReadinessIndicat

Stephens, C. and Cope, P. (2003) *European Educational Research Journal*, 2(2). Available at: http://www.wwwords.co.uk/pdf/viewpdf.asp?j=eerjandvol=2andissue=2andyear=2003andarticle=5_Stephen_EERJ_2_2_webandid=86.128.16.233 (accessed 7 November 2006).

Tizard, B. and Hughes, M. (1984) *Young Children Learning*. London: Fontana.

Webb, J., Schirato, T. and Danaher, G. (2002) *Understanding Bourdieu*. London: Sage.

Chapter 19

Listening to young children
Multiple voices, meanings and understandings

Elizabeth Wood

The development of the professional skills of observing and active listening are seen by Elizabeth Wood as essential for reflective practitioners working in integrated service provision for children and families. In this chapter she examines and discusses policy and theories underpinning developments in recognising children's rights and listening to their voices. Drawing on vignettes from research to exemplify how children are co-constructors of knowledge and meaning, she argues that developing a pedagogy of listening and observing, that is respectful of children's communications and understandings, informs practitioners own understanding and challenges them to reflect on their own perspectives, values and beliefs.

Introduction

Contemporary research and policy frameworks agree that reflecting in and on practice is essential to improving the quality of provision, and supporting professional development. However, the concept of reflective practice may be narrowly interpreted as a means of ensuring that teachers and practitioners are 'delivering' the curriculum and achieving defined learning outcomes. Wood and Attfield (2005) argue that effective educators need to be good researchers, and to develop inquiry-based approaches to their practice. Similarly, Rinaldi (2006) proposes that early childhood education should be based on a 'pedagogy of listening', which encompasses ethical and political commitments to children, families and communities. By integrating such approaches, Dahlberg and Moss (2005) argue that education settings can become sites for ethical practice, in which practitioners can confront injustice and inequity, and forms of domination and oppression. They can also challenge assumptions, which may be derived from their own professional and life experiences, and policy texts.

In this chapter I will demonstrate that the skills of observing and listening are integral to repertoires of professional practice, and that reflective practice can extend into critical engagement with policy, theory and practice, from which new possibilities for action can be generated. Reflective educators can become change agents and 'activist educators', who have the ability to transform, rather then merely implement policy frameworks (MacNaughton 2005). Such developments are particularly important in the context of *Every Child Matters* (DfES 2004a), because professionals have contrasting knowledge bases and ways of seeing young people and their families.

In the first section I examine the implications of contemporary policy frameworks for developing inquiry-based approaches. In the second section I discuss methodological trends towards incorporating children's voices in research, and the implications for practitioners. Vignettes from research studies are used to provoke reflective consideration of children's voices, meanings and perspectives, and how these can be used to develop ethical assessment practices.

Policy directions

Contemporary developments in early childhood provision and services are taking place within a dynamic framework of policy, research, theories, and changing images of children and childhood. Three policy frameworks are relevant to educational provision and practice: *Every Child Matters* (DfES 2004a), *The Early Years Foundation Stage* (DCSF 2008) and the *Primary National Strategy* (DfES 2004b). These frameworks can be interpreted narrowly to promote a culture of conformity to technical practices, 'outcomes' and 'standards', or more broadly to promote a culture of entitlement, empowerment and inclusion. Personalized learning and services, assessment for learning, children's well-being, the voices and rights of the child, are policy aspirations that are shared across integrated service providers – education, health, law and social care. Such practices also respect cultural and social diversity, and promote social justice by ensuring equal opportunities and equal access to provision and services. The development of integrated services is based on inter professional collaborations, which have the potential for creating new knowledge bases, practices and 'ways of seeing' children and their families. Therefore all practitioners need to develop active listening and observing, along with a language of critique and reflexivity.

Young children's voices and perspectives in research

Recent developments in research reflect a willingness to involve young people as research participants, and to access their voices and perspectives. These developments are supported by postmodern and emancipatory theories and methodologies, which recognize children's rights, agency and competences (MacNaughton 2005; Underdown and Barlow 2007). Children are seen as expert informers and witnesses, and practitioners in multi-professional contexts take account of their choices and perspectives. The role of researchers and professionals is to understand children's ways of representing and voicing their perspectives, by following their trails of thinking and meaning-making. Participatory approaches have also created methodological and ethical challenges (Wood 2005), not least because children are capable of challenging and resisting dominant discourses and power relations in classroom and research contexts. Drawing on their work in the field of special educational needs, Norwich and Kelly (2004) argue that eliciting children's perspectives is not just a technical matter, it also involves complex ethical considerations and contextual factors, including:

1 the child's and young person's competences and characteristics;
2 the questioner's competences and characteristics;
3 the purpose and use made of eliciting child and young person's views;
4 the setting and context: power, relationships and emotional factors;
5 ethical and human rights considerations.

(Norwich and Kelly 2004: 45)

Researchers are required to work within ethical frameworks in designing, conducting and reporting research; they acknowledge the socio-political context, and the power relations between the researchers and the participants. Researchers have developed more respectful views about young people, and more sensitive approaches to eliciting their voices and perspectives about issues that are of direct concern in their lives, such as their health, welfare, education and legal rights. Those concerns are situated in networks of influence, such as home and community cultures, practices and discourses. Two complementary principles underlie a contemporary rhetoric of empowerment: a belief in children's *rights* (including the right to be heard, to participate, to have control of their lives) and a belief in children's *competence* (to understand, to reflect, and to give accurate and appropriate responses) (United Nations 1989; Brooker 2002).

These principles are relevant to academic and practitioner researchers. Accessing children's thinking and understanding is pedagogically challenging because adults' perceptions of intent (particularly in play) are only ever partial. Similarly, interpretations of child- and adult-initiated activities may also be partial where defined learning goals and curriculum content are the main indicators of progress and achievement. Reifel (2007) argues for hermeneutic approaches to data collection and analysis, with researchers 'placing texts within multiple narratives, reflecting the multiple perspectives of participants' (2007: 26). In hermeneutic enquiry, '*texts* can be used to describe any number of productions: written words, oral discourses (a conversation, an interview), performances (staged, informal, impromptu), and works of art (language based or otherwise)' (Reifel 2007: 28). Therefore textual analysis in early childhood settings can capture complex and multiple meanings, and the contexts in which these are produced and negotiated. Small actions and interactions often have immediate significance for the child, and build towards increasing competence and participation. Such approaches are relevant to researchers and educators for exploring playful meanings and actions, for individuals and groups of children. Researchers (and practitioners as researchers) can go beyond the boundaries of developmental and curriculum goals, because observations can be used as texts for analysis, not merely as evidence of developmental milestones, learning outcomes and curriculum targets.

Multiple meanings can be understood through different modes of representation and communication, and not solely through spoken language. In relation to issues of power, Silin (2005) argues that a concern with children's voices should include a concern with silence and silences, and whether those silences are self-chosen or imposed by others. In researching equity and diversity in pre-school settings in Australia, MacNaughton (2005) documents the potential dangers of giving voice to young children in research, because this raises questions about relative power between children, and between children and adults. MacNaughton recommends that the following questions be asked in research (2005: 130–1).

- Which children's voices will come forth?
- What will the consequence be for each child who participates?
- How might one child's voice silence that of another?
- What can and should I do when the voices are racist or sexist?
- How might intervening as one child voices their knowledge enable another child to speak?
- How will I honour those children who struggle to make their voices heard?

These questions are equally pertinent for educators, particularly in the context of *Every Child Matters* (DfES 2004a), where there is a central concern with children's social and emotional well-being and not just their performance against curriculum targets.

Recent studies explore how listening to children's voices can challenge dominant policy discourses and practices in pedagogy, curriculum planning and assessment. These concerns are illustrated in the following learning story, which is taken from a study on progression and continuity (Wood 2002). Two cohorts of children were studied across one school year: one from nursery to reception (ages 3/4–4/5) and one from reception to Year 1 (ages 4/5–5/6). Liam's story shows how his teachers interpret his progress and achievements through the dual lenses of developmental theories and curriculum objectives. However, in conversations with the teacher and researcher, Liam reveals humorous and subversive perspectives, and his preference for activities where he perceives himself to be competent. The study took place at a time of policy intensification, with teachers being pressurized to 'raise standards' through prescribed pedagogical approaches and learning objectives in literacy and numeracy.

Liam's Story: Reception to Year 1

Diane (reception teacher) is concerned about the pace of Liam's development, particularly his problems with fine and gross motor skills, concentration and sitting still. In March, Liam is copying over Diane's handwriting and is struggling with recorded work. In contrast his oral language is imaginative and vibrant, as shown in Diane's transcription of Liam's version of 'The Gingerbread Man':

> To make a gingerbread man you need some crispy water and some ginger to make it tasty, and some cherries to help them stick on it and some milk to make it yummy. You make one with play-dough, you stick it on with PVA glue and put it in the oven.

Liam is 'much more interested in drawing than in writing', and in talking about (rather than recording) his work. His playful use of language is demonstrated in a numeracy session that focuses on counting backwards from five, using the rhyme of 'Five Little Ducks'. Liam is asked to draw five ducks on a pond, but draws four ducks. Diane asks 'Where is the fifth duck?' Liam draws a duck over the page and says 'It is swimming away.' In the plenary session, he shows his picture to the class and counts 'one, two, three, five'. When Diane asks again where the fifth one is, he turns the page to show the duck on the back and says 'Well, number four swam away', and tells an imaginative story about the duck getting stuck in quicksand, then the mummy duck came back, but was eaten by a fox, and the fox was eaten by a crocodile. Diane interprets this episode as Liam having partial understanding of counting to five, and plans further work before he can progress to numbers 5–10.

In a subsequent conversation with the researcher, Liam recalls that the fourth duck is missing: 'It's on the waterfall.' When the researcher asks 'How did you know what to do?', Liam describes the sequence of his drawing, rather than the one-to-one matching and counting:

> Started with the water . . . and the duck's beak orange, and the body blue and the . . . and at the front the ducks have got webs on their feet.

Liam continues to use stories to contextualize his learning, and as a subversive or humorous response to teaching. Diane comments that Liam 'has got a very good imagination'. However, she anticipates problems with writing because of Liam's difficulties with fine motor skills, although she notes his skills in drawing:

> . . . there is a really lovely picture of a duck, and it always amazes me as to how he can do such wonderful pictures because his hand control is just awful, and he's got such a really awkward grip as well.

In the first term of Year 1, Liam is focused on tasks, and responds to questions, but there is less time for making up stories or responding imaginatively to tasks. He continues to interpret tasks in his own way, and performs better orally than in writing and recording. In the research conversations, he talks about his interest in animals, and remains proud of his drawings. He follows his own agenda, expressing the achievements and competences that he values.

In December, Susie (Year 1 teacher) reviews Liam's portfolio of work, and judges his progress against the teaching objectives in the National Literacy Strategy. Susie has difficulty in getting him to focus on learning objectives:

> This year he is more focused on individual words. He knows how to write some words – for example, 'I' and 'zoo'. He can write his name . . . he can spell words, he knows that there should be spaces between words. He knows about direction, how to start a new line. He's put a full stop at the end of the sentence, so there's quite a bit of progression there.

Susie says that Liam is an intelligent boy who is being held back because of his difficulties with recording, behaviour and motivation. Liam's progress is good when he does what she expects him to do, but 'it's really hard to get him to do it'. Liam is easily frustrated, particularly in tasks that require fine motor skills. Diane and Susie see Liam as an imaginative, creative child who likes to go off at tangents, but this creates problems within the demands of the curriculum objectives. The more Liam resists and follows his own agenda, the more he is positioned as a naughty child who needs behaviour support.

Liam's learning story shows that he experienced and interpreted activities in ways that were not always understood by his teachers. For example, from observing and listening to Liam, the counting and drawing ducks episode could be interpreted differently. His knowledge about ordinal and cardinal numbers was so well embedded that he could play with the idea of the fourth duck being missing, while still holding its place value in the 1–5 sequence. In other words, Liam was able to represent a more sophisticated level of understanding than Diane recognized. This may be because her perceptions were influenced by the need to map Liam's performance against curriculum objectives. Within the framework of entitlement provided by National Curriculum policies, educators need to develop flexible and responsive pedagogies that respect the complexity of children's thinking and activity in different contexts.

The foregoing studies exemplify trends towards more respectful strategies for interviewing children, and away from high-control, adult-dominant, question-and-answer formats (Brooker 2002), or narrow testing and assessment regimes. New theoretical understanding of children's agency as learners highlights the importance of teachers and learners co-constructing knowledge and experience from positions of mutual engagement and understanding. Wood and Attfield (2005) argue that all professionals who work with children and their families should have an inquiry-based approach to improving the quality of their provision and engaging in professional development. But how can these approaches become embedded in practice?

From active listening to ethical practices

Dahlberg and Moss (2005) propose that the processes of active listening, reflecting, arguing, discussing and interpreting can contribute to ethical practices. These processes are integral to the Mosaic Approach (Clark and Moss 2001), which can include the perspectives of children and other people who have a role in their lives. In common with the hermeneutic approach to researching play (Reifel 2007), the Mosaic Approach uses pedagogical documentation as the evidence base for professional reflection and for generating questions about children and their experiences. There is a world of difference between seeing a child's performance in an activity as a 'unit of assessment', and understanding that performance within a broader pattern of interests, meaning-making, choices and representations.

Drawing on the work of pre-schools in Reggio Emilia, Rinaldi proposes a 'pedagogy of listening', which means:

> . . . listening to thought – the ideas and theories, questions and answers of children and adults; it means treating thought seriously and with respect; it means struggling to make meaning from what is said, without preconceived ideas of what is correct or appropriate.

> (Rinaldi 2006: 15)

For Rinaldi, a pedagogy of listening 'challenges the whole scene of pedagogy' because it demands that we see schools as places of ethical and political practice. Many contemporary theorists (Dahlberg and Moss, 2005; Ryan and Grieshaber 2005; Yelland 2005; Fleer 2006) contest established interpretations of children's learning and development that have been reified through developmental classifications and curriculum goals and objectives. Such frameworks are based on normative understandings of children, and serve to regulate their development and progress, thereby reifying what is considered valuable in terms of learning outcomes, behaviours and dispositions. Contemporary perspectives view learning and development as socially and culturally situated within complex cultural practices, belief systems, and relationships between the child, the home, early childhood institutions and wider society (Fleer 2006). Moreover, predominantly western, individually centred notions of child development are no longer acceptable within culturally diverse communities. Guttiérez and Rogoff (2003) argue that, by understanding cultural ways of learning, educators can move beyond theories that see learning as being influenced predominantly by individual traits, dispositions and learning styles. They propose that people develop repertoires for participating in a range of practices: they engage in activities according to how they have observed and interacted with other people in different communities (for example, home, playgroup, school, workplaces). Socio-cultural theories emphasize children's motivations to exercise agency and mastery in their social and cultural worlds. Therefore, rather than waiting for developmental readiness, culturally situated teaching and learning processes help children to participate with increasing competence in the activities of their communities, whether these are classified as work, leisure, play or formal education.

In socio-cultural theories, the challenge for children (and indeed for all learners) is how they move between different communities and practices, and how they choose from their personal repertoires of practice in order to perform in different contexts. They, too, have to be good listeners and observers in order to negotiate their ways into different contexts and practices, to understand rules, roles, rituals and expectations. By observing and listening to children, educators can go beyond narrowly conceived performance on individual tasks (as evidenced in Liam's learning story) to understand their repertoires of participation across a wide range of activities.

These issues are also relevant to developing a critical understanding of play. Contemporary researchers have contested the efficacy of play-based learning, and of developing a curriculum around children's needs and interests (Wood 2007). Ryan (2005) has argued that such approaches can sustain inequitable practices, and may privilege certain groups of children who are confident with exercising choice and know how to benefit from such freedoms. For example, in a study of 4–5-year-old children in a multi-ethnic school, Brooker (2002) has shown that free choice and play-based activities do not benefit all children, especially where these are not consistent with culturally situated child-rearing practices in homes and communities. The choices made by individuals or groups of children may be biased in terms of culture, social class, gender, sexuality, ability/disability, which may result in unequal power relations and detrimental power effects of free choice (MacNaughton 2005; Ryan 2005). Play-based approaches may actually militate against equality of opportunity and equal access to curriculum provision. Thus a pedagogy of listening and observing can enable practitioners to contest their assumptions about play activities, and to challenge stereotypical and discriminatory practices.

Using a pedagogy of listening to inform assessment

Detailed knowledge of children is developed through observing, listening to and interacting with them, across a range of contexts and activities. The processes of reflection involve mapping evidence of children's responses and performances across contexts, and building a 'credit' rather than a 'deficit' model of assessment (Carr 2001). In a credit-based model, educators take pedagogical decisions and actions on the basis of informed insights into children's competences, perspectives and meanings, and their unique interpretations of their social and cultural worlds. Pedagogical documentation (such as recorded observations, examples of children's representations and communications, video and still images) creates an evidence base that informs interpretive discussions between team members. Such professional conversations can ensure that decision-making takes place within and beyond curriculum frameworks, and that children's perspectives, knowledge and competence are acknowledged.

These processes are exemplified in the following vignettes, which were recorded in a Foundation Phase setting in a primary school in Wales (the Wales Foundation Phase includes children from 3 to 7, in contrast with the English Foundation Stage, which includes children from birth to 5). Around 87 per cent of children in the school are from minority ethnic groups, with seven to eight languages spoken in every class. The whole school team was involved in an action research project to improve the quality of teaching and learning through play, with each year group team choosing its own focus. The nursery team focused on improving the quality of language in imaginative play activities. Episodes of play were video taped for around ten minutes, and provided data for professional discussion and reflection. In the first episode, a teaching assistant (TA) is playing with the children in an outdoor role-play area, based on the story of 'Little Red Riding Hood'. The TA is supporting language development by playing alongside them. This vignette shows what happened when the TA's interactions did not flow with the children's play.

TA to Majida: Hello Little Red Riding Hood. Who are you going to visit today – to see today? Are you going to see grandma? What are you going to take her?
Majida to TA: Buns.
TA to Majida: Have you? Look at all that lovely food for grandma. That is super.
Majida to TA: Grandma not in there, not in there.
TA to Majida: Pardon? Grandma not in there? OK. It should be the wolf. Who's the wolf?
Rajiv to TA: He's already in the bed.
TA to Rajiv: But he needs someone to talk. Can you talk and be the wolf?
Rajiv to TA: It's not easy. I don't know what to think.

Rajiv leaves the area and the play finishes.

This episode provided much interesting evidence for reflection, focusing on whether the adult really listened to the children's meanings and the flow of the play. The team realized that it is all too easy to slip into question-and-answer mode when trying to understand what is happening in play, especially when they have not observed the beginning and the development of the episode. When adults were present (in this and other episodes), children tended to say very little, and relied on the adult to take the lead (even where the bilingual support assistants were involved). Rajiv's final comment – 'It's not easy. I don't know what to think' – indicated that he did not know what was expected of him by the adult, and perhaps did not have sufficient knowledge to further develop the role of the wolf. Rajiv's comment also provides valuable insights into his play skills: he is beginning to understand what it means to play in role, but needs to do this in his own way. Rajiv also understands that play takes place 'in the mind' as well as in social actions and interactions between players. What is 'in the mind' needs to be transformed into action for play to develop. His play skills were demonstrated in a subsequent observation of an energetic episode of outdoor play, where he leads two friends in a 'Spider-Man' game.

Rajiv to TA: Mrs L. I am Spider-Man. There are two Spider-Men and more Spider-Men.

He climbs the climbing frame, then gets a scooter and demonstrates jumping off the scooter while it is moving.

Rajiv to Jamil: Come on Jamil, we are Spider-Men. Spider-Man can do this. You do it Jamil.

This activity continues for a few minutes before the boys stop and run away.

Observing and listening to Rajiv showed the team that he could lead imaginative play with friends of his choice, and that he was willing to talk about his game and demonstrate his competence to an adult. Play provides many opportunities for 'out-loud thinking' as children reveal the purposes and direction of the action, and the imaginative context of their activities. By playing with meanings, they can also reveal quite sophisticated levels of understanding of their social and cultural worlds.

In a subsequent episode, listening to children involved observing their body language, facial expressions and symbolic activities, and, as Silin (2005) argues, listening to children's silences. Mohammed, a shy child, was reluctant to speak to peers and adults. It was difficult for team members to know how much he understood of spoken English, and how much he was able to communicate in his home and additional language. In the nursery, there was a 'three-way' puppet that was used to tell the story of 'Little Red Riding Hood' (the puppet could be transformed into the wolf, the grandmother and Red Riding Hood, to show each character). Mohammed approached the TA with the puppet, and she engaged him in the story. As she told the story, he revealed his understanding by showing each different character at the correct cue. After much encouragement, he did respond verbally (but in a very quiet voice), using individual words. His facial expressions and body language conveyed enjoyment and engagement with the adult. He was happy to participate on his own terms and was under no pressure to communicate verbally. The TA understood Mohammed's intentions and meanings through respecting his silence, while tuning in to his communicative competence.

This study had some valuable outcomes for the nursery team, particularly in informing how they could accurately read and interpret play activities. Interrogating these play texts, and reflecting on their own assumptions and beliefs, helped them to develop a collaborative pedagogy of listening and observing, and enhanced their understanding of children's interests, talents and capabilities. Their assessment practices became located within a process of understanding children as learners and players, based on sharing and building knowledge. The study also demonstrated how analysis of classroom texts captures complex and multiple meanings, and the contexts in which these are produced and negotiated (Reifel 2007). Even short observations (up to ten minutes) can provide much valuable evidence for critical reflection.

The vignettes in this chapter have exemplified how children create individual and personal responses within diverse contexts. Young children are not passive recipients of knowledge but are 'epistemologists' in their own right. Therefore a pedagogy of listening respects children's understanding of their identity and individuality, and helps educators to understand the influences of wider social systems such as class, culture, ethnicity, gender and sexuality. A pedagogy of listening also ensures that multimodal forms of communication are recognized and valued, and that children are not silenced by their inability to communicate in a dominant language, or within a dominant culture.

From reflective to activist educators

Contemporary researchers and theorists have extended the concept of 'reflective practitioners' to 'activist educators' who see their practice as inherently ethical and political. A pedagogy of reflexivity is synchronous with a pedagogy of critical engagement. These developments are essential as educators work in increasingly complex contexts, with diverse communities and within challenging policy frameworks. Activist educators can transform, rather then merely implement, policies; they go beyond the platitudes of 'facilitating' and 'enabling' children's development. Instead, they work towards greater equity and social justice, and become co-constructors of vibrant communities of practice, which draw on the perspectives, meanings and resourcefulness of all members. They are prepared to act as researchers, to generate knowledge, to engage critically in their practice and to sustain collaborative professional development. These approaches will always provoke more questions than answers. However, activist educators will welcome such questions, in order to sustain their commitment to children's well-being and to processes of educational change and transformation.

References

Brooker, L. (2002) *Starting School – Young Children Learning Cultures*. Buckingham: Open University Press.

218 Elizabeth Wood

Carr, M. (2001) *Assessment in Early Childhood Settings – Learning Stories*. London: Paul Chapman Publishing.

Clark, A. and Moss, P. (2001) *Listening to Young Children: The Mosaic Approach*. London: National Children's Bureau.

Dahlberg, G. and Moss, P. (2005) *Ethics and Politics in Early Childhood Education*. London: RoutledgeFalmer.

Department for Children, Schools and Families (DCSF) (2008) *The Early Years Foundation Stage*, http://www.standards.dcfs.gov.uk/eyfs/.

Department for Education and Skills (DfES) (2004a) *Every Child Matters: Change for Children in Schools*. London: HMSO.

Department for Education and Skills (DfES) (2004b) *Primary National Strategy. Excellence and Enjoyment: Learning and Teaching in the Primary Years*. London: HMSO.

Fleer, M. (2006) The cultural construction of child development: creating institutional and cultural intersubjectivity, *International Journal of Early Years Education*, 14(2): 127–140.

Guttiérez, K.D. and Rogoff, B. (2003) Cultural ways of learning: individual traits or repertoires of practice, *Educational Researcher*, 32(5): 19–25.

MacNaughton, G. (2005) *Doing Foucault in Early Childhood Studies. Applying Post-structural Ideas*. London: Routledge.

Norwich, B. and Kelly, N. (2004) Pupils' views on inclusion: moderate learning difficulties and bullying in mainstream and special schools. *British Educational Research Journal*, 30(1): 43–65.

Reifel, S. (2007) Hermeneutic text analysis of play: exploring meaningful early childhood classroom events, in J.A. Hatch (ed.) *Early Childhood Qualitative Research*. London: Routledge: 25–42.

Rinaldi, C. (2006) *In Dialogue with Reggio Emilia. Listening, Researching and Learning*. London: Routledge.

Ryan, S. (2005) Freedom to choose: examining children's experiences in choice time, in N. Yelland (ed.) *Critical Issues in Early Childhood*. Maidenhead: Open University Press: 99–114.

Ryan, S. and Grieshaber, S. (2005) Shifting from developmental to postmodern practices in early childhood teacher education, *Journal of Teacher Education*, 56(1), January/February: 34–45.

Silin, J.G. (2005) Who can speak? Silence, voice and pedagogy, in N. Yelland (ed.) *Critical Issues in Early Childhood Education*. Maidenhead: Open University Press: 81–95.

Underdown, A. and Barlow, J. (2007) Listening to young children, in A. Underdown (ed.) *Young Children's Health and Well-Being*. Maidenhead: Open University Press: 154–162.

United Nations (1989) *The United Nations Convention on the Rights of the Child*. New York: United Nations.

Wood, E. (2002) *Progression and Continuity in Language and Literacy*. Paper presented to the United Kingdom Reading Association annual conference, University of Chester, July.

Wood, E. (2005) Young children's voices and perspectives in research: methodological and ethical considerations, *International Journal of Equity and Innovation in Early Childhood*, 3(2): 64–76.

Wood, E. (2008) Conceptualising a pedagogy of play: international perspectives from theory, policy and practice, in D. Kuschner (ed.) *Play and Culture Studies, Vol. 8.* Westport, CT: Ablex.

Wood, E. and Attfield, J. (2005) *Play, Learning and the Early Childhood Curriculum* (2nd edn). London: Paul Chapman.

Yelland, N. (ed.) (2005) (ed.) *Critical Issues in Early Childhood Education*. Maidenhead: Open University Press.

Chapter 20

The role of grandparents in children's learning
Charmian Kenner, Tabera Arju, Eve Gregory, John Jessel and Mahera Ruby

The role of grandparents in children's learning is a neglected area of research but as the authors of this chapter, members of a research team at Goldsmith's College, University of London, discovered their contribution is worth further consideration. Grandparents often have a close and special relationship with their grandchildren and the research team found many examples of them involved in a range of learning events in the home where the grandparents sensitively joined with children in a process of discovery or shared their knowledge and experience.

Setting the scene

Sumayah, her cousin and her grandmother are showing our research team how they work together in the small garden of their terraced house in Tower Hamlets, London's East End. First there are leaves to be swept up. Five-year-old Sumayah is determined to do the job and begins pushing the broom. After letting Sumayah sweep for a while, her grandmother takes over and demonstrates the firm strokes needed, then leaves Sumayah to finish the task. Next there are trees and plants to be watered. In this tiny space, Sumayah's family grow apples, pears, lemons, pumpkins, tomatoes and herbs, using the agricultural knowledge brought by the grandparents from Bangladesh. This knowledge is now being passed on to Sumayah and her cousin; it is they who are left in charge of the garden when their grandparents are away on visits to Bangladesh.

Learning from experience

What do the children learn from this experience? As they do the watering with three sets of hands grasping the watering-can handle – Sumayah's, her cousin's and her grandmother's – they find out how much water to give each tree or plant. They also know that not every plant is watered on every occasion; some need more water than others.

Sumayah points to the growing tip of a lemon tree seedling, commenting that the leaves are a different colour from the others because they are new. Her cousin shows three plants in a line of pots and explains while pointing to each one that two of them are his uncle's and one is Sumayah's. Sumayah is responsible for her own particular plant and she will thus find out in detail how to nurture it. For example, she knows whereabouts in the garden the plant has to be placed to receive the right amount of light. Her knowledge goes beyond the classic primary school experiment of growing cress under different conditions in order to discover that plants need light and water to thrive. As well as being aware that these elements are essential, Sumayah also knows what quantities are necessary for each plant.

The project

Our research project with grandparents and grandchildren in English-speaking and Bengali-speaking families in East London revealed a wealth of such learning events taking place between the older and younger generations. We had suspected that this little-investigated inter-generational relationship was of special importance to children's learning, but we were surprised by the wide range of activities going on.

An initial questionnaire, answered by eleven Bangladeshi British families and three Anglo (English-speaking) families, offered a list of 20 activities and asked grandparents whether they engaged in any of these with their three- to six-year-old grandchildren. Figure 20.1 shows the spread of activities.

Firstly, the questionnaire demonstrated that Bangladeshi British as well as Anglo families took children on outings to the park, played and read with them, involved them in cooking and gardening, told them stories and recited rhymes together. This finding challenges the assumption often made that ethnic minority families do not offer their children these kinds of learning experiences.

Secondly, the Bangladeshi British families placed a high priority on 'visiting others' and 'talking about members of the family and family history'. These were categories which the Anglo members of our research team had not originally thought of including, until two of the researchers – themselves from Bangladeshi backgrounds – made the suggestion. They explained that family visits are of considerable importance in Bangladeshi culture. When children go to see relatives, often accompanying their grandparents, they learn how to greet each person appropriately and how to behave within the social group. They gain knowledge of each relative's place in the complex kinship network and where they themselves fit in, giving them a sense of their own identity. Conversations with grandparents enhance their understanding of family history. These are important types of learning experience often overlooked by main-stream educators, and largely absent from the National Curriculum. We need a wider definition of the term 'learning' in order to encompass the rich variety of knowledge children gain from spending time in family settings.

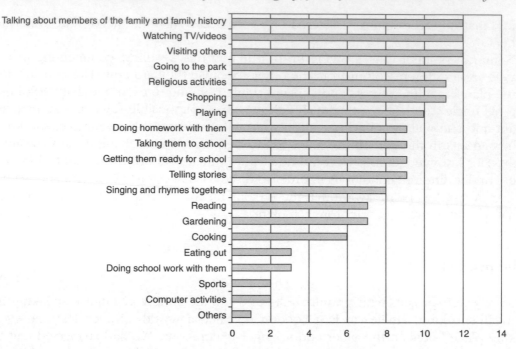

Figure 20.1 Activities carried out jointly by children and their grandparents, showing the number of grandparents reporting each activity

The study

Having gained an initial idea of the kinds of learning experiences happening between grandparents and grandchildren, we approached 12 families who agreed to participate further in the project. Six were Sylheti/Bengali-speaking of Bangladeshi origin and six were monolingual English-speaking. Four families had children in the nursery class, four in Reception and four in Year 1. In interviews with grandparents and video recordings of learning events at home such as cooking, gardening, storytelling and computer activities, we examined the following questions:

- In what ways do grandparents and grandchildren take the lead in the learning interactions?
- In what ways are the learning interactions co-constructed by the participants?
- What kinds of knowledge are exchanged between the younger and older learners?
- What is the role of the computer in the cultural, linguistic and technical aspects of learning?

A special relationship

Children's relationship with their grandparents involved a sense of mutual vulnerability. Grandparents were recognised as needing care due to age and a certain amount of frailty. Sitting at the computer with his grandmother Hazel and observing her hand as she held the mouse in front of him, three-year-old Sam suddenly raised his own hands and declared: 'I'm not getting old . . . I've not got old skin.' Hazel agreed with amusement, noting that she indeed had wrinkles while Sam did not.

The grandparents in the project were keen to take care of their young grandchildren, and expressed this through a supportive use of touch. The close physical relationship between the generations was noticeable in the events we video recorded: Sahil's grandmother Razia linking her arm through her grandson's as they talked about the books they read together, Hazel patting Sam's tummy while talking about the computer game they were playing. The children's response showed a reciprocal use of touch: Sahil's younger siblings climbed on their grandmother's lap as she and Sahil read a poetry book, while Sam rested his head against his grandmother's shoulder as he listened to her comments on the computer game.

Guidance through touch

Touch was an important means of communication between young children and grand-parents. As well as building children's sense of security and self-confidence, it was used by grandparents to guide kinaesthetic learning. The example was given above of Sumayah's grandmother helping her grandchildren to water plants in the garden. Through her touch, she indicated at what angle to hold the watering-can and how much water to give. We also observed Sahil's grandmother guiding his hand as he wrote in Bengali, enabling him to experience the flow of the pen on the page to inscribe the pattern of each letter. Once again, guidance through touch could be reciprocal. Moments later, Sahil placed his hand over his grandmother's to show her how to operate the mouse on the computer.

Learning exchanges around language

Grandparents often considered themselves responsible for particular areas of their grandchildren's learning. In the case of the Bengali-speaking families, one of these areas was language. For example, Sahil's grandmother Razia was seen by the family as responsible for maintaining the children's knowledge of Bengali. Sahil's mother, having grown up in Britain, tended to speak English as well as Bengali to her children, but wanted them to develop their family language in order to retain a link with their heritage and culture. Razia entered into her task with considerable energy. She used books brought by the children's mother from Bangladesh, including stories such as 'Snow White' in Bengali which she knew the children would enjoy.

Sahil was able to identify diffcrent categories of Bengali book – alphabet primers, 'chora' (poetry) books, and the 'Snow White' storybook – realising that each had a different purpose. When reading the 'chora' book with his grandmother, he closely followed her lead. The oral recitation of poetry was enjoyed by Sahil and also by his younger sisters, who ran into the room to join in when they heard the rhythm of their grandmother's voice. As well as developing their vocabulary and expression in Bengali, the children were receiving an introduction to rhyme – a skill considered very important by early years educators.

Meanwhile, Razia was learning English from her grandchildren, in an inter-generational language exchange. Along with other grandparents in the study, Razia mentioned that contact with her grandson added to her knowledge of English. When Sahil was asked by the researchers whether his grandmother knew English, Razia (understanding the question perfectly) told her grandson in Bengali 'say Granny doesn't speak English'. She was maintaining her role as the resource person for Bengali within the family, but throughout the video recorded event her knowledge of English was evident. When Sahil was asked what he most enjoyed doing with his grandmother, he thought for a few moments and then replied in English 'I enjoy she telling me what the word means in Bangla' ('Bangla' is the term often used for Bengali). Contented, Razia smiled and kissed him, once again showing her understanding.

Several of the Bengali-speaking grandparents were also introducing their grand-children to Arabic for the purposes of reading the Qur'an. Sumayah and her grandmother spread out a prayer mat on the carpet and sat together on the mat, with Sumayah reciting verses of the Qur'an after her grandmother. This early introduction to the sounds and intonation of classical Arabic was a prelude to a gradual understanding of the content of the verses, just as children participating in hymn-singing or prayers in an Anglican church would be inducted into the richness of language which they would later comprehend more fully.

Learning exchanges around computers

It can be seen from the questionnaire results that few grandparents engaged in computer activities with their grandchildren. For the Bangladeshi grandparents particularly, computers were unfamiliar and there were language constraints – computers operate in English script unless special software is obtained.

The potential for learning from computer activities was emphasised by our video observation of Hazel with her grand-daughter Lizzie. Hazel and Lizzie frequently used the Internet at Hazel's house to search for information to enhance the other learning activities they did together. For example, they often looked at wildlife in the garden and once discovered an unusual moth which they could not then find in Hazel's reference book. Via the Internet, they identified its picture, with the name 'Quercus' and information about the male and female moths and egg-laying habits. They then printed out this page and glued it into Lizzie's scrapbook.

Hazel's support for Lizzie's learning was sensitively given, allowing Lizzie to take the lead when doing the typing or clicking the mouse on the appropriate spots. At some moments, Lizzie's responses preceded those of her grandmother. While Hazel was working out what step to take next on the search engine 'Google', Lizzie had already pulled out the keyboard ready to type the search word. Hazel stated that she was less confident about word processing than her grandchildren, 'but now that Lizzie is learning at school, hopefully she'll teach me'.

In this exchange of competencies, Hazel helped to structure the stages of the learning event for Lizzie and supplied alphabet letters to complete the word 'moths' when Lizzie was unsure. Lizzie's eager confidence in using the word processing commands suggested that she would indeed soon be instructing her grandmother in this area. Her desire to go beyond the limits of this particular investigation by printing out information about another moth on the same website (despite her grandmother's attempts to keep to the original task) would exploit the possibilities of hypertext and introduce new areas of learning for them both.

A different form of support

In comparison, the activities conducted by Bangladeshi grandparents (when the research team supplied a laptop computer for them to use with their grandchildren) at first seemed more basic. The children were unfamiliar with a laptop although they had used other types of computer at school, and for most of the grandparents it was their first chance to use the technology. The children mostly typed their names, working out how to use the different from of mouse incorporated in the laptop keyboard.

However, a closer examination of these events reveals that the grandparents, sitting quietly beside their grandchildren, were playing an important role similar to that of Lizzie's grandmother. Through their presence they helped to structure the event, for example by ensuring that the child was the main actor and an older cousin did not take over, or by suggesting the activity of typing the child's name and supporting the child's efforts through their own knowledge of English letters. By giving their attention through gaze or pointing, even though they did not touch the computer, they helped the child maintain concentration and accomplish the task.

Furthermore, the grandparents showed a growing interest in what was happening on the screen. Their curiosity indicated a potential to develop knowledge and expertise if they were to have access to software or websites, which operated in their own language, as Lizzie's grandmother did. One aim of the research project is to increase family involvement with computers at our partner school in the study, Hermitage Primary School in Tower Hamlets. If Bangladeshi grandparents can attend family workshops with tutoring and resources in Bengali, this could lead to positive outcomes for their own learning and that of their grandchildren.

Grandparents may need special encouragement to come into school and share their wisdom and experience. When invitations were issued to a 'Grandparents' Coffee Morning' at Hermitage School, a number of grandparents attended, some having dressed in their best clothes for the occasion. The grandparents were proud that the school had acknowledged their importance in their grandchildren's education – and the children were delighted to bring to school these key figures in their learning lives.

Conclusion

This research project has begun to open up a fascinating world of learning between grandchildren and grandparents, hitherto little-known to schools, particularly with regard to ethnic minority families. Our findings suggest the potential benefits if teachers widen their links with 'parents and carers' to ensure that the significant role of grandparents is recognised and built upon in home-school interactions.

Chapter 21

What can we learn from listening to girls and boys talking about their play?

Naima Browne

How does children's understanding of gender influence who they choose to play with and what they choose to play? In this chapter Naima Browne draws on children's conversations with her, carried out as part of her research, to explore children's perceptions of masculinity and femininity and what children consider boys' games and girls' games and why. The chapter focuses particularly on Superhero and weapons play and the debates that have taken place over whether or not to allow such play in early years settings.

Introduction

Listening to what children have to say provides an insight into their concerns, how they are making sense of the world and how they are positioning themselves and others. It is very apparent from conversations with young children that they are conscious of gender, and as practitioners we need to be sensitive to and acknowledge how children's ideas about gender impact on how children position themselves and are positioned by others in the early years setting.

As part of my research into young children's ideas about gender I interviewed children in a number of early years settings and primary schools. All the children were aged between three and seven and every child was absolutely clear about whether they were a girl or a boy, they were able to categorise other children in the setting and were also certain that one's gender is constant and unchanging. My research also highlighted how important it is for practitioners to support children in exploring what it means to be a girl or a boy and to introduce children to different ideas about femininity and masculinity.

Children's friendship patterns: 'boy games . . . girl games'

Gender-based friendship patterns are a feature of life in early years settings The majority of 3–7 year olds tend to play in same-sex groups for most of the time that they are in the early years setting (Thorne, 1986, Lloyd and Duveen, 1992, Macoby, 1998, Browne, 2004). Many of the children were able to clearly articulate their reasons for their gender-based pattern of friendships. Interestingly, none of the children's comments hinted at parental or explicit peer group pressure (i.e. fear of being bullied). Most of the children identified differences in interests as the reason for not playing with certain children. Emma, aged four, explained why she didn't play with boys:

> Because I don't want to run about I just think of playing with girls . . . Because they just play boy games . . . Like fightin' and I don't like playing it. I like playing girl games. Girls just like playing dogs, cats. I just like playing cats and dogs.
>
> (Browne, 2004)

Four-year-old Neil was also able to explain about how he thought girls' and boys' interests differed and the effect this had on his friendships:

> Because I'm not their friend . . . They don't like playing Power Rangers. I play Superman, Power Rangers and Batman and that's why I don't want to play with them.
>
> (Browne, 2004)

The views and attitudes of these young children were echoed by slightly older children who, when asked whether girls and boys liked playing with different things, responded with comments such as:

> 'Boys like Power Rangers, football, tennis and cricket.' (Boy aged 6.2)

> 'Girls like playing with Barbies and My Little Pony. Boys play with scary things and cars and trains.' (Girl aged 6.2)

> 'Most boys like football. I don't really know what girls like.' (Boy aged 6.1)

> 'Yes of course! Girls like pink stuff and yellow and Barbie and Sindy and boys like bluey [sic] stuff and Action Man and cars and trains. I like Power Rangers . . . I like the pink one. Boys and girls can play together like with Pokemon.' (Girl aged 6.5)

> 'Girls like Barbie and things. Boys like Batman.' (Boy aged 5.9)

The children's comments about 'boy games' and 'girl games' was a very clear echo of children's views almost two decades ago about certain toys and activities being 'girls' stuff' or 'boys' stuff' (Browne and Ross 1991: 39). Clearly, if we are to make any headway in developing gender equity in our settings we need to know more than simply who and with what children play.

Dealing with gender 'deviance'

The dominant gender discourse places females and males as different and in opposition to each other. Hegemonic masculinity is this form of masculinity that is the dominant or culturally accepted from of masculinity (Connell, 1995, 2000). Hegemonic masculinity emphasises, among other things, men's (and boy's) superiority to women (and girls), competitiveness, physical strength and rationality. Other styles of masculinity can, and do, co-exist with the hegemonic form but it is the dominant form of masculinity that determines what it means to be a 'real' man or boy. The prevailing conceptualisation of gender in binary and polarised terms means that femininity is not masculinity and vice versa. The dominant form of femininity emphasises conformity, nurturing, compassion and empathy (Connell 1987: 187–8). The girl/boy divide is not innate and the power relations between women and men and girls and boys is not 'natural', and yet dominant discourses are construed as providing us with taken-for-granted 'truths' about the world. In order to retain a sense of psychological and intellectual balance and maintain the 'reality' constructed by the dominant discourses, children (and adults) need to develop strategies for dealing with instances when they themselves, or others, deviate from the 'norm'.

One strategy is to ignore the deviations in order to retain a clear distinction between girls and boys or women and men (Davies, 1989). This ability to clearly categorise according to binary gender divisions whilst simultaneously ignoring contradictions and deviations is evident in the following comments made by a five-year-old girl:

> Boys like Action Man and Spiderman. Girls like soft animals, they like Pokemon but it's really a boy thing.

> (Browne, 2004)

Children who operate effectively within the dominant discourse and 'correctly' position themselves are likely to be praised ('What a lovely strong boy!'), which provides positive emotional feedback to children. In view of this it is not surprising that many strategies aimed at encouraging children to deviate from the 'norm' have proved to be unsuccessful.

Providing children, for example, with models of adults or children who 'do' gender in a way which diverges from the dominant norm (e.g. inviting female fire-fighters or male nurses to talk to the children) has had limited success for three main reasons. First, insufficient account has been taken of the processes by which children learn to position themselves as girls and boy. Secondly, there has been little acknowledgement of the emotional investment in these positions and thirdly, children's tendency to ignore or discount instances of deviations from the norm and to 'other' (or to treat as 'different and not one of us') those who cross the gender boundaries has been disregarded. Another explanation for the difficulty adults experience in broadening children's play choices and playmate preferences could lie in the tendency in young children to conceptualise gender in terms of clear and sometimes extreme, categories. Paley has noted:

> Kindergarten is a triumph of sexual self-stereotyping. No amount of adult subterfuge or propaganda deflects the five-year-olds passion for segregation by sex. They think they have invented the differences between girls and boys and, as with any new invention, must prove that it works. . . . [The doll corner] is not simply a place to play; it is a stronghold against ambiguity.

> (Paley, 1984: ix)

When I asked children what girls and boys liked to play the majority talked about girls liking Barbies and playing mummies and daddies and boys liking cars, fighting and superhero play. Only a few children mentioned activities that both girls and boys enjoy.

Maintaining the binary gender divide and upholding the dominant styles of masculinity and femininity leads to what Davies has referred to as category maintenance work (Davies, 1989). Children who deviate from the norm are likely to experience disapproval from both adults and other children.

This category maintenance work is not confined to older children, even very young children will tease or criticise other children who do not conform and who seem to have disregarded the gender categories (Davies, 1989; Browne, 1999).

Adults engage in category maintenance work with girls and boys. During the course of my research I found that although girls were less likely to rigidly enforce gender boundaries adults sometimes did. For example, in a nursery where playing with guns and other weapons was not discouraged by the staff, two four-year-old girls were showing me something they had constructed out of two pieces of wood and one of the girls said it was a sword and the other said it was a gun. A nursery assistant then said, 'I don't think so. I thought it was an aeroplane.' It would appear that these two girls were being told that playing with guns and other weapons was really something for boys and that their interest in such activities suggested that the girls had not 'correctly' positioned themselves.

Not all boys adopt the style of hegemonic masculinity. Stephen was one such boy. He was very articulate and cheerfully spent a long time talking to me about his interests and his friends. He told me that he liked playing tennis and doing jigsaw puzzles. He also talked about playing at pirates and explained why Hercules was his favourite video:

> Um . . . 'cos he's very strong and I pretend to be strong. 'Cos I've got big muscles as well as him [flexes muscles] . . . but I'm not as strong as him.
>
> (Browne, 2004)

He also talked about having girls as friends and was at pains to correct me when I suggested that he seemed to play only with boys.

Stephen appeared to be a good example of a child who, having rejected total adherence to the hegemonic style of masculinity, is successfully negotiating the various positionings that are an inherent part of different styles of masculinity and femininity. He is able to do this by ensuring that he engages in activities which are associated with hegemonic masculinity (for example superhero play) and is friendly with boys who have clearly positioned themselves as 'real boys'. This means that his masculinity is not an issue and enables him to also engage in more 'feminine' activities such as playing mummies and daddies.

In view of the ruthless way in which the categories are maintained children, especially boys, may pay a high price if they move away from the norm. This could explain children's resistance to strategies aimed at enabling boys to participate in activities traditionally associated with girls and vice versa.

Imaginative play

In conversations with young children it was very apparent that there was a sharp gender divide in terms of imaginative role-play. The girls talked time and again about playing mummies and daddies and the boys told me about their games of Batman, Superman,

Spiderman and the Power Rangers. This echoes the findings of numerous other researchers (e.g. Paley, 1984, Thorne, 1993, Jordan and Cowan, 2001).

In the past, boys have been discouraged from toy weapon and superhero play but in recent years concerns about boys' underachievement at school and the ways in which early years settings were not meeting boys' needs has led to a reconsideration of the value of such play (Gurian, 2001; Jones, 2002; Holland, 2003). This has resulted in a shift in many educators' response to superhero and gunplay in early years settings. Such play is now being tolerated, and in some settings encouraged, rather than being forbidden.

Do children need superhero play?

One argument is that the high levels of physical activity that characterises superhero play and weapon play is what young boys 'need'. Because of their particular brain structure Gurian (2001). This justification is problematic, as insufficient research has been undertaken to support this claim.

It has also been argued that superhero play enables boys who are learning English as an Additional Language to develop relationships and play with their peers (Holland, 2003) but research has suggested that superhero play based on television characters and programmes tends to be very limited in terms of variety of plot, situations and dialogue which leads to rigid play scripts (Cupit 1996). While the rigidity or predictability of the playscripts would enable participation by children who are familiar with the characters and stories, in other words children who have watched superheroes on television or video, it could be argued that the play itself is of limited value due to its repetitive nature.

A third justification for superhero and weapon play is that such play develops children's self-confidence and social skills. It is worth remembering that it is mainly boys who engage in these types of activities, so if this view is valid then we should be asking why we do not encourage girls to engage in these types of play activities.

Psychoanalytical theory crops up when discussing superhero play and is frequently drawn upon to explain or justify children's 'need' for imaginative role play and stories in which good is pitted against evil and which provide children with the chance to explore and eventually conquer their fears and anxieties. Bettelheim has argued that fairy tales deal with universal fears and anxieties and therefore play a vital role in young children's emotional development (Bettelheim, 1978). Bettelheim was unconvinced about the value of modern children's literature and the superhero stories on television but others have extended his argument about fairy tales to include stories about Batman, Superman and other superheroes. Boyd (1997: 25), for example, has argued that 'superhero play offers a sense of power to children in a world dominated by adults' and that through superhero play children can work through fears about their own safety.

The various arguments outlined above have made it difficult for practitioners to continue to be critical of activities that supposedly develop children's confidence, social skills, language and emotional resilience. There is, however, a need to examine the issues more closely as the arguments tend to refer to 'children' and in so doing mask the gender dimensions of the issues.

Who wants to play Batman?

The majority of children that engage in play-fighting and superhero play are boys. If, however, we accept the argument that children 'need' such play it is not clear why there is a discernible gender divide in weapon and superhero play.

A dominant theme in children's imaginative role play is that of 'good' overcoming 'evil' and in so doing children's fears are conquered. Young children feel strong, empowered and secure through pretending to be good fairies defeating wicked witches or 'flying' to the rescue as Batman or pretending to be brave princesses chasing monsters or Spiderman imprisoning 'baddies' with a magic web. The various possible roles and stories, however, do not seem to appeal equally to all children. The vast majority of girls that I spoke to were adamant that superhero play and weapon play was not something they did:

> Emma: I don't like Power Rangers.
> NB: Why?
> Emma: Because it's a boys' thing

(Browne, 2004)

Much of the girls' imaginative role-play seems to draw on fairy tales:

> Sameena: Sometimes . . . sometimes I be Sleeping Beauty's mother and then the princess sleep for a hundred years and great big forest grew around and some prince came and chopped the forest away. So then they would get married.

(Browne, 2004)

The vast majority of boys, on the other hand, seemed to take on superhero roles in their imaginative role-play:

> Jamal: I be Batman. Batman flies to . . . at night and not on a sunny day and Superman come in a sunny day and Superman doesn't like night time . . . They find baddies to kill them . . . With the gun.

(Browne, 2004)

Some of the boys, such as five-year-old Orlando, are unable to explain why they enjoy superhero play:

> NB: Why do you like playing Spiderman?
> Orlando: Because we all of us like it.
> NB: All of the children you play with?
> Orlando: No, Finlay and William and Toby
> NB: What's so good about playing Spiderman?
> Orlando: I don't know.
> NB: What do you do when you play Spiderman?
> Orlando: We get baddies . . . there's nothing else.
> NB: What do you do when you've got them?
> Orlando: Tie them up, that's all.

(Browne, 2004)

A possible explanation for the differences in the imaginative role play of girls and boys lies in the fact that imaginative role play does not only function as a means through which children can explore and overcome fundamental fears and anxieties. Imaginative role play or dramatic storying is also a way in which children can explore who they are, what and who they would like to be and how they would like others to see them and position them.

From talking with the boys it soon became very apparent that superhero play is about the exercise of male power and the celebration and exploration of hegemonic masculinity. Three five-year old boys explained that a superhero is 'the person who saves the world, and then went on to say:

. . . . They can fight all the world. They help the baddies not to fight all the world.

. . . A superhero has got special powers.

. . . They are really strong and really fast.

. . . They fight with their feet and their hands

. . . Spiderman fights with his web and his hands

(Browne, 2004)

The boys I talked to were working hard at developing an understanding of what it meant to be a superhero and although they felt it was possible for a woman to be a superhero they were hard pressed to name more than one. They were clear that superheroes are strong, are physically agile, are morally 'good', will use violence to achieve their ends and powerful enough to 'save the world'. The characteristics these young boys highlight are remarkably similar to those characterising hegemonic masculinity. At this point it is worth noting that it would appear that the young girls I spoke to had not thought much about superheroes, and although they could name a few superheroes they found it hard to recognize the essential characteristics of superheroes.

Interesting research with older children's analyses and understanding of traditional folktales in Canada (Mello, 2001) has shown that older children also defined male heroes as brave and physically strong. Female heroism was not linked to physical prowess but to effort, creative problem solving and endurance. Mello also argued that the children's comments revealed much about how they saw themselves in gender terms.

Male heroes and superheroes seem to encapsulate the essential characteristics of unambiguous and traditional 'masculinity' while heroines, despite their brave deeds and resourcefulness remain essentially 'feminine' in that they are kind and caring. It would seem therefore, that the stories children have experience of and the imaginative role play that arises out of these stories can have far-reaching consequences for how children position themselves as 'feminine' and 'masculine', what they understand as characterising the positions they adopt and the emotional satisfaction they experience from these gendered positions.

In Mello's study the boys talked about their conflicting feelings about war and violence but also talked about how reading about and fantasising about physically active heroism 'felt good' (Mello, 2001: 551). The boys that I talked to did not explicitly talk about superhero play making them 'feel good' but it was clear from their keenness to discuss what they did when pretending to be Batman or Superman or one of the Power Rangers, and the excitement with which they narrated various superhero storylines, that this was definitely an activity that captured their interest. The emotional satisfaction the boys experienced through such play may help explain why many boys persist in this form of play even in settings where it is discouraged.

None of the girls I interviewed expressed a desire to participate in superhero play. It is probable that even if the girls did want to become involved in the boys' superhero play the boys would resist their involvement and certainly would not allow them to be a superhero or have any real power or authority within the game. It would seem that superhero play is something that boys do:

NB: What about Spiderman? Can girls pretend to be Spiderman?
Robbie: No. Spiderman has a girlfriend.
NB: Can Spiderman's girlfriend do what Spiderman does?
Robbie: No
NB: So who can girls pretend to be if they want to pretend to be really strong?
Robbie: Mummy.
Robbie: Batman can be a Daddy!
Ashok: Girls can be a baby.
[The boys laugh.]
James: They [points to a picture of the Powerpuff Girls] can pretend to be Batman 'cos they can fly but they're not really Batman . . . they are fairies'.

                                                                                          (Browne, 2004)

This conversation was fascinating as it revealed that not only did the boys not think girls could be superheroes but also that they perceived mothers to be 'really strong'. Walkerdine and Lucey (1989) have argued that it is only in the domestic context that women are seen to have any real authority. The boys' comments would suggest however, that they could not tolerate the thought of the girls being placed in a powerful position and instantly added that Batman could be the Daddy thus effectively reducing the girls' power as 'mother'. After all, what match for Batman is a mother? Ashok diminished the girls' power still further with his suggestion that the girls could pretend to be babies. Robbie acceded that girls could pretend to be the Powerpuff Girls but James was not impressed by the Powerpuff Girls who appear to have superhero powers and very effectively neutralised their power by locating them in the 'feminine' world as fairies.

Girls it would seem can be girlfriends, mothers, babies or fairies. The boys' view that girls could be Batgirl rather than Batwoman is also revealing as they were assigning the girls a less powerful role than a woman. The boys themselves never pretended to be Batboy or Superboy. If, as Davies (1989) has argued, language perpetuates existing social structures, the young boys' positioning of young girls as girls rather than women in fantasy play while positioning themselves as men in their fantasy play serves to preserve boys' superior status.

When one considers the manner in which boys talk about their superhero and weapon play it becomes more evident that the play is inextricably linked with their exploration of 'masculinity'. While talking to children about superheroes it was very noticeable that not only had the boys thought carefully about what constituted a super-hero but also that they became very animated and physically active when discussing what superheroes do. Four-year-old Stephen talked about Hercules and flexed his arm muscles, while numerous other boys leapt up from their seats and adopted superhero stances and demonstrated how their favourite superhero moved and fought, while they talked excitedly about their superhero play. Such behaviour, I would suggest, is a prime example of the process of bodily inscription. One's adoption of particular forms of 'masculinity' and 'femininity' is not merely something that occurs inside one's head. From a young age one's ascribed sex (i.e. the sex others assign you on the basis of your observed biological sex at birth) becomes inscribed on your body and this is evident in the way one stands, sits and moves.

A major way in which we indicate our gender position is through how we use and present our body. It is possible to argue that young boys are exploring and learning a particular form of 'masculinity' through adopting exaggeratedly 'strong' poses, flexing their muscles, running, leaping, occupying large amounts of space with their bodies and engaging in physically aggressive, albeit playful, episodes. The bodily inscription that results from such activity serves as a potent signifier of gender and as such not only influences how others begin to position the boys, but also develops the boys' under-standing of what their bodies have the potential to do and what their bodies can and should do to reflect their positioning as 'masculine'. Girls' imaginative role play involves the girls in different types of physical activity and leads to them developing a different understanding of how they can and should physically interact with the environment and with other people.

Consequences of superhero and weapon play

I would suggest that many educators' unhappiness about boys' superhero play is not that it is violent, as children rarely hurt each other when playing, but what educators may find unsettling is the realisation that superhero play is essentially a display of hegemonic masculinity and therein lies the appeal for boys. Recurring episodes of superhero play enables boys to repeatedly experience a specific type of masculine power and the emotional high that goes with this experience of power.

While the boys are experiencing power, the girls and women are experiencing being dominated. The boys' superhero play, for example, reduces the girls' access to a safe area to play in which they do not risk being knocked over by a gang of Power Rangers intent on saving the world. Adults may also be affected by this display of masculine power. An experienced nursery assistant told me that she sometimes felt 'intimidated' by the boys when they were running around in a group and 'shooting' at her from the climbing frame. The question educators have to face is how to deal with this superhero play.

It could be argued that boys' fascination with superhero play is simply a very visible manifestation of their exploration of a particular form of masculinity which will include developing judgements about the desirability of adopting such a form rather than another.

236 *Naima Browne*

Guns and magic wands

Much of the superhero play involves the use of an array of weapons that include guns, lasers, swords, light sabres and knives. As with superhero play, the issue of whether to allow young children to play with toy weapons has recently become the subject of debate. Holland (2003) has shown that from around 1960 to the early 1990s early child-hood settings in Britain adopted a 'zero tolerance' approach to weapon play. Holland has argued that allowing interested children, the overwhelming majority of whom are boys, to engage in play scenarios involving imaginary weapons, does not encourage violence and aggression. She has documented how in some of the settings in which the 'zero tolerance' to such play was relaxed the boys' play became more imaginative and in none of the settings was there an increase in violence.

When talking to young boys it is clear that they seem to be aware of the difference between their toy guns and real guns. One child, living in an area of London with a high rate of gun crime, seemed to be very aware of the fact that even pretend guns could be mistaken for real ones:

NB: Is it OK to point your toy gun at somebody?
Robbie: No, not at a policeman. They might take their real gun and point it at you.
NB: When you are playing with your toy guns do you like to pretend to shoot other people?
Robbie: Yeah, but not policemans. [sic]

(Browne, 2004)

While children seem to be aware of the difference between toy weapons and real weapons the fact still remains that using weapons, especially guns, are seen to be signifiers of male power, because the majority of male heroes and superheroes rely on weapons to vanquish their foes. Heroines, in contrast, tend to rely on other means such as magic. Girls from a very young age associate guns with boys and the vast majority of the girls I spoke to claimed to have no interest in playing with weapons on the grounds that guns were 'for boys'.

It has been argued that toy guns empower and 'embolden' the children who play with them (Jones, 2002: 53). The majority of children who play with guns are, however, boys. The question we need to ask ourselves is, what merit is there in encouraging boys to rely on imaginary weapons to injure or annihilate their 'enemies' when they could be encouraged to think of more creative ways of overcoming their foes and fears? Running around shooting down your enemies may be exciting and emotionally satisfying in the short term but does such play enable boys to face the underlying issues? Paley has observed that:

Boys [play] has already masked sensitive issues. Storytelling for them is primarily a recall of superhero themes. When something makes a boy sad, he simply becomes a more powerful superhero. He is not compelled to act out confusing events, face to face, as are the girls.

(Paley, 1984: 111)

By enabling boys to simply deal with difficult experiences and emotions by whipping out a toy gun, surely we are inhibiting boys' opportunities to acknowledge and deal with their emotions?

Holland has argued that magic wands should perhaps be viewed in the same light as guns since they can inflict fantasy pain and even death (Holland, 2003) but I think that the difference between guns and magic wands lies in the fact that magic wands can be instruments of 'good' as well as destruction and furthermore, are not gender-specific. Magic wands therefore, are less likely to reinforce unequal gender-based power dynamics within the classroom and in the playground.

Conclusion

Young children's play is a powerful medium for young children's exploration of 'femininities' and 'masculinities', what it means to be 'feminine' and 'masculine' and for coming to understand the gendered nature of society. Listening to children and watching them play raises a number of questions for practitioners who are keen to encourage and support all children in exploring different ways of 'being' a girl or a boy:

- Are there ways in which practitioners can help children become more confident about exploring new roles and identities?
- How does the ethos and/or practice within a setting need to change or develop to enable young children to talk about gender issues?
- Can practitioners ensure that superhero play does not endorse the view that men and boys are more powerful than girls and women?
- How can practitioners extend children's understandings of 'femininity' and 'masculinity'?
- How can practitioners talk to parents and carers about gender issues?

The way in which children maintain their categorisation of themselves as boys and girls through their friendship patterns and choice of activities, the children's emotional investment in the positions they adopt and the way in which particular beliefs about gender are woven into the fabric of this society means that it will not be easy to encourage children to explore new and different ways of 'being' a girl or boy. Ensuring that children have access to a wider range of discourse (ways of seeing the world and ways of being) is, however, a necessary aspect of work aimed at disrupting gender divisions. Children who decide to explore new roles and different positions that do not conform to accepted models of 'femininity' or 'masculinity' will need to be supported as they move outside the current gender norms. MacNaughton has taken up this theme and has suggested that practitioners will need to:

> . . .work hard to provide boys with understandings of masculinity in which dominance is not always seen as positive. They will need to work equally hard to provide girls with understandings of femininity that enable them to assert their rights.

> (MacNaughton, 2000: 125–6)

References

Bettelheim, B. (1978) The Uses of Enchantment: *The Meaning and Importance of Fairy Tales*. London: Penguin.

Boyd, B.J. (1997) Teacher response to superhero play: to ban or not to ban? *Childhood Education*, 74(1): 23–8.

Browne, N. (1999) *Young Children's Literacy Development and the Role of Televisual Texts*. London: Falmer Press.

Browne, N. (2004) *Gender Equity in the Early Years*. Maidenhead: Open University Press.

Browne, N. and Ross, C. (1991) 'Girls' stuff, boys' stuff: young children talking and playing.' In N. Browne (ed.) *Science and Technology in the Early Years*. Buckingham: Open University Press.

Connell, R.W. (1987) *Gender and Power*. Stanford, CA: Stanford University Press.

Connell, R.W. (1995) *Masculinities*. Berkeley, CA: University of California Press.

Connell, R.W. (2000) *The Men and the Boys*. St. Leonards: Allen and Unwin.

Cupit, C.G. (1996) Superhero play and very human children, *Early Years*, 16(2): 22–5.

Davies, B. (1989) *Frogs and Snails and Feminist Tales: Pre-school children and gender*. Sydney: Allen and Unwin.

Gurian, M. (2001) *Boys and Girls Learn Differently. A Guide for Teachers and Parents*. San Francisco: Jossey-Bass.

Holland, P. (2003) *We Don't Play with Guns Here: War, Weapon and Superhero Play in the Early Years*. Maidenhead: Open University Press.

Jones, G. (2002) *Killing Monsters. Why Children Need Fantasy, Super Heroes and Make-believe Violence*. New York: Basic Books.

Jordan, E. and Cowan, A. (2001) 'Warrior narratives in the kindergarten classroom: renegotiating the social contract?' In M.S. Kimmel and M.A. Messner (eds), *Men's Live*. Needham Heights, MA: Allyn and Bacon.

Lloyd, B. and Duveen, G. (1992) *Gender Identities and Education: The Impact of Starting School*. New York: St. Martin's Press.

MacNaughton, G. (2000) *Rethinking Gender in Early Childhood Education*. London: Paul Chapman.

Macoby, E.E. (1998) *The Two Sexes: Growing Up Apart, Coming Together*. London: Belknap Press.

Mello, R. (2001) Cinderella Meets Ulysses, *Language Arts* 78(6) 548–55.

Paley, V.G. (1984) *Boys and Girls. Superheroes in the Doll Corner*. Chicago: University of Chicago Press.

Thorne, B. (1986) 'Girls and boys together, but mostly apart'. In W.W. Hartup and Z. Rubin (eds) *Relationship and Development*. Hillsdale, NJ: Erlbaum.

Thorne, B. (1993) *Gender Play: Girls and Boys in School*. New Brunswick, NJ: Rutgers University Press.

Walkerdine, V. and Lucey, H. (1989) *Democracy in the Kitchen*. London: Virago Press.

Chapter 22

Watching and listening
The tools of assessment

Cathy Nutbrown

Assessment is a key feature of the work of practitioners in early years settings. However, all too often external demands and considerations can mean that the focus is on outcomes and measurable achievement – assessment *of* learning rather than assessment *for* learning. Cathy Nutbrown argues that we need to reconsider why we assess young children's learning and to develop assessment practices that begin with respect for children and that will provide us with information to engage with and support children's learning and understanding. She suggests that listening to children and observation are essential tools in achieving this.

This chapter focuses on how early childhood educators can understand young children's capabilities and learning needs. It asks what is assessment and why assess young children's learning and development? It considers values and vision underpinning assessment, and discusses current national policy on early assessment of learning in England. In discussing assessment for teaching and learning the chapter emphasizes the importance of observation as one of the most effective 'tools of the trade'; it discusses some key aspects of assessing young children and the importance of assessing with due respect for young children.

What is assessment?

The word 'assessment' is used in different contexts and taken to mean different things. It refers to at least three different purposes, and there is no single shared understanding in policy or practice. Nutbrown (2006) has suggested three different purposes for assessment in the early years, arguing that different tools are needed for different purposes. *Assessment for teaching and learning* is the process of identifying the details of children's knowledge, skills and understanding in order to build a detailed picture of a child's development and subsequent learning needs. *Assessment for management and accountability* prefers scores over narrative accounts of children's learning. Such assessments included the Baseline Assessment system which measured children's progress in predetermined objectives (SCAA, 1997) and allowed the 'value added' by the school to be calculated. *Assessment for research* includes those assessments (and often tests of 'scales' involving numerical outcomes) which are used specifically in research projects where quickly administered measures are needed and where uniformity of approach is necessary. One such example is the Sheffield Early Literacy Development Profile (Nutbrown, 1997), which was developed to measure aspects of early literacy of 3–5-year-olds. Table 22.1 summarizes the characteristics of these three purposes of assessment.

Assessment of young children raises a number of concerns in relation to their well-being and self-esteem. Roberts writes:

> Assessment and recording arrangements carry a world of hidden messages for children and parents. Is a positive model used, one which identifies children's special strengths as well as areas for support? Is there accurate and detailed information about children? Do adults make sure that children share their successes, both with their parents and with each other? These questions raise some of the issues which have a direct bearing on how children learn to see themselves.
>
> (Roberts, 1995: 115)

Why assess young children's learning and development?

This is a fundamental question in teaching young children. Children's learning is so complex, so rich, so fascinating, so varied, so surprising and so full of enthusiasm that to see it taking place every day, before one's very eyes, is one of the greatest privileges of any early childhood practitioner. The very process of observing and assessing children's learning is, in a sense, its own justification. Watching young children can open our eyes to the astonishing capacity of young children to learn, and shows us the crucial importance of these first few years in children's lives. But there is much more to say about assessing children's learning. Watching young children learn can, at times, make us marvel at their powers to think, to do, to communicate and to create. But observation points to more that our awe at young children's capacities. There is also an important piece of work for early childhood practitioners to understand, to really understand what they see.

Several pioneers (Froebel, Piaget, Vygotsky and Isaacs) and more recent figures such as Donaldson (1983), Athey (1990), Elfer et al. (2003) and Nutbrown (1997) have illuminated children's learning and development and provided practitioners with strategies for reflecting upon and interpreting their observations of children. The rich resource of research and commentary opens up to educators the meanings of children's words, representations and actions. Educators' personal experiences of individual children's learning can help them to see more clearly the general principles that other researchers and educators have established as characteristic of that learning. For example, those who work with babies and young children under 3 can draw on the work of Elfer, Goldschmied and Selleck (2003), Goldschmied and Jackson (2004),

Table 22.1 Some characteristics of the three purposes of assessment

Assessment for teaching and learning	Assessment for management and accountability	Assessment for research
Focus on individuals	Focus on age cohort	Focus on samples
Concerned with details about each individual learner	Concerned with a sample of group performance	Concerned with performance of the sample
Is ongoing	Occurs within specific time frame	Takes place at planned points in a study
'Takes as long as it takes'	Is briefly administered or completed from previous assessment for teaching	Can be brief, depends on assessment and ages
Needs no numerical outcome to be meaningful	Numerical outcome provides meaning	Numerical outcomes often essential
Is open-ended	Often consists of closed list of items	Often consists of closed items
Informs next teaching steps	Informs management strategy and policy	Informs research decisions, and findings – measures outcomes
Information relates primarily to individuals	Information relates primarily to classes, groups, settings or areas	Information relates to the sample, not to individuals or schools
Assessments required for each child	Some missing cases permissible	Some missing cases permissible
Main purpose is teaching	Main purpose is accountability	Purpose is to add to knowledge
Only useful if information is used to guide teaching	Only useful when compared to other outcomes (of other measures of cohorts)	Only useful as evidence of effectiveness of research study
Requires professional insight into children's learning	Requires competence in administration of the test	Requires competence in administration of the test
Depends on established relationship with individual children to be effective	Can draw on information derived through interaction with individual children, but not dependent on relationship	Often requires no previous relationship, but the ability to establish a rapport with the child at the time of the assessment
Requires ongoing professional development and experience	Requires short training session, learning the test and practice	Requires short training session, learning the test and practice.

Source: Nutbrown, 1999: 127.

Abbott and Moylett (1997) and the *Practice Guidance for the Early Years Foundation Stage* (DfES, 2007) in order to embellish their own understanding of the children with whom they work. When early childhood educators hold up the work of others as a mirror to their own, they can see the essential points of their own work reflected more clearly and better understand the learning and development of the children with whom they work.

The published observations of some of the earlier pioneers can be useful to educators now as tools for reflection on children's processes of learning and as a means of moving from the specifics of personal experiences to general understandings about children's thinking. Susan Isaacs, for example, ran an experimental school, The Malting House, in Cambridge from 1924 to 1927. Her compelling accounts of the day-to-day doings of the children in the school show clearly how her analysis of children's intellectual development is the product of a mass of detailed anecdotal insights. For example, she describes (Isaacs, 1929) the development of the basic concepts of biology, change, growth, life and death, and illustrates the process with a rich body of observational evidence as the following show:

18th June 1925
The children let the rabbit out to run about the garden for the first time, to their great delight. They followed him about, stroked him and talked about his fur, his shape and his ways.

13th July 1925
Some of the children called out that the rabbit was dying. They found it in the summerhouse, hardly able to move. They were very sorry and talked much about it. They shut it up in the hutch and gave it warm milk.

14th July 1925
The rabbit had died in the night. Dan found it and said: 'It's dead – its tummy does not move up and down now'. Paul said, 'My daddy says that if we put it in water it will get alive again'. Mrs I said 'shall we do so and see?' They put it into a bath of water. Some of them said. 'It's alive, because it's moving.' This was a circular motion, due to the currents in the water. Mrs I therefore put a small stick which also moved round and round, and they agreed that the stick was not alive. They then suggested that they should bury the rabbit, and all helped to dig a hole and bury it.

15th July 1925
Frank and Duncan talked of digging the rabbit up – but Frank said, 'It's not there – it's gone up to the sky.' They began to dig, but tired of it and ran off to something else. Later they came back and dug again. Duncan, however, said, 'Don't bother – it's gone – it's up in the sky' and gave up digging. Mrs I therefore said, 'Shall we see if it's there?' and also dug. They found the rabbit, and were very interested to see it still there.

Isaacs's diary entries about the play and questioning of young children formed the basis of her analysis of children's scientific thinking and understanding, and offer rich evidence of the development of children's theories about the world and the things they find in it. Isaacs was able to learn about children's learning through her diligent and meticulous study of her own detailed observations of their play and other activities. Observation as a tool for assessing children's learning is not new, though for some who have not had the opportunity to continue to practise their skills of observation or had time to reflect with colleagues on those observations, these tools may have become a little blunt and may need to be sharpened and polished. However, many researchers and practitioners have followed Isaacs's observational practices; indeed, my own work on young children's learning has been informed by my daily journal jottings (made while working with young children) of children's words, actions and graphic representations (Nutbrown, 1999). Similarly, the pioneering practice of Reggio Emilia in northern Italy is developed largely through careful documentation which includes observations, notes, photographs and reflections upon the children's work as it unfolds in their learning communities (Filippini and Cecchi, 1996; Abbott and Nutbrown, 2001).

Goldschmied's (1989) work with babies illustrates the importance of close observation. Watching babies playing with the Treasure Basket can give the adult valuable insights into their learning and development and interactions with others. The following extract from an observation of Matthew shows the fine detail of this 9-month-old's persistent interests:

> Kate places Matthew close enough for him to reach right into the basket. He immediately reaches in with his right hand and selects a long wooden handled spatula. 'Oohh, ahh,' he says and looks directly at his mother. She smiles at him in approval. Still holding the spatula he proceeds to kneel up and lean across the basket in order to reach a long brown silk scarf. He pulls at the scarf and squeals in delight as he pulls the fabric through his fingers, 'oohh, ahh' he repeats. He lets go of the spatula and abandons the scarf to his side, his eyes rest on a large blue stone, he picks up the large stone with his right hand and turns it over on his lap using both hands. Still using both hands he picks the stone up and begins to bite it, making a noise as his teeth grind against the hard surface. He smiles; looking at his mother as he repeatedly bites the stone over and over again. He stops, holds the stone up to his face and looks at it intently then puts it to his mouth once more. He then picks up the wooden spatula again and whilst holding it firmly in one hand, he turns the contents of the basket over with his other hand, squealing loudly with delight as he discovers the matching long handled fork. Matthew looks at his mother and waves both items in the air smiling and rocking on his knees saying 'oohh, ahh'. He turns away from the basket and waves the long handled implements up and down in his hands, first one then the other then both together. He turns back to the basket with a puzzled expression and for a few seconds stops waving the items. He drops the fork and reaches back into the basket and randomly picks up items one at a time, looks at them and then discards them on the floor beside him. He continues this pattern for several seconds until he comes upon a long handled brush. He picks up the brush, pauses and then waves it in his left hand, all the time continuing to hold the wooden spatula in his right hand. For several seconds he proceeds to bang the long handled items together, smiling as the two wooden items make a sound as they came together. He then spots the wooden fork he had disposed of earlier and letting go of the brush picks up the wooden fork and bangs it together with the spatula. 'Baba, baba, da, da, da' he says, then a little more loudly he repeats 'baba, baba, da, da, da'.

(Nutbrown, 2005: 153)

Elfer et al.'s sensitive (2003) observations of babies in day care also show how so much can be learned about babies' interests and needs if observations are made and reflected upon.

Other reasons for observing and assessing young children centre around the adults' role as a provider of care and education. Young children's awesome capacity for learning imposes a potentially overwhelming responsibility on early years practitioners to support, enrich and extend that learning. When educators understand more about children's learning they must then assume an even greater obligation to take steps to foster and develop that learning further. The extent to which educators can create a high-quality learning environment of care and education is a measure of the extent to which they succeed in developing positive learning interactions between themselves and the children such that the children's learning is nurtured and developed.

'Quality' is often culturally defined and community specific (Woodhead, 1996) but whatever their setting and wherever they are located, where educators watch the children they teach with a view to using those observations to generate their own understandings of children's learning and their needs, they are contributing to the development of a quality environment in which those children might thrive. Where educators observe young children they are using a tool that plays an important part in achieving high-quality pre-school experiences, shaping their present, daily learning experiences – whatever the type of setting. The evaluative purpose of assessment is central for early childhood educators, for they cannot know if the environments they create and the support they provide for children as they work are effective unless they watch and unless they learn from what they see.

- *Observation can provide starting points* for reviewing the effectiveness of provision and such observational assessments of children's learning can be used daily to identify strengths, weaknesses, gaps, and inconsistencies in the curriculum provided for all children.
- *Assessment can be used to plan and review* the provision and teaching as well as to identify those significant moments in each child's learning which educators can build upon to shape a curriculum that matches each child's pressing cognitive and affective concerns.
- *Observation and assessment can illuminate the future* as well as provide information with which to improve the quality of the present. This forward-looking dimension of assessment is the means by which early childhood practitioners can explore the possibilities offered through the provision they create in the settings in which they work. Curriculum, pedagogy, interactions and relationships can all be illuminated and their effectiveness reviewed through close observation of adults' work with children. Despite the introduction of the Foundation Stage and the Foundation Stage Profile, formal assessments continue to be used routinely to diagnose children's abilities and there is a danger that over-formalized assessment at the age of 4 can limit the opportunities children are offered rather than opening up a broad canvas of opportunity for learning. It is important, however, to use the active process of assessment to identify for each child the next teaching steps so that learning opportunities in the immediate future are well matched to the children for whom they are offered.

This focus on the next steps in teaching and learning takes us into the 'zone of proximal development' – a concept developed by Vygotsky (1978) who argued that assessment does not end with a description of a pupil's present state of knowing, but rather begins there. Vygotsky (1978: 85) wrote: 'I do not terminate my study at this point, but only begin it.' Effective assessment is dynamic, not static, and can be used by educators as a way of identifying what s/he might do next in order to support children's learning. Assessment reveals learning potential as well as learning achievements.

Observation and assessment are the essential tools of watching and learning with which practitioners can both establish the progress that has already taken place and explore the future – the learning that is embryonic. The role of the adult in paying careful and informed attention to children's learning and reflecting upon that learning is crucial to the enhancement of children's future learning.

Values and vision

Against the backdrop, in England, of the Early Years Foundation Stage Profile, and an emphasis on the acquisition of some identified elements of knowledge, skills and understanding, it remains the case that early childhood educators can assess children in ways which are appropriate to their age and learning stage. As devolution gathers pace around the UK, it is possible to see the way in which different policies are being developed to allow, to varying degrees, a freedom of practitioners to decide how and what to assess. Whatever the national policy, practitioners' own personal and professional values underpin their assessment practices. Those who work with young children bring to the processes of assessment their implicit values and their beliefs about children. Whatever the framework for national assessment, the ways in which adults assess children depend upon their views on the nature of childhood, children's behaviour, children's feelings, and their personal approaches to living and learning. Whenever, wherever educators observe, assess and interpret young children's learning, they are influenced by personal beliefs and values.

Policy documents since the early 1990s show a shift in the language about children and childhood and the purposes of early education and care which perhaps indicate a change in the dominant political view of childhood. The language in policy documents of the 1990s suggested that 'childhood' had been reconstructed for policy (or perhaps *through* policy) with very young children becoming 'pupils' and early 'experiences' designed to promote learning gave way to 'outcomes' (Nutbrown, 1998). In 2000, there was a re-emergence of a more appropriate language within early education with talk of 'foundations', 'play' and 'children'. However, target-driven assessment dominated until 2002 when the Foundation Stage Profile and subsequently the Early Years Foundation Stage Profile, held out the hope of a more flexible approach to ongoing assessment of young children's learning and needs through observation. It is crucial that early childhood educators are supported in the appreciation and articulation of their own personal vision of early experiences for children (how things might be) as such vision derives from the values they hold, their own constructions of childhood. It is important, too, that early childhood educators challenge the language of policy when it is at odds with a holistic and developmental view of children's early learning. Target oriented assessment remains but such targets are only useful if they match children's learning and development needs.

National policy on early assessment of learning

The *Early Years Foundation Stage Profile Handbook* (QCA/DCSF 2008) brought a further shift in the language of early education and policy. The following example is taken from this Profile and illustrates how one of the items on the assessment scale for Knowledge and Understanding of the World is assessed, through indirect observation, for a number of children.

Scale point 6 Finds out about past and present events in own life, and in those of family members and other people s/he knows. Begins to know about culture and beliefs and those of other people:

After a visit by her grandmother, Grace talks to a group about the old toys she has brought for display and explains how they were used by her grandmother when she was a girl.

Zara and Helen lay out the laminated pictures in the correct sequence – baby, toddler, child, adult. Then they sort the basket of objects (keys, baby bottle, picture book, lipstick, etc.), putting them next to the appropriate picture.

Sanjay takes Toby (the diary dog) home for the weekend. In circle time on Monday he describes what he did with Toby and his family during his stay.

Sally explains to her mum that her friend is having a special family dinner because her uncle is going to Australia.

(QCA/DCSF, 2008: 72)

Assessment for teaching and learning

Effective and meaningful work with young children which supports their learning must be based on appropriate assessment strategies to identify their needs and capabilities. The fine mesh of learning requires detailed, ongoing and sensitive observations of children as they play.

Observation is crucial to understanding and assessing young children's learning. The following example demonstrates the importance of involving parents in assessing their children's learning.

Sean was three and a half years old. He attended a nursery class each morning, where he spent much of his time playing outdoors, on bikes, in tents, climbing, gardening and running. His nursery teacher was concerned that he did not benefit from the other activities available indoors – painting, writing, drawing, construction, sharing books, jigsaws and so on. Even when some of these opportunities were placed outside, Sean still seemed to avoid them. The nursery teacher spoke with Sean's mother who said: 'We don't have a garden and there's nowhere for Sean to play outside – he hasn't got a bike and there's no park for climbing, or swings around here, or a space to do outside things, but we have lots of books and jigsaws, Lego, playpeople, we draw and make things.' Sean was balancing his own curriculum but the adults involved needed to share what they knew in order to understand his learning needs and current capabilities.

(Nutbrown, 1996: 49)

Key aspects in assessing young children

Several aspects need to be addressed if assessment is to work for children (Box 22.1).

Box 22.1 Issues in assessment

- *Clarity of purpose* – why are children being assessed?
- *Fitness for purpose* – is the assessment instrument or process appropriate?
- *Authenticity* – do the assessment tasks reflect processes of children's learning and their interests?
- *Informed practitioners* – are practitioners appropriately trained and supported?
- *Child involvement* – how can children be fittingly involved in assessment of their learning?
- *Respectful assessment* – are assessments fair and honest with appropriate concern for children's well being and involvement?
- *Parental involvement* – do parents contribute to their child's assessment? (Adapted from Nutbrown, 2005: 14)

Respectful assessment can include the development of inclusive practices which seek to allow children to 'have their say' in the assessment of their own learning. Critchley (2002 – Box 22.2) explored ways of including children in the assessment of their achievements.

Box 22.2 Including children in assessment of their own learning

Critchley (2002) carried out a study in the United Arab Emirates, to explore 4–5-year-old children's abilities to assess their own learning. She talked to 18 children in their classrooms, some in small groups, others on an individual basis. Some children were Emirate with Arabic as their first language, others were children of expatriate families with English as their home language. Some children spoke both English and Arabic. The first interview focused on their progress and the second on their reasons for learning. Children were asked to review their own work and to comment on what they 'thought they were better at now'.

One child compared two similar pieces of work and, because she saw progress in terms of visual data such as neatness of letter shape, perceived the neater work to be of better quality. In another instance where a child compared his two pieces of writing, he declared that the earlier piece was better because he thought it looked neater – it did – but the earlier work had been copied from a slip of paper and the later piece had been written independently and had clearly been concentrating more on words and meaning than letter formation. That the independent effort did not represent progress in his eyes can be a problem for teachers, and they need to ensure that their views do not dominate children's opinions when they select work to represent children's progress.

When asked, 'What have you learnt this year that you're pleased about?' one child answered 'Doing work like adding' and when asked 'Is there anything you need to practice more?' he replied 'Take away'. Another child expressed her progress in terms of playground activity and swimming, 'I can now open my eyes under water' – rather than the adults' perspective of the distance she could swim. Most children, however, viewed their progress in terms of drawing, as the following, fairly typical, conversation illustrates:

DC: What have you learnt this year that you're pleased about?
Danny: Drawing zebras.
DC: Anything else?
Danny: [drawing] Jumping rabbits.
DC: Anything else that's not drawing?
Danny: Colouring clowns.
DC: Is there anything you need to practise more?
Danny: [drawing] beds!

The children's perspective suggested that for them progress in drawing was important and desirable – often forming part of their classroom and out of school experience and being also something they could see and feel – so progress was immediately visible.

The mismatch between the child's perspective and the adult's perspective represented by the school report is stark. The fact that the child's view is neither elicited nor considered in many such situations could lead a child to abandon his or her view of progress and achievement in favour of the accepted, adult view of progress – and this would not be because of reaching mutual ground but because the child's view had gone unnoticed.

With due respect . . .

This chapter has considered why early childhood educators should observe and assess young children in the context of assessment policy in England. Answers to remaining questions depend upon the principles on which early education and assessment are based. The principle of respect is crucial. Assessment must be carried out with proper respect for the children, their parents, carers and their educators. Respectful assessment governs what is done, what is said, how relationships are conducted and the attitudes which practitioners bring to their work. Those who watch young children – really watch and listen and reflect on their learning – will know that time to watch and reflect is essential to really understanding what young children are doing. Observations which are never reflected upon are wasted effort. It is only when practitioners seek to under-stand the meanings behind what they have seen that the real worth of observational practices is realized.

Whatever the future of the Foundation Stage Profile and future policies and practices, two things are essential: the involvement of parents and practitioners in generating

Table 22.2 What is a respectful educator? What is respectful teaching? What is respectful assessment?

Respectful approaches	Disrespectful approaches
Taking account of the learner – 'children as as participants' in learning	Ignoring the learner – 'children as recipients' of knowledge
Building on existing learning	Disregarding/unaware of existing learning
Based on tuning into learners' agenda	Based on predetermined teaching
Responsive/adapted to learners' needs interests	Unresponsive/unadaptive to learners and needs and interests
Informed by children's developmental needs	Informed by targets/key stages/ages
Curriculum based on children's identified needs	Curriculum based on external definitions of needs
Includes/embraces issues of children's rights	Ignores/disregards issues of children's rights
Clarity for learner	Lack of clarity for learner
Authentic assessment to inform teaching	Contrived assessment used to track progress of cohort
Challenge	Unchallenging
Opportunity for extension and diversity	Little or no extension and diversity
Holistic	Compartmentalized
Involves parents	Excludes parents
Evaluative	No evaluation
Revision in the light of experience	'Carrying on regardless'
Recognizes all achievement	Values achievement of specific, prespecified goals
Purposeful	Lack of purpose
Knowledgeable practitioners	Practitioners with limited knowledge
High-quality professional development for practitioners	Lack of/limited professional development opportunities
Appropriately qualified early childhood educators	Unqualified/poorly trained/qualified early childhood educators
Every learner matters uniquely	The cohort/group/majority is the main focus
Equality for *all* children	The 'same' for all children
Inclusive practices	Segregated/exclusionary practices
Sufficient and appropriate equipment and resources	Insufficient and inadequate equipment/resources
Sufficient/appropriate space and access to learning areas/experiences	Insufficient/inappropriate space and limited access to learning areas/equipment
Key workers	No key worker system

respectful understandings of children's learning, and professional development for educators which is worthy of children's amazing capacity to learn. The Reggio Emilia model of documentation and reflection shows the benefits of practitioners talking together about children's learning and their role in it.

Time for teaching and assessment, *confidence* in educators' capabilities, *recognition* of the judgements practitioners make, can create the important climate of *respectful early education*. The concept of respect can underpin and inform the way adults work and how policies are developed and implemented, but the notion of respect in education can be misunderstood (Nutbrown, 1996; 1997). 'When advocates of respect for children are accused of being "idealistic", of "romanticizing early childhood" – their meaning is misunderstood. Respect is not about "being nice" – it is about being clear, honest, courteous, diligent and consistent' (Nutbrown, 1998: 14).

In 2005 Prime Minister Tony Blair announced his desire to see respect restored to the classroom. A clear way to ensure that children respect their teachers is for them to experience respect in their early years. The concept of respectful assessment and respectful teaching could be dismissed by some as an over-romanticizing of early education. Therefore, the careful articulation of meanings is important, as is the examination of what the concept of respectful work with children might mean. Table 22.2 suggests what might constitute respectful approaches to teaching, and identifies the characteristics of the opposite – *disrespectful* approaches to teaching (who would want to endorse such a term!).

Teaching young children requires clarity, honesty, courtesy, diligence and consistency. It means identifying what children *can* do, what they *might* do and what their educators need to do next to support and challenge them in their learning. Despite repeated policy attempts to keep it simple teaching young children can never be other than complex. Watching young children as they learn, and understanding their learning moments, is complex and difficult work and places the highest of demands upon their educators.

References

Abbott, L. and Moylett, H. (eds) (1997) *Working with the Under-Threes: Training and Professional Development*. Buckingham: Open University Press.

Abbott, L. and Nutbrown, C. (eds) (2001) *Experiencing Reggio Emilia: Implications for Preschool Provision*. Milton Keynes: Open University Press.

Athey, C. (1990) *Extending Thought in Young Children: A Parent-Teacher Partnership*. London: Paul Chapman Publishing.

Critchley, D. (2002) 'Children's assessment of their own learning', in C. Nutbrown (ed.), *Research Studies in Early Childhood Education*. Stoke-on-Trent: Trentham Books.

Department of Education and Skills (DfES) (2007) *Practice Guidance for the Early Years Foundation Stage*. Nottingham: DfES Publications.

Donaldson, M. (1983) *Children's Minds*. Glasgow: Fontana/Collins.

Elfer, P., Goldschmied, E. and Selleck, D. (2003) *Key Persons in Nurseries: Building Relationships for Quality Provision*. London: Early Years Network.

Filippini, T. and Cecchi, V. (1996) (eds) *The Hundred Languages of Children: The Exhibit*. Reggio Emilia: Reggio Children.

Goldschmied, E. (1989) *Infants at Work: The Treasure Basket Explained*. National Children's Bureau, 8 Wakley Street, London ECIV 7QE.

Goldschmied, E. and Jackson, S. (2004) *People Under Three: Young Children in Day Care*. 2nd edition. London: Routledge.

Isaacs, S. (1929) *The Nursery Years*. London: Routledge and Kegan Paul.

Nutbrown, C. (1997) *Recognising Early Literacy Development: Assessing Children's Achievements*. London: Paul Chapman Publishing.

Nutbrown, C. (1998) *The Lore and Language of Early Education*. Sheffield: USDE.

Nutbrown, C. (1999) *Threads of Thinking: Young Children Learning and the Role of Early Education* (2nd edition). London: Sage.

Nutbrown, C. (2005) *Key Concepts in Early Childhood Education and Care*. London: Sage.

Nutbrown, C. (2006) *Threads of Thinking: Young Children Learning and the Role of Early Education*. London: Paul Chapman Publishing.

Nutbrown, C. (ed.) (1996) *Respectful Educators, Capable Learners: Children's Rights and Early Education*. London: Paul Chapman Publishing.

Qualifications and Curriculum Authority/Department for children, Schools and Families (2008), *Early Years Foundation Stage Profile Handbook*. London: QCA/DCSF.

Roberts, R. (1995) *Self-esteem and Successful Early Learning*. London: Hodder and Stoughton.

School Curriculum and Assessment Authority (SCAA) (1997) *National Framework for Baseline Assessment: Criteria and Procedures for the Accreditation of Baseline Assessment Schemes*. London: DfEE and SCAA.

Vygotsky, L.S. (1978) *Mind in Society*. Cambridge, MA: Harvard University Press.

Woodhead, M. (1996) *In Search of the Rainbow*. The Hague: Bernard van Leer Foundation.

Chapter 23

'It's not like anything Joe and I have experienced before'
Family workshops at Tate Modern

Roger Hancock with Alison Cox and Synthia Griffin

Art galleries are often not seen as places to take young children but there are indications that they wish to change this perception. Roger Hancock has been involved with Alison Cox and Synthia Griffin, Curators of Family and Community Programmes at Tate Modern, in a project to involve parents and children in joint learning experiences around works of art in the gallery. In this chapter they describe what this involved using both words and a series of images to tell the story.

Introduction

Tate Modern, a major national gallery of international modern and contemporary art, is located on the border of the London boroughs of Southwark and Lambeth and is close to the borough of Tower Hamlets. All three boroughs have some of the most diverse communities in the UK and contain areas of extreme social deprivation.

One of the major challenges for Tate Modern is to develop links with communities and groups that have not visited museums or art galleries, especially those living and working locally. The gallery's family programme is one way in which it has approached this challenge. The programme is aimed both at first time and repeat visitors, and attracts families from all over London, the rest of the UK, and overseas. The programme offers a range of events, some bookable, some not, but all are free of charge. The gallery has proven to be a popular venue for family visitors and this is reflected in the success of 'Start' which uses games and other self-directed activities to introduce children and their accompanying adults to exhibited artworks.

Tate's website also provides a welcome and suggestions to family groups for making the best use of the gallery. But clearly, such written guidance hopes that families are sufficiently confident to make a visit. Many local families, it seems, do not have this confidence and they continue to be under-represented in visitor surveys. These families feel Tate is not a place relevant to them, or they worry that prior knowledge of art and artists is important in order to use the gallery.

Figure 23.1 Tate Modern: 'A gallery rooted in its context' (*Architects' Journal*, 1993, cited in Barker, 1999, p. 198).

A second challenge for Tate Modern is to address the specific need for increased provision for children under five years, since experience suggests that provision for this age range is often poorly met by galleries. Like the majority of family events at Tate Modern, 'Start' is aimed at children aged five to twelve years rather than those under five. Nevertheless, as well as bringing children within this age range, a substantial number of these families do bring children under five and some provision is made for them, for example there is a 'soft trail' and a simple sketch book with activities related to art works.

One way in which Tate has addressed these two needs is to provide specifically designed workshops for families with very young children. These – run as a series of three weekly workshops when families could attend all or some – first began in 2002 and are collectively known as 'Small Steps in a Big Space'.

The workshops

Outreach to the local community

Well before a 'Small Steps' workshop takes place, a local parent with a background in art and community participation is employed by Tate to visit nearby playgroups and libraries to spread the word and invite potential participants. This outreach work is conceived as a process rather than an event, however, in which this visit is only a beginning. Following this initial contact there is further consideration in terms of how best to make the journey to Tate and how to ensure that those parents who might be a little anxious are linked with others who are more confident travellers. Reassuring telephone calls are sometimes made and, where necessary, the outreach worker agrees to meet a group a parents on the morning of a workshop and accompany them to Tate.

Without wishing to patronise parents, it's important to recognise that, for those unused to travelling with their children even a little way from their locality, an unfamiliar journey to a public gallery can present an obstacle. Despite such outreach under-standings, there have been parents who said enthusiastically that they would like to come to a workshop who, on the day, did not actually make it. These parents serve to emphasise that outreach work is far from straightforward and highlight the complexity of increasing social inclusion in an art gallery.

The nature of the workshops

A workshop lasts for two hours and consists of the following structure:

Time	Activity
10.30	Welcome and refreshments
10.40–10.50	Warm up song/game/activity
10.50–11.10	Initial studio based activity linked to an overall theme
11.10–11.50	Gallery visit to look at selected art works linked to the theme
11.50–12.00	Return to the studio for refreshments
12.00–12.30	Final studio activity linked to the overall theme

These are approximate timings as each workshop needs to adjust to the specific needs and interests of parents and children who attend, and particularly their ability to move easily and safely from the art studio to the gallery and also around the gallery.

The artist educators who lead the workshops work to an overarching theme arising from, perhaps, two or three gallery exhibits and make decisions about how these art works might be made interesting and meaningful to children and their parents. This interest is kindled through preliminary activities – playful songs, games, and exploratory tasks in the art studio; and then, on visiting the gallery itself, viewing and responding to what is seen there. This response can involve an art activity while sitting in front of an artwork, but sometimes participants might be asked just to look while, for instance, the artist educator tells a story related to the content of the exhibit.

Examples of themes that have been successfully used in workshops include the following.

1. 'Making your mark'

Figure 23.2 Learning in tandem: 'If you give adults a way of engaging with their child, you set up a circle of learning' (Young, 2004).

This workshop drew on the works of Lucio Fontana, Henri Matisse and Barbara Hepworth. The 'making your mark' theme involved participants in sand drawings in the studio and a collage activity in the gallery based on Matisse's 'The Snail'.

2. 'Topsy turvy world'

Figure 23.3 Waiting for the performance: A piano that doesn't follow the rules. Every five minutes it unfolds, playing discordant music ('Concert for Anarchy', 1990, Rebecca Horn).

This workshop, in particular, used Rebecca Horn's 'Concert for Anarchy' and, on return to the studio the participants used foam and card to make their own versions of Horn's upside-down piano.

3. 'Shapes in space'

Figure 23.4 Exploring the gallery space: 'Unique Forms of Continuity in Space, 1913' by Umberto Boccioni. 'It's not easy for an adult to be so playful in public but I think what we did was very supportive of children's learning' ('Small Steps' parent, 2004).

In the gallery, this involved parents and children making shapes with their bodies around Umberto Boccioni's bronze sculpture, a figure that is aerodynamically changed by speed.

The art studio

The art studio provides an important social base for workshop participants as well as a place where activities related to the chosen art works can be done. Occasionally, when a child becomes tired in the gallery, a parent may feel that there's a need to return to the studio given that it offers a more private and secure space. When children and parents engage well with an activity the art studio can be buzzing with creative energy and also enables 'messy' activities that could not be done on the gallery floor.

Artist educator's approach

It's very important that I am an artist and that I know something about how artists express things. An artist educator is a creative person wishing to educate others.

(Artist educator, 30.3.07)

Figure 23.5 Art studio: making still life prints: '. . . museums must accommodate the family's social agenda first, so that learning can take place,' (Forman and Landry, 2000, p. 164).

Since the inception of 'Small Steps' in 2002, the group of artist educators who have led the many workshops to date have evolved a shared approach and practice which takes into account the needs of both adults and young children when learning together. There are four principles that guide their pedagogy:

- the selected art works always provide the main stimulus for the workshop activities and the focus of the learning;
- 'plural responses' and 'open readings' of artworks are expected and encouraged from children and adults;
- workshop activities like games, movement, music, drama, drawing and painting can help participants make their own conceptual links with art works;
- relaxed, socially inclusive and enjoyable workshops enable participants to interact and learn from the artist educators but also each other.

Underlying these principles is a theory of learning that places learners and their responses at the centre. As indicated above, there is a planned content to each workshop linked to specific art works, but the meaning of this content is not pre-defined nor 'delivered' to participants as appears to be the case with much of the curriculum in schools. The personal interpretations of parents and children are encouraged at all times and the artist educator is also a learner with members of a workshop as an 'interpretive community' (see Hooper-Greenhill, 2004).

Participants' responses

'Small Steps' evaluations have involved collecting a range of data arising from end-of-session questionnaires to parents, parent comments during a workshop, in-depth telephone interviews, observations of children, photographs of workshops in process, and discussions with Tate artist educators, outreach worker, and curatorial staff (see Hancock et al., 2004; 2007). In the main, these have highlighted three areas of benefit.

First, with regard to the children, there has been confirmation from parents that their children have become more confident at being in a large gallery and more able to look at specific art works and show interest in them.

Figure 23.6 Echoing a Henry Moore: It seems that we can safely assume that a sculpture has a pedagogical force but we cannot say exactly what its impact will be for those who relate to it.

The structure of the workshops (see table above) was considered by most parents to be very appropriate for their children and the flexibility of those running the sessions was seen as essential to the inclusion of young children. Some parents reported that their children were helped, by this structure, to achieve in ways that were not expected. For instance, one parent said:

> I was surprised at the way Fergus picked up on things during the workshops. I think it helped him to be part of a big group doing practical things together.
>
> ('Small Steps', 2004)

The social benefits for children were similarly highlighted by parents, and particularly the way in which the younger children (say 18 months) could be drawn productively into the collective life and energy of a workshop.

Secondly, there were benefits for parents themselves in terms of adult learning. For many, 'Small Steps' was a new and unfamiliar gallery experience even if they had already been to Tate on a family visit. The expectation that parents would work closely with their children seemed particularly effective. In a sense, they were asked to be 'intermediaries' between artist educators and children, helping their children to participate in the workshop and also supporting the leadership of the artist educators.

Many parents reported that this insider role enabled them to enjoy and learn from activities primarily designed for young children, gain new knowledge of their children's skills and abilities, and also to learn about the selected artists and art works.

Figure 23.7 Joint participation in the art studio: There were times when both adults and children were totally absorbed – everyone seemed purposeful.

Thirdly, some parents reported spin-offs from the workshops with regard to what children wanted to do at home and how they might support this. Children, for instance, might ask if they could repeat a song or a game, or request to do a similar art-making activity. For those parents who, following a workshop, visited Tate independently with their children, some reported that this could trigger children's memories in terms of gallery objects and spaces – the escalators, the lifts, toilets, a walkway, an entrance to a gallery room. Some children also remembered specific art works that had been the focus for a group experience and wanted to see them again. A mother who had attended a 2004 workshop commented:

> When I'd taken Emily back again after the programme, she actually was pointing lots of things out to me . . . she even did some of the actions that we'd been doing, so I was really surprised because I didn't realise that she'd taken all that in.
>
> ('Small Steps', 2004)

Conclusion

> It's difficult to measure the benefits. My intuitions tell me that he takes it all in and it's kind of stored inside him somehow. Whether he really understands exactly what spirals are or not is not so important as the experience of being in an art gallery and looking at art and being surrounded by art.
>
> ('Small Steps' parent, 2004)

This comment from a parent of a two-year-old child captures well the potential personal benefits for very young children when they spend enjoyable and meaningful time with adults in a public gallery.

Hooper-Greenhill et al. (2004) have highlighted that, 'visitors and users remain unaware of the great changes that have taken place in museums in recent years' (p. 541). 'Small Steps' seeks to address this need for updating and to increase local community access to the rich resources on offer in an internationally renowned gallery. Families with children under three, who may not normally visit Tate Modern, are encouraged to participate in workshops designed to give them an enjoyable way of being in the gallery and relating in personal ways to the art works. The belief is that these families will be stimulated to return independently so that Tate becomes a natural place for them to visit. In the period that the 'Small Steps' workshops have been running there is evidence that a very significant number of families have been helped to feel they can do this.

In many ways, 'Small Steps' is an ambitious programme for a gallery to take on. It not only aims to reach out to local families who may not see Tate as being for them, but also to include children under three, a category of visitor still very unrepresented in gallery surveys. Accommodating to the ever-shifting physical, social, and psychological needs of such young children as well as their learning in a dynamic public space is difficult, but it seems that, in many very significant ways, 'Small Steps' is achieving this.

Acknowledgements

Grateful acknowledgement is made to the following people who have shared their practice with us and discussed many of the ideas contained in this chapter: Kate Bagnell, Joleen Keizer, Michèle Fuirer, Michaela Ross, Eden Solomon and Bridget Virden.

References

Barker, E. (1999) *Contemporary Cultures of Display*. London: Yale University Press in association with the Open University.

Forman, G. and Landry, C. (2000) 'The constructivist perspective on early education: applications to children's museums', in Roopnarine J. L. and Johnson J. E. (eds) *Approaches to Early Childhood Education*, Third Edition, Prentice Hall, New Jersey.

Hancock, R., with Cox, A., Fuirer, M., Griffin, S., Solomon, E. and Virden, B. (2007) Small Steps in a Big Space: workshops for children under three and parents at Tate Modern. Available from: alison.cox@tate.org.uk or w.r.hancock@open.ac.uk

Hancock, R., Ross, M., Virden, B., Keizer, J., Bagnell, K., Cox, A., Jarra, A. and Powell, S. (2004) Small Steps in a Big Space: workshops for parents and children from birth to three at Tate Modern. Available from: alison.cox@tate.org.uk or w.r.hancock@open.ac.uk

Hooper-Greenhill, E., Dodd, J., Philips, M., Jones, C., Woodward, J. and O'Riain, H. (2004) *Inspiration, identity, learning: the value of museums*. Research Centre for Museums and Galleries/DfES, London.

Young, C. (2004) Personal communication from a home-educating mother.

Chapter 24

Parents and practitioners
Sharing education

Vicky Hurst and Jenefer Joseph

A close relationship between the child and parents or carers is seen by Vicky Hurst and Jenefer Joseph as being fundamental to children's emotional well-being and early learning. They see this early experience as being crucial to successful transitions in 'the world beyond the familiar one'. They make the case for an inclusive approach to working with children and families which recognises and responds sensitively to diversity through a partnership approach.

[. . .] In all but a very small proportion of families, parents (and carers who fulfil that role) are the agents who provide the context of each child's first learning. Writers such as Trevarthen (1993) and wide-ranging analyses of many research studies (e.g. the Carnegie Corporation of New York 1994) show the formative role of the parent's engagement with the child. This offers both the stimulus that presents the child with something new to deal with, and also the response which shapes the child's learning from the encounter. To give an example:

> Two babies, Eleanor and Mark, are cousins. Mark is 18 months old and Eleanor is three months. They live quite close to each other and to their grandmother, whose daughter is Eleanor's mother; and whose son is Mark's father. The grandmother is delighted to help the young families by caring for the children when she is free. She finds the babies fascinating in their differences and similarities. One thing that particularly interests her is that she can always calm and reassure Eleanor by singing to her the songs that she sang to her own children when they were little, but she has noticed that, at the same age and now, Mark's response is not the same. He responds to the songs and comfort strategies that his own mother and her mother use, which she herself, his paternal grandmother, has now learned. The babies have learned to be comforted in different ways.

Research such as that of the Carnegie Corporation (1994) shows that it is not only the particular kinds of initiative and response that parents use with their babies that are important, but rather the levels and suitability of the interaction. The closer the relationship between parent and child, the more likely it is that there is a good match between the communications of each side, and that the child's growing understanding, know-ledge and skills are rooted in experience shared with the parents. Emotional well-being, which [. . .] affects learning, is also founded on the relationship between child and parent.

When it comes to educational and care settings outside the home, a new stage begins. There has to be an opening up of this parent and child world to other influences, and the practitioner has to learn something of what has gone on so far in order to help the child make a transition into the world beyond the familiar one.

We have to think what it means for the practitioner that parents are the first in the field with their influence on children's development and learning. We have to ask ourselves what it means for parents that they know the child best but that the practitioner has a responsibility for decisions about the child's learning. We need to reflect on what can happen when to this basic difference of responsibility is added a contrast of culture and experience of life. Working in partnership is not just about the two very different spheres of home and educational setting. It is also about people from different cultures learning to work together for the good of the child.

Human beings live in divided societies. People who appear to be different from the so-called mainstream are often looked down upon by members of the dominant group. Judgements by practitioners about parents as members of particular social groups or about parents as partners in their children's education, are sometimes based on beliefs about particular groups. If parents as individuals belong to groups that are not part of the dominant group in society, stereotyped views of such ethnic minority groups can affect how the parents are perceived and what the expectations are for their children. Decisions have to be made fairly, but also with sympathy.

> An African-Caribbean mother and father obtained a part-time place for their daughter Sarah in a nursery school, but they really wanted one of the full-time places that they knew were available. The head explained to them that only in real emergencies, such as illness at home or concern for the child's safety, were children allowed to go straight into a full-time place. These places, which were valued highly because they made it easier for parents to work, were usually offered after the child had spent one or two terms in a part-time place. Sarah's parents were upset because they needed both incomes to support the family, and another child was expected. The interview was rather an uncomfortable one.
>
> Later, Sarah's mother asked if she could leave Sarah until mid-afternoon on the days when she had to go to the clinic at the hospital, as she found it a strain looking after Sarah while she waited and during the examination. The head refused, explaining that while she could do this for one family, she could not do it for the many who would ask if they thought it was a possibility. Towards the end of the pregnancy the mother asked again, hesitantly. The head and another member of staff felt that the mother was tired and low in spirits, so it was agreed.
>
> On another occasion, a white mother living in bed and breakfast accommodation had her daughter in a part-time place (there were no full-time places) when her baby boy was born. The baby was suspected of having a genetic disorder and had to be taken to various hospital appointments. The mother explained she might not be able to bring her daughter every day because she could not collect her at the end of the morning. The head offered to keep her daughter with her between the part-time sessions and have lunch with her. Every day that the baby went to hospital, and every day for the following three months that it took the family to adjust to the care their son needed, the head and Stacey lunched together.

We often expect children and parents to be able to make do with what is offered to the main group, whatever their circumstances. It sometimes appears that the degree of conformity can determine whether family or individual shall have access to the rewards available. The same can be true on a much wider scale. Patterns of speech and pronunciation, private/local authority schooling, income, where one lives, skin colour, religion, family history, marital status and sexual orientation – all give signals to others about whether people are in a favoured group or not. We all need to guard against our prejudices and misconceptions.

[. . .]

There are also individuals in society who are not able to build a viable life for all sorts of reasons including illness, domestic disasters, unemployment and so on. People in these situations need and deserve as much help as possible, and their children's rights to an appropriate education must be upheld with particular care. High standards are vital; it has been shown that children are by no means destined for a life of failure, even when their early lives are full of difficulties and deprivations. What they need was clearly identified by a study based at the National Children's Bureau (Pilling 1990). She showed that, of a group of children from the most disadvantaged backgrounds of all, some children succeeded to a marked extent in later life in spite of their early disadvantages. The parents of the successful ones retained high ambitions for them and spent time with them, playing with them, reading to them, taking them to the park. Practitioners can help if they can find ways to show their appreciation and support for the relationship between parent and child, and if they can contribute their own understanding of what the parent is trying to do. However, as it is quality of relationships that is the crucial factor, practitioner intervention needs to be very sensitive to family relationships and situations, and to cultural differences.

Parental confidence is the key to much of their children's success (Pugh *et al.* 1994). What helps children to make a success of their lives is the value of good child-rearing at every level of society, and practitioners should show awareness of this at every stage of education. This can happen as long as we recognise the importance of not having one rigid picture of good child-rearing practices; we have to be culturally adaptable and respectful, with criteria for effectiveness based on children's progress.

Practitioners and parents sharing intentions

A young father, Chris, is pleased that his daughter Christina has made a smooth transition into the infant school from the nursery class. He and his wife have been teaching her to recognise her letters. The teachers has asked them not to use upper case only, but to show her lower case when it is appropriate. This is quite a surprise for the parents; they had assumed that they would start with all one kind of letter because it was easier, and that capitals were best because of the way that shop signs and names on packets of food are so often in capitals.

Chris is willing to follow the teacher's request, however. He appreciates that she has been trained in how to teach and that there will be differences between the way he and she see things. While his daughter was settling into the nursery class he noticed that there was little direct teaching going on, and a lot of learning through play. He says 'It wasn't the way I thought, at first, but now my wife has explained that the children are supposed to learn through doing, I can see the way the school is thinking.'

But there are also things that happen at home that would change the way the teacher sees this little girl if she knew about them. For instance, Chris is bilingual; he was born in Greece and speaks Greek with his parents and family friends. He would very much like to pass this inheritance on to his daughter, but he worries about her having to learn a language she cannot use in her daily life. 'There's a Saturday school attached to the church where my father goes . . . My mates try to teach their kids, but when I try and talk to them they don't seem to want to answer. One of them told me it was dead boring and she didn't see the point of it.'

Even if there was no other way to give support, the teacher could show her interest in Christina having a bilingual parent and be sure to include Greek in the languages and scripts available in the classroom. There might be other things she could do to help, like telling Greek stories among the folk tales and fairytales, and asking Christina to teach the other children Greek words for familiar people and objects.

Some might wonder how much difference it would make if the teacher knew about Chris's wish to teach Christina Greek. With all the other things she has to do, is it a good use of her time? Two significant aspects are:

1. Understanding of this part of the relationship between Christina and her father and grandfather is helpful at times when the teacher, Mrs S., wants to make a particular effort to help Christina feel at home in the classroom. It can also help with Christina's understanding of others who are or are not able to speak more than one language.
2. Sharing this part of their home life will help Chris and his wife feel more 'in tune' with Mrs S., and will make them feel that their perspectives on Christina are valued.

But the sharing of intentions and perspectives between parents and practitioners is not easy in a busy classroom. There has to be a rationale for it, and it needs links with a curriculum model which sets a value on children's experiences at home with family and friends. It requires just as much commitment as sharing intentions with children does.

Contacts with the home should be seen as a part of the curriculum, and a part of the practitioner's responsibility to provide for children's learning in ways that suit them. The first step is to consider what kind of contact with parents is most valuable, and to find out what kind of contact with the setting is needed by parents.

We have begun with practitioners' wishes for contact because there is a lot of work that may have to be done on their side before contacts, however much wished for, can be successful. Practitioners need to establish in themselves what they believe about home-setting partnership and how important they think contacts with parents are for their work. They also need to think about how to overcome barriers that may be causing some parents to hold back. Comments such as 'these parents wouldn't really under-stand' show that sometimes practitioners feel completely out of their depth in relating to parents; this can happen for all sorts of reasons and is a definite sign that something is going very wrong. Similarly, 'You only see the parents of the good children – you never see the ones you really want to see' is a warning that the children who most need help are getting the least. Somehow barriers must be overcome, and differences made into a source of strength.

In the early years, home and community culture are extremely influential on learning and children do not leave their culture behind them as they come in through the doors of the setting. This gives practitioners the challenge of planning a curriculum that embraces children's culture and draws on its strengths. Perhaps the most demanding task practitioners face is to make links for children between their current understanding and knowledge and the more advanced learning that the practitioner wishes them to progress to. We have described already the difficulties presented by a curriculum which seeks to be standardised and is therefore not able to reflect the experiences and cultures of minority groups. A curriculum with its aims set out in broader and more flexible terms would make it easier for early years practitioners to draw in all their children. However, it is also the task of the practitioner to be flexible and creative in interpreting the requirements of the existing curriculum and adapting it to children's circumstances. Nothing makes the case for well-educated practitioners more obvious. In the end, it is the quality of practitioners' understanding of the nature of the different subject disciplines that determines how well they do this, just as it is the quality of their understanding of child development and of the children as individuals that determines how they construct and implement the curriculum as a whole so as to give all children the opportunities for learning that they need.

Practitioners need to know the children and to understand enough of their cultures to be able to construct an appropriate curriculum. This is where they gain one great benefit from contacts with parents and where the parents also have much to gain since, while practitioners are learning what they need to know, they are also sharing information about how they work, which is invaluable to parents when they help their children at home. However, for these contacts to take place, time is needed, whether for home visits or for conferences in the setting. Parents and practitioners need time to talk together because the educational value of these contacts is clear. The setting will gain from sharing such concerns as:

I worry about underestimating children when they are so young and come from a great range of different backgrounds and experiences.

I need their help with monitoring progress.

I can learn a great deal from the parents, who have known the child from birth.

The closer the partnership the more consistency of handling for the child – we can share our intentions for children's behaviour.

The child needs to feel secure, that parents and practitioners are working together.

Parents need to know what goes on in the setting in order not to be panicked by political or media manipulation.

It helps parents to make judgements about the quality of what is provided by the setting if they have real experience of what happens in their child's class or group.

Parents have a lot to offer to the setting; not just any special talent, but just as ordinary supportive adults who will tell or read a story, chat to children, help with puzzles, share games and work with children generally.

Practitioners may not be the victims of society's prejudices against particular groups, yet they may be resistant to sharing their professional domain with parents. Practitioners may be understandably concerned about encroachments on their area of responsibility. The meaning of professionalism is that you have an area of expertise which is acknowledged as being highly specialized, and rightly so. Lawyers, doctors and architects are in the same position. All professionals have to ask themselves two questions:

1 To what extent is it right for me to share my specialised knowledge, for which I received many years of training by experts? Would it weaken or dangerously undermine the real value and meaning of this knowledge if I shared a small area of it with those who did not have access to an informed starting point?
2 If it *is* right, to what extent can I convey this knowledge to others in such a way that they can use it to make informed decisions for themselves or their children?

In the case of practitioners, it is appropriate to explain and share as much as possible because it is best for the child, who is their professional responsibility. Unlike a lawyer, they depend on the parents of their 'client' to support their professional intentions. But it is not easy to explain all the professional issues, and we have to help practitioners to become better able to articulate their work to parents and others.

But these are not the only issues at stake. There is a question which is even more important and which should come before the others. The care and education of young children is personally sensitive. As in many other professions, early years practitioners need to have good ongoing relationships with the families (parents and children) and a constant flow of communication between themselves and parents. How is this to be fostered and shaped to include what both sides need to share and to know? There is much information that practitioners can only have access to through parents, and they need practical ways in which to learn it – occasions for easy exchanges of view. It is important also that parents share just as much as they feel able to; practitioners must be careful not to exercise pressure or push people in directions that are not suitable or even possible for them. Conversely, practitioners need to be able to hear and understand parents' communications when they do happen, and it may be personally quite challenging to respond appropriately.

The following example illustrates both the nature of the partnership between practitioners and parents, and how a structure based on respect for the parent-child relationship can support it.

The nature of partnership in education in the early years

Life is one long transition for the under-6s; if parents do not offer constant well-informed support, who else can do this job? Sometimes parents are in serious trouble and need support themselves. The setting can help them and be a kind of buffer area for parent and child without turning the relationship into a social work one. Sensitivity and self-awareness are essential for this (Whalley 1994: 28–33).

> Adam was 5 when his parents parted, after some very painful months. Soon his mother was dealing with his sense of rejection, his anger and his grief. His outbursts were hard to contain,

and his behaviour deteriorated in other ways too, becoming very distractible and aimless. His mother asked his teacher whether he showed any signs of disturbance at school, but apparently there were none. She felt that the teacher and headteacher did not understand how serious the problem was; the head told her that a firm hand was all he needed. After a few days with no improvement she sought help through her doctor and was referred to a local hospital's child guidance clinic. Gradually, Adam's behaviour at home improved. It therefore came as a bombshell to learn a few weeks later that the school was now experiencing the same behaviour that had so concerned her, and that if it did not improve they felt that they would have to exclude the child. His level of achievement had dropped, and he was falling behind the other children in his work. His mother did her best to get Adam to behave at school, and somehow he came through the behaviour difficulties in the end, but she felt very let down by the way the problem had been handled. She felt strongly that if the school had taken Adam's difficulties seriously when she first reported them there could have been a joint approach instead of a fragmented one which seemed to give him little sense of consistency and prolonged his unhappiness. It had also caused him to miss several months of his schooling and to have a sense of himself as a failure. Over a year later she was oppressed by a sense that Adam had been failed when he most needed help.

Ways and means

Children and parents can go through very difficult times together in the early years, and practitioners can do much to help or hinder them. How can we help practitioners to help parents? We have to recognise that practitioners need proper training, and they need a pedagogy that accepts the importance of understanding children's development. [. . .] A new understanding of the care and education of such young and emotionally vulnerable children will permit practitioners to work with the support of a curriculum that is founded on child development theory as well as on subject knowledge. [. . .]

References

Carnegie Corporation of New York (1994) *Starting Points: Meeting the Needs of our Youngest Children*. New York: Carnegie Corporation.

Pilling, D. (1990) *Escape from Disadvantage*. Lewes: Falmer.

Pugh, G., De'Ath, E. and Smith, C. (1994) *Confident Parents, Confident Children*. London: National Children's Bureau.

Trevarthen, C. (1993) *Playing into Reality: Conversations with the Infant Communicator*. Winnicott Studies, No. 7, Spring 1993: 67–84. London: Karnak Books Ltd.

Whalley, M. (1994) *Learning to be Strong: Setting up a Neighbourhood Service for Under-Fives and their Families*. London: Hodder and Stoughton.

Chapter 25

Working with parents
Lucy Draper and Bernadette Duffy

It is widely agreed that partnership with parents should be central to early years provision. Lucy Draper and Bernadette Duffy draw upon their work at Thomas Coram Children's Centre in London to explore the challenges and benefits of working in partnership with parents, and consider why such partnership is important in achieving positive outcomes for children and their families.

Partnership with parents should be a key aspect of provision. Parents should be recognised as children's first and enduring educators, and should be seen as key partners in supporting children's learning and development.

(DfES, 2003d: 10)

In this chapter, we draw on our work in Thomas Coram Children's Centre in London to look at the central importance of parents and practitioners working in partnership together in early years settings.

We ask '*Why* is it important that we work in partnership with parents?' and 'What are the benefits and challenges of working together?'. We then describe our work at Thomas Coram and some of the lessons we have learnt about different groups of parents and what partnership means to them. While using our own centre as an example, we hope that this chapter will have relevance to practitioners working in a wide range of settings.

When we use the term 'parents' we are referring to all those who take on this role in children's lives, whether or not they are the child's biological parent. When we use the term 'practitioner', we are referring to the wide range of adults who support children's learning and development, whether paid or unpaid.

Families are changing, as they always have done. Parents are not a homogeneous group; their views and beliefs will be diverse. Our views about what constitutes a family and the roles these different individuals take, need to reflect this and, in turn, will influence the way we work with parents.

Why is partnership important?

There is a long tradition of working with parents in early childhood settings. At the beginning of the twentieth century, Margaret Macmillan included lectures for parents and parent groups as part of the nursery schools she established. However, by the 1960s, parent involvement programmes tended to focus on parents whose children's achievements seemed low, and parental involvement was seen as a way of compensating for the limitations of home. In recent years, models of parental involvement have moved from being largely compensatory to participatory (Whalley and the Pen Green Centre, 1997).

Today, working in partnership with parents is interpreted in a number of ways. These can include parents working with staff in settings, practitioners visiting families in their own homes, parents as governors or on management committees, parents attending workshops and courses, and parents running services such as toy libraries.

For the past 20 years, government legislation and guidance has strongly encouraged working in partnership with parents. The Education Reform Act 1988 emphasized schools' accountability to parents and parental choice, while the Children Act 1989 introduced the concept of parental responsibility.

The Sure Start programme, launched in 1998 and now integrated into the rapidly expanding national programme of children's centres, recognized the centrality of parental involvement from the start. *The Statutory Framework for the Early Years* (DCSF 2008) emphasizes that effective practice involves using the knowledge and expertise of parents and other family adults, while the *Every Child Matters: Change for Children* framework (DfES, 2004b) stresses the importance of parents, carers and families in meeting the desired outcomes for children.

What are the benefits and challenges of working in partnership with parents?

Benefits for children

There is growing evidence of the long-term benefits of preventive work with parents and young children within mainstream open access services (Pugh, 1999). In the USA, the High Scope Project found that high levels of parental involvement were one of the keys to a successful early years programme (Schweinhart and Weikart, 1993). Projects such as Peers Early Education Partnership (PEEP) in Oxford demonstrate the significant and lasting benefits of working with parents and children from babyhood onwards (Evangelou and Sylva, 2003), while Flouri and Buchanan (2004) looked specifically at the role of fathers and showed that a greater level or frequency of fathers' interest and direct involvement in their children's learning and education is associated strongly with better educational outcomes for children. The Effective Provision of Pre-School Education (EPPE) research project (Sylva et al., 2004) has identified the key role of home learning environments in children's achievements.

Many of these findings were cited in a review of research carried out for the DfES by Desforges and Abouchaar in 2003, which confirmed the view that both parental involvement in the early years setting and the educational environment of the home have a positive effect on children's achievement and adjustment, even after other factors (such as social class) have been taken into account.

In a survey of parents we carried out at Thomas Coram on parents' views of their children's transitions into nursery, it was clear that their main worry was whether the nursery staff would *understand* their child in the way that the child had up until then taken for granted that they would be understood. They listed their worries:

- 'Will my child be able to go to the toilet?'
- 'Will they give extra time to the new children?'
- 'Are there any other children from my ethnic background?'
- 'Will there be someone who speaks my child's language?'
- 'He asked if they'd cook him pasta if he doesn't like the dinner!'

It is important to children that the adults in their lives share an understanding of who they are, what matters most to them and what they are capable of. They mind very much about whether the adults they care about – first their parents and, later in their lives, their nursery workers – seem to like and respect each other. Continuity between home and setting benefits children's learning. Parents and staff who are focusing together on the child's learning are able to share insights and to understand the child more fully. This involves the practitioners going to some degree of trouble to get to know the family and in showing an interest (without being off puttingly intrusive) in a child's home circumstances and life history to date, in their interests and achievements, hopes and fears, likes and dislikes. It will also entail staff sharing with parents the details of a child's life in the nursery, and the sometimes familiar and sometimes entirely new facets of a child's personality that reveal themselves in the early years setting.

Benefits for parents

Parents' first and most important motivation to have a good relationship with staff in their child's early years setting is that they can see that the better the practitioner understands their child, the happier their child is likely to be. They are also intrigued to know about what their child is doing and learning during the hours they are apart from them, and children, frustratingly, are not always able (or willing) to explain this themselves. ('What did you do at nursery today?' 'Played.') Parents may also welcome a different (and less intense) perspective on the rewarding, but often challenging, experience of bringing up a child. Practitioners bring a broader view of the different developmental stages young children go through, what is 'normal' and, perhaps, what really is concerning, and parents are grateful to learn from this. They are often fascinated to find out a bit more about the ways in which early years settings provide learning opportunities and the particular ways in which their own child responds to these.

Some parents also welcome the chance to develop themselves as individuals; if they are asked to contribute their particular ideas, knowledge or skills to share with children in the setting, they will feel respected and valued. Involvement of this kind can release untapped potential – many early years practitioners have started out this way. Other parents have got involved in courses, which have led on to further and higher education. Involvement in management committees and governing bodies empowers parents and gives them a voice in their community, as well as ensuring that their perspective informs the thinking of the setting. Programmes designed to bring practitioners and parents together also bring parents together, reducing parental isolation and helping to build support networks in the wider community.

Benefits for practitioners

Parents and practitioners need each other and have useful differences in their approach that can complement each other. Parents are experts on their own individual child and their family culture, and practitioners offer expertise in this stage of children's development and learning. By combining these, the best opportunities can be provided for each child. For many staff, the opportunity to work closely with parents adds a new dimension to their work. Practitioners can assume that their experience of family life is the only way it can be, and working with parents from diverse communities widens their views on families and family life. Differences can be shared, respected and explored. The children's life at home provides many opportunities for learning, on which the setting can build.

At Thomas Coram, we have tried to make our partnership focus include all these elements and thus benefit children, parents and practitioners. We believe that, though there are different roles and responsibilities, there is not such a great separation between staff and parents. Many practitioners *are* parents, and all have been children. Everybody shares a concern for the welfare of the children, and this is also true of the wider community.

The challenges of partnership

Studies looking at parental involvement from the point of view of the parents (for example, Ghate and Hazel, 2001; Quinton, 2004) show that parents want to have their views taken seriously, to be listened to, to be respected and to be treated as partners in the upbringing of their children.

However, working together in partnership is not always easy for either parents or practitioners, and partnerships are not necessarily equal. Both may have anxieties about the relationship; for example, if practitioners have a view of themselves as the experts on children's learning they may find it difficult to value the parents' views. Often, practitioners who feel confident in their work with children feel less confident in their work with parents, or with parents who are very different from them. On the other hand, parents may have negative memories of school, or may have questions about some aspect of the curriculum, but find it hard to find the courage to express this.

Settings may find it harder to work in partnership with some groups of parents than with others. Our discussions about so-called 'hard to reach' parents made us question who it was that was having the difficulty in 'reaching'. Exciting work has taken place at

Thomas Coram with both very young parents and with fathers, both groups who are as keen to support their children as any other parent, but who may want to get involved in different ways.

A lack of shared language (both literally or metaphorically) can make communication harder. Family circumstances (lack of time, pressures of work, no crèche facilities for younger children) may make it difficult for parents to participate in programmes or events organized by the setting. Practitioners are often busy, and where children are transported long distances to attend, or where there is a rapid turnover of children, opportunities to build relationships can be limited.

Such situations bring constant challenges to good partnership working. However, none of these problems is insurmountable and, in the following section, we will be describing some of the ways in which we have tried to put partnership into action at Thomas Coram.

Thomas Coram Children's Centre

Our centre is situated in the King's Cross area of London and is a partnership between Camden Local Education Authority, Coram Family – a children's charity – and the local King's Cross Sure Start programme. Already having to think about working in partnership as different professionals, we draw on many of the same understandings in our work with parents. The centre is part of Coram Community Campus, which houses a wide range of providers from the maintained and voluntary sectors. It consists of the Early childhood centre – often referred to as 'the nursery' – which provides 106 places for children from 6 months to 5 years; and (adjoining it in the same building) the Parents Centre, which provides support and training for parents from the nursery and the wider community, health and mental health services, as well as a drop-in centre, crèches and out-of-school childcare. The activities in the Parents Centre are accessible to both the parents of children attending the nursery and to families in the wider community. Potentially, therefore, a family can have a connection with the whole centre for many years, spanning the child's transition from home to nursery to school. The centre as a whole offers a training and dissemination programme, including training for practitioners in working with parents.

When we are thinking about partnership with parents, we need to think about what we wish to achieve in our particular setting. What are the characteristics and needs of the community we serve and how will we reflect this in what we offer? At Thomas Coram, we have tried not to assume that the practitioners' agenda for partnership is necessarily shared by parents (Henry, 1996), but that trust, sharing information, sharing decision-making, sharing responsibility and accountability are all important.

A successful partnership involves a two-way flow of information, and flexibility and responsiveness are vital. We want to create a centre that reflects our ethos that everyone is welcome, that parents can express their views and feelings, that diversity is valued and that the centre is seen as part of the wider community.

In the following section, we will be giving examples that highlight different aspects of our work with parents:

- working with parents around children's learning
- support for parents
- access to further training
- parental involvement in management.

Working with parents around children's learning

In any early years setting, the 'settling-in' process is a crucial arena for the establishment of a good partnership between parents and practitioners. We know from attachment theory that if a child feels securely attached to their parent or carer, they will also have more confidence to be able to learn from new experiences. The Parents Centre gives the opportunity for parents and children to 'practise' small amounts of separation, without the stress that is sometimes felt when a child is starting nursery full time and a parent perhaps needs to get back to work. In the drop-in, which parents and children attend together, a child may start by taking a few small steps away from his or her parent or, sitting on their lap, simply start to show an interest in an activity in which other children are involved. Later, parents may attend groups or classes, while the children stay in the crèche for an hour or two. In the nursery, some children will already have visited from the Parents Centre drop-in before they are offered a place, but our first contact with others is during weekly visitors' mornings, when prospective families come to look at the centre.

Once children are offered a nursery place, the family is invited to join our induction programme, which consists of visits to the centre, home visits by the key worker, and a settling in period. During this time, we get to know the family and they get to know us. Part of this process is a detailed parent conference during which parents tell us about their child in a semi-structured interview. The information we get from this covers all areas of the child's development and learning, and provides the foundation for our planning for the individual child. At the same time, parents and children are starting to make a relationship with the key worker – if they feel that they like and trust them (which often comes from feeling that the key worker has a genuine and open interest in the child), this is a sound basis for good communication in the future.

Feedback from parents – what do we look for in a practitioner?

- Listening very carefully.
- Being understanding.
- Not quick to judge.
- Giving time for us to explain.
- Finding a way out of turmoil – a chance to calm down.
- Never say 'you are not doing it right'.
- Take time – get to know the children. If our children like you, we will like you.
- Don't compare the children unfavourably to others – say 'some children do this, some children do that'.
- It's important to discuss cultural and religious issues in parenting.
- Understand that it's hard for us when one worker leaves, but you can slowly build up trust in a new person.

(Comments from parents contributing to a practitioner training programme.)

Arrival and collection times are crucial for communication between parents and practitioners, though in a nursery as large and busy as ours, they can also be quite pressured. We organize the sessions to ensure that staff, especially key workers, are free at these important times of day to welcome families and exchange information. As well as daily informal contacts, there are regular times for parent and key worker to meet and review the progress of individual children. As part of this review, parents and key workers jointly decide the next priorities for learning and discuss how they can work together to support the child. Key workers in each base room also hold regular meetings with parents to discuss what is going on in the room and possible new developments.

As our work with parents developed, it became clear that being available for parents was a priority. In a review of the nursery management structure, it was decided that we should free up one of the deputies specifically to work with parents and to encourage involvement and inclusion. This has proved to be particularly important for, and valued by, the parents of children with special needs.

The centre makes full use of video footage to share children's nursery experiences with parents; parents love to come in and talk about their children's lives in more detail. While key workers have been privileged to learn a little more about the child's family life from the home visit – perhaps seeing a child they have thought of as quiet showing confident fluency in their home language – parents watching a video of the child's day in nursery will often be struck by the ways in which their children are different in this other setting – passing food around at lunchtime, for instance, might be something they've never done at home. In this way the child's two worlds are brought together, with the adults in each having a greater understanding of the child's experiences in the other.

We have tried to develop ways of ensuring that busy parents who work or are students are also offered accessible ways to be involved. One method has been the use of home/centre books where parents and key workers enter into a dialogue by recording observations of the child's experience at home and at the centre. Another has been the use of regular newsletters and information sheets about the current work of the centre. Our website contains a wide range of information about the centre and offers opportunities for parents to get involved in current projects. The toy and book libraries also provide opportunities to bring centre and home life together.

There are also opportunities for parents to get involved in specific programmes. Peters and Kostelnik (1981) point out that practitioners often present irrelevant and ineffective materials in these situations, because they have neglected to find out more about the strengths and needs which parents are bringing to the programmes in the process. We have tried to ensure that we consider this when planning what to offer. In the groups, there is a strong focus on the children's learning and development, drawing on our in-house skills, reflecting the cultural and linguistic diversity of the community we serve, and again often using video. Workshops might be entitled 'What does a 2-year-old do all day?' or they focus particularly on interactions between adults and children. The discussion that has resulted has been rich and has offered parents and staff new insights to the children. Another group – again using video observations – has been used to consult with parents on what they would like to see for their children at the beginning and end of the 'extended day'. They fed back to staff that the priority for them was that their children should have as relaxed and calm a time as they might have had at home if they were there.

Parents, who first became interested in the question of how their children learn, have sometimes gone on to train as practitioners through the 'Introduction to Childcare' and then the accredited 'Level 2 Certificate in Childcare' courses, which we offer in partnership with the local college. For us, this also brings the opportunity to employ our practitioners from among parents in the local community, with all the benefits that brings. Other parents have trained with us as community interpreters or outreach workers, again building on the skills and knowledge of their communities.

Support for parents

All our work rests on an acknowledgment of the importance of parents and carers in their children's lives, and of the rewards – as well as the challenges and difficulties – involved in the parenting task. (In a 1998 survey of parents, 87 per cent of parents named joy as the emotion they felt most often – Barnardo's, 1998.) The staff are privileged to have come to know an enormous amount about families' lives; in the relatively informal setting of the drop-in, we have watched babies grow and develop, eat and sleep and – both literally and metaphorically – take their first steps. We have listened to their parents' worries and concerns, heard about their pregnancy and childbirth experiences, been part of workshops where they have shared a wide range of cultural expertise concerning children and childcare, and music sessions where songs and lullabies from many different languages are shared and learnt. Sometimes we have heard about difficulties with housing or money or immigration status and at times, hopefully, have been able to give useful advice in these areas. It is also not unusual for parents to share their worries about conflict with partners or other family members.

Two mornings a week, we are lucky enough to have a psychologist and psychotherapist, provided by the local Primary Care Trust, available in the centre to see parents who have particular concerns about their children. Parents who have worries about their children's behaviour often find it very hard to seek help, and may worry they will be blamed for these difficulties or 'reported' to Social Services. The service has worked very well and proved to be helpful to parents with a variety of concerns about their children's sleeping, eating or behaviour. It seems that because the service, though specialized, is based in a community setting, parents find it much easier and less threatening to use. An early evaluation showed that 93 per cent of parents attended their first appointments, compared with 68 per cent who are referred to psychologists in clinical settings. The psychology staff also co-run parents' group with centre practitioners, provide help for staff wanting to think about the needs of particular children or groups of children, and teach on courses for parents and practitioners.

There are very wide variations in beliefs (held by both practitioners and parents) about what is 'good for children'. Thomas Coram is situated in a culturally very diverse neighbourhood, and families attending the centre speak 48 different languages. Working in effective partnership with parents from different ethnic backgrounds requires both knowledge of and respect for these differences, and a commitment to provide a service of equal quality to all their children. Parents who were not themselves educated in the UK may be unfamiliar with the British education system and possibly are not confident it will serve their children well.

Having information and knowledge about parents' points of view is crucial. At a meeting of Bangladeshi parents brought together to discuss their perspectives on their children's education, they were for the first time given the information that as a group, Bangladeshi children – especially boys – were doing less well in school than most other ethnic groups. There was, understandably, a great deal of anxiety about their children's progress.

> This anxiety had several causes: ignorance of the methods and expectations of English schools; embarrassment that as parents they lacked the education needed to support their children; and confusion about the English belief in learning through play. Parents were torn between trying to implement the kinds of learning they had experienced as schoolchildren, and trying to follow the advice of English practitioners. This confusion and contradiction was only slowly discussed and understood, through initial visits from outreach workers, visits to the toy library, recruitment to parents' classes in primary schools (part of the wider work of the Parents Centre) and continual discussion in groups at the Centre. Some parents remained uncertain of the benefits of the English school system, but all knew that they had to put their faith in it, and most became quite confident in dealing with schools and teachers, as well as in supporting children's learning at home.
>
> (Brooker, 2004)

At a series of 'International Parenting' workshops, groups of parents made presentations about their home cultures, particularly in relation to pregnancy, childbirth and child-rearing. Childcare practitioners who attended these workshops found them particularly valuable and the material was published in a booklet entitled 'Sharing our Stories'.

Research in the UK has shown that black and ethnic minority parents are less likely to attend family centres or 'parenting skills' classes than white parents, even though they have similar needs for support (Butt and Box, 1998). We looked for particular models of parenting support that would meet the needs of all parents and have for some years been running a programme called *Strengthening Families: Strengthening Communities* (Steele, 2000). This has many things in common with better known models, but two of its features are unique. One is that it emphasizes the strengths in a family's cultural history and looks at ways in which parents can pass these on to their children (rather than focusing on problems). The other is that it includes discussion of a 'spiritual' component in parenting, which can mean a variety of things from formal religious teaching to creating a moral framework for children's lives.

This has been eagerly welcomed by parents, who have taken from it not only new ideas about children's learning and behaviour, but also a determination to make the local neighbourhood a safer and happier place for their children to grow up.

The bombings in London in July 2005, some of which took place very close to Thomas Coram, not only made local families very fearful, but also presented a challenge to the community's capacity to tolerate the differences within it. Only a few days after the bombings, a large community festival – Bangladesh Mela – had been planned in a local park. Staff and parents from the centre had long been involved in the preparations for this event, and though there was talk of postponing it, it was agreed that it would make an important and positive statement if it went ahead. In the event, over 2,000 local families took part, including many from Thomas Coram.

Like the wider group of families, our Teenage Parent Project includes young parents from many different backgrounds, including some who are refugees from war-torn countries, as well as those who grew up in the UK. There are as many individual stories as there are individual young parents, including 16-year-old married couples, young care-leavers, and teenagers who arrived in this country pregnant having experienced severe trauma. The project has an educational focus and the young parents are given an opportunity to study, while keeping their children close by them (some in the same room, some in crèches and some given nursery places, according to their parents' wishes). Their successes have challenged the stereotype of feckless teen parents; their motivation to take part in various photographic and film projects about the lives of young parents have stemmed from their desire to put the record straight and to demonstrate their serious commitment to their children.

We have learned that it is important to provide specific services targeted at the particular needs of certain groups (such as young parents); after a while, though, they may welcome the opportunity to take part in more general activities. The same is true of fathers, whose particular needs and interests often get forgotten, even while we are talking about work with 'parents'. We have for some years employed a specially designated Fathers' Worker to co-ordinate particular activities for fathers and also to raise the general level of awareness among staff of 'the man's position' – important in such a generally female environment. To ensure that the Fathers' Worker does not become professionally isolated (in a mirroring of the father's role in the young family), he is part of a wider team of men employed by Coram Family's Boys2Men Project, who work with fathers in different children's centres across London.

Access to further training

The centre offers a number of ways in which parents can access further training. There is a well-resourced information technology room, in which we offer a range of courses as well as individual access to computers, and classes are also offered in sewing, first aid, ESOL and return to work. Ongoing support and encouragement from staff are important as a return to study can be daunting but, when parents are ready, we also offer accredited professional training in childcare, interpreting and outreach. Teenage parents, whose studies may have been interrupted by the birth of their babies, are able to continue to study, while keeping their children close to hand, and are also given support with their other concerns.

Since the recent publication of the new *National Occupational Standards for Work with Parents* (Lifelong Learning, 2005), we have offered a new training course for practitioners linked to these standards, drawing on the range of different kinds of work with parents at Thomas Coram. Parents – fathers and mothers – are regular contributors to this course, bringing the perspectives of different ages, backgrounds and needs.

Parental involvement in the management of the centre

Parents can also, if they wish, become involved in the management of the centre. The development of the local Sure Start programme has particularly supported them to gain the skills and confidence necessary to contribute to the planning and delivery of services. There are five parents on the governing body, one of whom is the deputy chair, and parents are represented on each of the sub-committees, chairing two of them. The parents' forum, which is organized and chaired by the parent governors, offers an opportunity for those parents who wish to get involved with the management of the centre. In order to get the views of as wide a range of parents as possible, the parents forum and others organize surveys of parents' views on key issues.

Conclusion

At Thomas Coram, we see one of our professional tasks as being to use our knowledge about what parents want and need – both individually and more generally – to work together with early years practitioners in the best interests of all. Parents' involvement with the centre will vary over time and from family to family, as will the nature of that involvement. We would argue that the opportunity to be involved, especially in their own child's learning and in the management and development of the centre, must be open to all, and that not only they, but also early years practitioners, will benefit from this partnership.

References

Department for Children, Schools and Families (DCSF) (2008) *The Statutory Framework for the Early Years Foundation Stage*. Nottingham: DCSF.

Department for Education and Skills (DfES) (2003d) *Sure Start Children's Centre Start up Guidance*. London: Sure Start Unit.

Department for Education and Skills (DfES) (2004b) *Every Child Matters: Change for Children*. Nottingham: DfES Publications.

Desforges, C. and Abouchaar, A. (2003) *The Impact of Parent Involvement, Parent Support and Family Education on Pupil Achievement and Adjustment: A Literature Review*. Research Report 433. London: DfES Publications.

Evangelou, M. and Sylva, K. (2003) *The Effects of the Peers Early Education Partnership (PEEP) on Children's Developmental Progress*. London: DfES.

Flouri, E. and Buchanan, A. (2004) 'Early father's and mother's involvement and child's later educational outcomes', *British Journal of Educational Psychology*, 74: 141–53.

Ghate, D. and Hazel, N. (2001) *Parenting in Poor Environments: Stress, Support and Coping*. London: Policy Research Bureau.

Henry, M. (1996) *Young Children, Parents and Professionals*. London: Routledge.

Lifelong Learning UK (2005) *National Occupational Standards for Work with Parents*. London: Lifelong Learning UK.

Peters, D. and Kostelnik, M. (1981) 'Current research in day care personnel preparation', *Advance in Early Education and Day* Care, 2: 29–66.

Pugh, G. (1999) 'Young children and their families: a community response', in L. Abbot and H. Moylett (eds), *Early Education Transformed*. London: Falmer Press.

Qualification and Curriculum Authority (QCA) (2000) *Curriculum Guidance for the Foundation Stage*. London: QCA.

Quinton, D. (2004) *Supporting Parents: Messages from Research*. London: Jessica Kingsley.

Schweinhart, L.J. and Weikart, D.P. (1993) *A Summary of Significant Benefits: The High Scope Perry Pre-School Study Through Age 27*. Ypsilanti, MI: High Scope Press.

Steele, M. (2000) *Strengthening Families: Strengthening Communities: An Inclusive Parent Programme*. London: Racial Equality Unit.

Sylva, K., Melhuish, E.C., Sammons, P., Siraj-Blatchford, I. and Taggart, B. (2004) *The Effective Provision of Pre-School Education (EPPE) Project: Technical Paper 12 – The Final Report: Effective Pre-School Education*. London: DfES and Institute of Education, University of London.

Index